ELEMENTS OF FOLK PSYCHOLOGY

ELEMENTS
OF
FOLK PSYCHOLOGY
OUTLINES OF A PSYCHOLOGICAL HISTORY OF THE DEVELOPMENT OF MANKIND

(In Two Volumes)

(Volume 2)

by

WILHELM WUNDT

Authorised Translation
by

EDWARD LEROY SCHAUB

Introduction by

SILA BASAK

Publications

KALPAZ PUBLICATIONS

DELHI - 110052

Elements of Folk Psychology

ISBN : 81-7835 - 606-6 (Set)
ISBN : 81-7835 - 608-2 (Vol. 2)

Rs. 1800 (Set)

Published in 2007 in India by
Kalpaz Publications
C - 30, Satyawati Nager,
Delhi - 110052
Phone : 9212729499
E-mail : kalpaz@hotmail.com
First Published : 1921, London : George Allen & Unwin Ltd.

Laser Typesetting at : Rudhra Computer, Delhi
Printed at : Vishal Kaushik Printers Delhi - 110093

CHAPTER III

THE AGE OF HEROES AND GODS

CHAPTER IV

THE DEVELOPMENT TO HUMANITY

CHAPTER III

THE AGE OF HEROES AND GODS

1. General Character of the Heroic Age

THE expression 'the age of heroes and gods' may meet with objection no less than may 'totemic age.' The latter has an air of strangeness, because the conceptions of totem and totemism, borrowed from modern ethnology, have as yet remained unfamiliar to historians, and especially to the historians of civilization. The former expression may be objected to on the ground that the conceptions 'heroes' and 'gods' are altogether too familiar to be extended beyond their specific meaning and applied to an entire age. The word 'hero' suggests to us perhaps the Homeric Achilles, or Siegfried of the Niebelungen saga—those mighty, victorious warriors of epic song who, as we have already seen, gradually evolved out of the heroes of primitive märchen. It is self-evident, however, that, when applied to a great and important period of culture, the expression 'hero' must not be limited to the narrow meaning which it possesses in hero-lore. True, we must not go so far as does Carlyle when, in his "Heroes and Hero Worship," he begins the race of heroes with Odin of the Northmen and ends it with Shakespeare and Goethe, thus extending the heroic age from prehistoric times down to the present. Nevertheless, if we would do justice to the significance of the conception 'heroic' as applied to an important period of human development, we must be permitted to include under the broader conception 'heroic age,' not merely the heroic hero but also the hero who has factored in the spiritual realm, as the founder of cities or states, or the creator of religions. These latter heroes were gradually evolved, in the course of political and religious development, out of the ancient epic heroes ; in them, the heroic age continues its existence after the heroes of the powerful and crafty types have disappeared. In this broader significance of the word, a hero is any powerful individuality whatsoever, and the general characteristic of this new age, therefore, is the predominance of the *individual personality*. Externally, this expresses itself primarily in the fact that the age regards even all past events as the deeds of individual persons. Bound up with this is a progressive individualization of human personalities, and a constant refinement of the crude distinctions that characterize the tale of adventure and the older hero-lore.

The gods of this age are likewise patterned entirely after powerful human personalities. They are anthropomorphic in every respect—human beings of a higher order, whose qualities, though found only among men, are magnified to infinitude. Just as the hero is a man endowed with more than ordinary human capacities, so the god is a hero exalted above the measure of earthly heroes. This itself implies that the hero necessarily precedes the god, just as man antedates the hero. Any fairly detailed account of this period, therefore, must deal with the hero before considering the god. The god is created after the image of the hero, and not as traditional mythology still believes, the hero after the image of the god. It would, indeed, be a strange procedure for man first to create the ideal conception of his god and only subsequently to transform this into human outlines, and thus produce the hero. In the advance from man to the anthropomorphic god, the hero would surely already have been encountered. This, of course, does not imply that gods may not occasionally be transformed into heroes ; it simply means that in the development as a whole the hero must have preceded the god. The relation here is precisely the same as that found everywhere else in connection with the development and degeneration of mythological conceptions. The fact of sequence, however, must not be interpreted to mean that we can point to a time in which there were heroes but no gods. Hero and god belong together. Both reflect an effort to exalt human personality into the superhuman. In this process, no fixed line may be drawn separating the hero, whose activity still falls within the human sphere, from the god, who is exalted above it. (In fact, the differences between hero and god are by no means merely quantitative, measurable in terms of the elevation above the plane of human characteristics; the differentiating marks are essentially *qualitative*. The hero remains human in all his thought and action. The god, on the other hand, possesses not merely human capacities raised to their highest power, but also characteristics which are lacking in man and therefore also in the hero. Especially noteworthy among the latter is the ability through his own power to perform magical acts, and thus to interfere at will in the course of nature as well as in human life. True, the hero of saga and poetry also employs magical agencies. The means of magic which he controls, however, have been bestowed upon him by some strange demoniacal being, either by one of those demons which, in the form of a man, an animal, or a fantastic monster, are recognized even by the early mythical tales as magical beings, or by a god, who, as such, combines the highest qualities of the hero with those of the demon. The conception of an anthropomorphic god, therefore, results from a fusion of hero with demon. Of these, the hero is a new creation, originating in the mental life of this later age. He was long foreshadowed, however, first by the animal ancestor (especially in so far as the latter brought blessings and good fortune), and then by the subsequent cult of human ancestors. But the figure of the hero is not completely developed until the human personality enters into the very forefront of mythological thought; then, through regular transitions, the value placed on personal characteristics is enhanced until the ideal of the hero is reached. Doubtless the hero may still incidentally be associated with the ancestor, yet personality as such has now come so to dominate the interest of the age that in comparison with it the genealogical feature is but secondary.

Not so with the demon-idea. Though it has come down from very remote times and has assumed many forms as a result of varying cultural conditions, the demon has always remained a magic being, arousing now hope, now fear and terror. This was its nature up to the very time when the ideal of the hero arose. This new idea it then appropriated, just as it did, in earlier times, the ideas of a soul that survives the deceased, of the totem animal, of the ancestor, and of other mythological figures. The very nature of the demon has always been constituted by such incorporated elements. From this point of view, the god also is only a new form of demon. In its earlier forms, however, as spirit-demon, animal-demon, and, finally, even as ancestor-demon, the demon was an impersonal product of the emotions, and possessed characteristics which underwent constant transformations. When it became a hero, it for the first time rose to the level of a personal being. Through the enhancement of the qualities of the hero it was then elevated into the sphere of the superhuman. Thus it came to constitute a human ideal far transcending the hero. This accounts for the uniqueness of the god-conception, and for the fact that, though the god assumes the essential characteristics of the demon, the two are nevertheless more widely distinct than were any of the earlier forms of demon conceptions from those that anteceded them. The rise of the god-idea, therefore, ushers in a new epoch of religious development. Just because of the contrast between personal god and impersonal demon, this epoch may be designated as that of the *origin of religion*, in the narrower and proper sense of the word. The various forms of pure demon-belief are preparatory to religion; religion itself begins with the belief in gods. The relation which the belief in demons sustains to the belief in gods is another evidence that hero and god must be grouped together, for there can be no clearly marked temporal difference in the origin of these two ideals of personality Just as soon as the figure of the human hero arises, it assimilates the demon-conception, which was already long in existence and which continually underwent changes as a result of the various ideas with which it came into contact. Alongside of the being that arose from this fusion, however, there continued also the hero in his purity, as well as the demon, whose various forms were at most crowded into the background by the appearance of the gods. To however great an extent, therefore, the age of heroes and gods may introduce a completely new spiritual movement that proves fundamental to all future culture and religion, it nevertheless also includes all the elements of previous development. These elements, moreover, are not merely present in forms that have been altered and in part completely changed by the processes of assimilation ; side by side with such forms, there are always also the original elements, which may be traced back to the earliest beginnings of mythological thought. The dominant factor determining the character of this new age, however, is the *hero*. The ideal of human personality which the hero engenders in the folk consciousness conditions all further development, and especially the origin of the god. For this reason the 'age of heroes and gods' might also, and more briefly, be called the *heroic age*.

As the direct incarnation of the idea of personality, it is the hero about whom the new development of myth and religion centres. Similarly, the hero also stands in closest relation to the transformations that occur in all other departments of human life. Enormous changes in economic conditions and in the forms of life dependent upon them, new social institutions, with their reactions upon custom and law, transformations and creations in all branches of art—all give expression to the new development upon which this age has entered. Here also, just as at the beginning of the anteceding age, there are numerous reciprocal relations between these various factors. The hero and the god cannot be conceived apart from the *State*, whose founding marks the beginning of this period. Custom and law are just as much results of the new political society as they are themselves essential factors in its creation. Neither the State nor the worship of gods protected by it could survive apart from the great changes in economic life that took place at the beginning of this period, and that were further established and perfected in the course of time. Thus, here also each element reinforces every other : all the factors of life are in constant interaction At the beginning of the totemic period, as we have seen, it was the new creations of mythological thought that constituted the centre from which radiated all the other elements of culture. At the beginning of the age of heroes and gods it is the creative power of the *religious* consciousness whose activities most accurately mirror the various spiritual achievements of the period.

2. The External Culture of the Heroic Age.

The heroic era is so comprehensive and comprises so large a part of human history that any attempt to arrive at even the barest outlines of its external culture makes it clear that this culture is even less unitary than is that of the preceding period. The differentiation of phenomena naturally increases with advancing development. Even the various forms of totemic culture manifest wide differences in detail ; indeed, when taken as a whole, they represent distinct stages. When we come to the heroic age, however, whose beginning is practically coincident with the beginnings of history in the usual sense of the term, and which includes within itself a large part of the succeeding course of events, the multiplicity and diversity of the forms of culture are incomparably greater. Every nation has its particular heroes, even though there are also certain general hero-types which everywhere recur. Even more does each nation have its gods. Heroes and gods are ideals created in the image of men, and therefore they always reflect—if possible, in a heightened degree—the characteristic differences of peoples. Nevertheless, amid all these differences of times and peoples, there are certain constant features that distinguish the heroic period both from the preceding age and from the era that follows. Most important of all these features is the establishment of the *State*. It was a long step from totemic tribal organization to political institutions. In the surge and press of the folk migrations which occurred at the beginning of the heroic period, traces of the preceding tribal organization were still everywhere present. Tribes did not change suddenly into States. Nevertheless, along with the emergence of the heroic age and its concomitant phenomena, there was a noticeable tendency towards the formation of a political order. This development pursued different courses, depending on the character of the nations or of their heroes and gods. It is primarily the resultant differences in political organization which, when considered in connection with the parallel changes in mythological and religious development, clearly show that in this period, just as in the totemic age, all other aspects of culture were closely dependent upon mythological and religious ideas. 'Totemism' connotes not merely a complex of mythological beliefs in which a certain stage of culture had its setting, but also a unique form of tribal organization, which, in spite of many differences of detail, remained constant in its general features. Similarly, political society, in the original form in which it long survived, was closely bound up with the heroic age, even though the increasing differences between national cultures led, from the very outset, to a greater diversity of forms than were to be found in the case of totemism. In spite of these differences, however, the factor fundamental to political society remained the same. The formation of States was always conditioned by individual *rulership*. This itself is indicative of the character of the age as a whole: its typical expression is to be found in the personalities of heroes and of gods. Again it was the migrations and wars of peoples that brought about the dissolution of the old tribal organization and the creation of political society. But these migrations and wars were on an incomparably broader scale and had more intimate interconnections than had previously been the case. This gave them a correspondingly greater significance, both intensively and extensively. As a matter of comparison, we may refer to the migrations of the Malayan race during the totemic age. It would be difficult to conceive of more extensive migrations. But they took place gradually, in separate waves, and left no traces, for the most part, beyond changes in the physical characteristics and in the languages of peoples. These migrations, which frequently involved long voyages across the sea, were carried on by but small numbers of people, who set out from restricted groups. It cannot be doubted that these migrations exercised an influence on the character and the culture of the resulting mixed races. They were never able, however, completely to transform the culture as a whole. Even when these tribal migrations occurred in oft-repeated waves, they never resulted in more than such imperfect beginnings of a political organization as we find among the Polynesians or, in other parts of the earth, among many of the semi-cultural peoples of America and Africa.

Quite different are the *folk migrations* that occur at the very dawn of the history of the great cultural peoples. The difference between tribal and racial migrations is an important one. When a race migrates, it retains its peculiar characteristics, its traditions, its heroes, and its gods, and transplants these into the new territory. True, these various elements do not remain unchanged. They inevitably become fused with the culture of the original inhabitants, and it is from these fusions, when they are at all deep-going, that new peoples arise. None of the great cultural nations that mark the beginning of this age of heroes and gods, from the Babylonians down to the Greeks, the Romans, and the Germans, is homogeneous. Indeed, recent Babylonian investigations have shown that the Semitic immigration into Babylon was preceded by that of other peoples who were probably of different origin—namely, the Sumerians. We know of the latter only through linguistic traces in Babylonian inscriptions, of which, however, the religious parts, especially, show that the Sumerians exercised a great influence upon later civilization. Similarly, the settlement of the Greeks, Romans, and Germans in the territory which they eventually occupied, followed upon great earlier migrations to these regions. The people that finally formed the Greek race left the mountain country of

Thrace and Thessaly in prehistoric times; wandering towards the sea, they fused with the original inhabitants of the regions into which they entered. In view of these migrations of early history, the theory of the desirability of racial purity, which has recently been so ardently championed in many quarters, is scarcely tenable. Political organization, on the one hand, and mythology and religion, on the other, represent important creations which for the most part sprang into existence only in the wake of migration and of the resultant fusion of peoples of different races.

Though political organization has been mentioned as the first important feature distinguishing the heroic age from the preceding era, there is a second and not less significant differentia. This relates to the material conditions of life. Two things are of outstanding importance for the new culture. The first of these consists in what we ordinarily call agriculture—that is, the tilling of the soil by the aid of the *plough*, or, as it is therefore more properly called in contrast to the earlier hoe-culture, plough-culture. In addition, there is the *breeding of domestic animals*, particularly of food-supplying cattle, and, later, of sheep and goats.

It is even to-day widely believed that, of the various modes of procuring food, hunting came first. The hunter is thought to have been seized, one fine day, with an impulse to domesticate animals instead of hunting them. He tamed the wild creatures, and thus turned from a hunter into a nomad. In the course of time, the nomad is then supposed to have tired of his wandering life and to have settled down in permanent habitations. Instead of obtaining milk by herding his cattle, he hitched the ox to the plough, after having (with that wisdom and foresight which such theories always attribute to primitive man) invented the plough. This theory is an impossible fiction from beginning to end. It is just as intrinsically improbable as is the above-mentioned hypothesis that in prehistoric times the Australians invented totemic tribal organization and exogamy for the purpose of preventing the marriage of relatives. We have seen, on the contrary, that the prohibition of such marriages was a consequence of exogamy, and that the latter, in turn, was not a deliberate invention but the natural result of certain conditions inherent in the culture of the age. All these institutions were originally due to influences whose outcome could not possibly have been foreseen. The same is true of the subject under discussion. In the first place, the assumed order of succession of the three stages of life is contradicted by facts. It is hardly correct to speak of a hunting life which is not supplemented by a certain amount of agriculture in the form of hoe-culture—an industry which, as a rule, is carried on by the woman in the immediate vicinity of the hut. This primitive agriculture existed even at a very early age. We find it widely prevalent among the American aborigines, who possessed no domesticated animal whatever except the dog, and the dog, as was above observed, was never tamed at all, but domesticated itself at the very dawn of prehistoric times. The supposition that the nomadic life followed upon that of the hunter is impossible, in the second place, because the animals that are hunted are not identical with those that form the care of the nomad. Cattle were never objects of the chase ; the closely related buffalo, on the other hand, was never domesticated, but has remained exclusively a game animal down to the present day. Game animals have never been domesticated and utilized for the purpose of supplying milk and drawing the plough. No doubt the domestic animals of the nomad at one time existed in a wild state. Wild cattle, of course, preceded tame cattle. But the latter did not develop from the former by the indirect way of the hunted animal. Nor does agriculture at all presuppose a nomadic life. There are vast stretches of the Old World, as, for instance, all of China, Indo-China, and Indonesia, where the production of milk was never engaged in but where agriculture in the form of plough-culture has existed, in part, since early times. Agriculture, however, involves the raising of cattle, particularly of oxen. These male cattle are castrated, usually when very young. They are thus made tractable, so that they may be hitched to the plough and used for agricultural purposes more easily than is possible in the case of bulls, which are never completely manageable. What, then, were the motives which led to the raising of cattle, an occupation which, in many places at least, is carried on solely in the interests of agriculture? What motives led to the castration of male cattle, a practice which everywhere obviously serves agricultural purposes?

The traditional mode of explanation would lead us to suppose that man foresaw the effects of castration, that he knew beforehand that if the bull were subjected to this operation he would become an animal fitted to draw the plough. The impossibility of this supposition is evident. Such an effect could be learned only from experience, prior to which, therefore, it could not have been known. The problem relating to the cultivation of the soil by means of the plough, therefore, divides into two questions: How may we account for the ox? How for the plough? These questions are closely related, and yet they lead us back to divergent explanations. For in all probability the plough was originally drawn by man. Moreover, the plough was not the first implement to be thus drawn; it was anteceded by the *wagon*. Even on the early Babylonian and Assyrian monuments there were figures of a wagon bearing either an image of a god or else the king or chief priest, both of whom were probably regarded as uniting in *one person* the function of their offices with that of representative of the deity. Thus, the question as to the origin of the plough carries us back directly to that of the origin of the wagon. Now, the earliest wagon had but two wheels; the four-wheeled wagon came as a later discovery or as an improvement. The two-wheeled wagon, however, presupposes the wheel. But how did the wheel come to be recognized as a useful object of locomotion? The first traces of a wheel or of wheel-like objects are to be found in the latter part of the stone age. A number of such objects have been discovered in Europe; in their centre is a hole, and there are spokes that radiate to the circumference. The fact that these wheels are of small size indicates that they may have been worn about the neck as amulets. But even in early culture the wheel was also put to an entirely different use. Widely prevalent over the earth and probably connected with ancient sun worship, is the custom of kindling a fire to celebrate the festival of the summer solstice. In ancient Mexico, tradition tells us, this fire was started by turning a notched disk of wood about a stake until the heat thus generated gave rise to fire—the same method of producing fire by friction that is still in use among primitive peoples. This fiery wheel was then rolled down a hill as an image of the sun, and later, when the custom had lost its original magical significance, as a symbol of the sun moving in the heavens. According to the report of W. Mannhardt, a remarkably similar custom existed in East Prussia not so very long ago. Perhaps the wheel that was worn about the neck as an amulet or article of adornment likewise had some connection with the idea that the sun was a celestial wheel rolling across the heavens. After the early sun cults had once created the rolling wheel in imitation of the sun and its movements, it was but a short step to the idea of securing regular, continuous movements by means of which some sort of work might be performed. An early application of this idea is to be found in the practice of spinning with distaff and whorl. This invention was credited even by the ancients to prehistoric times. Doubtless its origin belongs to the beginnings of the heroic age. This same early period, however, probably also used the wheel for transporting heavy articles. This was the original purpose of the one-wheeled barrow. It alone enabled the ancient Babylonians and Egyptians to overcome the difficulties of transporting by human agencies the mighty blocks of stone required for their temples and pyramids. From this it was not a far advance to the two-wheeled wagon. The barrow was pulled or pushed by men. The wagon, in contrast to the barrow, was apparently from the beginning an aristocratic mode of transit, never used by the common people. The two-wheeled wagon was in the first instance a vehicle of the gods. Later it served as the vehicle of the ruler, the terrestrial counterpart of the deity. Finally, the nobleman employed it in war, in going forth to battle. A vivid portrayal of battles in which such two-wheeled wagons played a part is presented in the Iliad. True, the wagon is here also, as a rule, only a means for carrying the hero to the scene of combat. The fighting itself is seldom done from it. Upon its arrival at the appointed place, the warrior dismounts, to try his strength, shield against shield, with his opponent. The general populace, however, always goes on foot.

This sketch gives us the main outlines of the history of the wagon. But how did the animal, first the ox and later the horse, come to be hitched to the wagon? Originally, the wagon bearing the image of the god was very probably drawn by men, as was likewise, in imitation of this, the chariot of the king. But the breeding of animals soon changed matters. Oxen were used for the purpose of drawing wagons much earlier than were horses. The horse did not appear until late in the history of civilization. There are no Egyptian pictures of horses that date back farther than the fifteenth dynasty, whereas those of cattle occur considerably earlier. In Oriental civilization, furthermore, the ass antedates the horse. In harmony with ancient custom, the ass even to-day continues, in the Orient, to be a favourite beast of burden as well as a riding animal. The horse seems to make its first appearance in history along with the Indo-Germanic tribes, who were probably indebted for it to the Turanian peoples of the Asiatic steppes. As a result of its superior speed, it then superseded its rivals in all the civilized countries of the ancient world. The Assyrian king went forth to the chase and the Homeric hero proceeded to battle in a chariot drawn by steeds. It was only later that the Greeks used the horse for saddle purposes, and not merely to draw the chariot. When this took place, equestrian combat came into favour among the aristocracy.

This development, however, was preceded not only by the taming of cattle but probably also by the use of the ox for drawing the wagon. How the latter came about may, of course, only be conjectured. The bull has remained unmanageable even to the present day; the attempt to hitch him to a wagon, therefore, must always have failed. The cow was not forced into this service—at least, not in those places where milk was valued. On the other hand, the castrated male animal is thoroughly suited to the task of drawing the wagon. It is stronger than the cow, and also more tractable. It is inconceivable, however, that castration was originally performed with the purpose of engendering these characteristics. Before there could be such a purpose, the results must already have been known—that is, the operation must already have been performed for other purposes. Eduard Hahn has offered a suggestion with reference to our problem. He has called attention to the ancient Asiatic cults of the Phrygian Cybele and the Syrio-Phœnician Astarte. These cults are similar to the vegetation festivals which, as was mentioned in the preceding chapter, may be found among the Pueblo peoples of America. Similar orgiastic phenomena recur wherever peoples are primarily concerned with agriculture and are anxious for the welfare of the grain. The beginnings of vegetation cults, found in the earlier period of hoe-culture, were succeeded by more developed deity cults, connected with plough-culture. The ecstatic motives associated with the tilling of the soil then extended their influence beyond the limits of vegetation cults proper and became universal elements of the deity cults. The powers shared by the numerous demoniacal beings of the more primitive cults were now centralized in a *single* goddess mother. The life-giving activity of the deity in connection with human procreation came to be of focal interest. The exaggerated development of cult ecstasy caused the orgy to become a form of self-mortification. The cult associates, especially the priests, lacerated and emasculated themselves in the fury of religious excitement. By becoming a permanent custom, this gave rise to a group of eunuchs consecrated to the service of the deity. These were doubtless the earliest eunuchs of history. In the guardians of Turkish harems and in the singers of the Sistine Chapel, survivals of these unrestrained cults of the past still exist. Now, when the group of emasculated priests paced beside the chariot of the goddess, they might easily have hit upon the idea of hitching a castrated animal to the wagon. But, however plausible this hypothesis may appear, in that it avoids the impossible assumption of an invention, it nevertheless leaves one question unanswered. Even though the castration of the priest may be understood as the result of the well-known effects of extreme religious excitement, the castration of the bull is not yet accounted for. Are we to suppose that the priest merely aimed to render the animal similar to himself? Neither ecstasy nor reflection could account for such a purpose. But there is another factor which has always been significant for cult, and which attained to increased importance precisely in the worship of the deity. I refer to *sacrifice*. In its highest stages, sacrifice assumes new forms, in that man offers either himself or parts of his own body, his blood, his hair, or a finger. A late survival of such sacrifices is to be found in a custom that is still prevalent in Catholic countries. Here it frequently occurs that a sick man lays a wax replica of the diseased part of his body upon the altar of the saint. This idea of sacrificing parts of one's own body is also exemplified in the self-emasculation practised by the Russian sect of Skopzi even in our own Christian age. Such sacrifice, moreover, may receive a wider application, so as to include, among the sacrificial objects, parts of the animal. Now at one time the kidneys with their connected organs were regarded as vehicles of the soul, and, as such, were sacrificed to the gods. The castration of the bull, therefore, may originally well have been regarded as the sacrifice of the most readily accessible of the favourite vehicles of the soul. Thus, it may have been in the case of the animal whose generative organs had been sacrificed to the deity that man first observed the change of characteristics which fitted the animal to be hitched to the chariot of the deity, and finally, through an extension of its sphere of usefulness, to draw the plough across the fields. This hypothesis, which presupposes the joint influence of orgiastic vegetation cults and ancient sacrificial usages, is, of course, not susceptible of positive demonstration. Nevertheless, to one concerned with the transition from ancient field cults to the agriculture of later times, the combination of conditions just indicated may reasonably be regarded as affording the basis of an hypothesis that is psychologically not improbable.

Whether the raising of the milch cow was coincident with the taming of the ox for the purposes of agriculture, and whether it came about as the result of a similar transformation of motives, it is hardly possible to determine. Though such changes are of more importance for the development of culture than are many of the campaigns and ancient folk wars of which history has preserved a record, no positive clue as to their origin has anywhere survived. All that we know with certainty is that the taming of the ox to draw the plough and the raising of the milch cow are not necessarily bound up with one another. For plough-culture and the milk industry are by no means always to be found together. In spite of his highly developed agriculture, the Chinaman loathes milk, whereas the Hindoo regards it as a valuable gift of civilization, prizing it not only because of the butter which he secures from it but especially as a food and as a sacrifice to the gods. The Israelites received the promise that Canaan was to be a land "that floweth with milk and honey." The latter expression suggests the cultural conditions of two widely different periods. Milk represents the most valuable product of later culture, while even primitive man regarded the honey which he gathered from the hives of wild bees as his most precious article of food.

Whatever may be the relation of the two factors in the domestication of cattle, whether the taming of the ox preceded the raising of cows or vice versa, the production of milk, at any rate, represents the more difficult and slower task. The taming of the ox is essentially an act that affects only the particular animal in question; even to-day it must be repeated in the case of every male calf ; the inheritance of acquired characteristics is here not operative. The cow, just as all female mammals in their natural condition, produces very little milk except during the period of suckling, and then only so much as is necessary for the support of her young. Only through efforts continued throughout generations and as a result of the inheritance of acquired characteristics could she be brought to that tremendous over-production of her secretion of which she has become capable. In this case, therefore, there must from the very outset have been a systematic striving toward the desired goal. It is not absolutely essential to assume a change of motives such as occurred in the taming of the ox ; from the very beginning there may have been an attempt to make personal use of the milk which Nature intended for the calf. Nevertheless, it is not impossible that religious motives here also played a part. This is made all the more probable by the fact that the cow, no less than the bull and the ox, was worshipped by many peoples even in the earliest period of deity cults. Such worship is particularly noteworthy, inasmuch as cattle were never favourite totem animals as was, for instance, the buffalo among the hunting peoples of the American prairies. Even though the general idea of animal cult was carried over from the totemic period to the beginnings of the agrarian deity cults, this animal cult was essentially changed, and it became associated with different objects. The latter are now no longer connected with the old totem beliefs that sprang, in part, from primitive animism ; they are determined entirely by the conditions of a later culture, one of whose essential elements is the domestication of cattle. The two fundamental constituents of this later culture, agriculture and the milk industry, are not everywhere equally prized. Hence there is a difference as regards the relative importance of the male and the female member of the species in the cult worship that is accorded to the most valued domestic animal of the new economic era. In the Opis-worship of the Egyptians, as well as in the Persian cult of Mithra, the bull was regarded as an incarnation of the supreme deity. In many sections of Northern Europe it is even to-day customary, at harvest-time, to bedeck an ox with ribbons and wreaths of flowers and to lead him in a festal procession. On the other hand, we find that the Vedas and the Avesta, in harmony with the high value which the ancient Indian and Iranian peoples place on milk, extol the cow as the most sacred of animals. In the first stages of the domestication of cattle, it was possible to gain only a small supply of milk, since its over-production could be developed but slowly; just for this reason, however, milk was all the more valuable. This may probably also throw light on the high value which was long placed on butter as a sacrificial gift. The attempt to secure this valuable product for sacrificial purposes may then itself in turn have reacted upon the milk industry. Thus, the two great advances in material culture that attend the heroic age—the tilling of the soil with the plough and the systematic endeavour to secure milk and its products—seem to be, in part, directly due to, and, in part, closely bound up with, motives of cult. External culture and inner religious impulses have always attested themselves to be elements of a totality all of whose parts are interrelated.

Of the new forms of industry which thus arose, the cultivation of the soil by means of the plough led to a further important change. This change was just as much an effect of the new conditions of life as it was an expression of the altered spirit of the times. The guidance of the plough is a task which prevents the field work from being any longer done in common, as it was at the height of hoe-culture and during the time of the origin of the great vegetation festivals of totemism. The individual must guide his own plough. The appearance of plough-culture *individualizes labour*. Just as the individual comes to the fore in political development and is extolled in legend as the founder of cities and States, so also is it the individual who cultivates the land. This individualistic tendency also gradually makes itself felt in the raising of domestic animals. Plough-culture gives rise to *private property* as regards both the soil and its products.

Here again, however, the new social order influences economic life, and both together produce further changes in external culture. Individual activity receives emphasis not alone in the cultivation of the soil but also in *warfare*. Primitive man was not at all familiar with war. He slew his enemy from an ambush, attacking him but seldom in open combat. In the totemic age, when actual weapons of war first made their appearance, tribal war was a strife of many against many. As yet the individual combatants were not sharply differentiated from one another. The masses clashed with each other in unregulated strife, without definite leadership or fixed system. Only with the dawn of the political era do we find regulated single combat. Such combat then becomes the decisive factor in warfare. Consider the Homeric description of the battles before the walls of Troy. The battle is decided by champions (*promachoi*). These alight from their chariots of war and fight, man against man. The masses stand in the background, hurling lances or stones. Their actions, however, have little importance. They flee as soon as their champion falls. The result of the battle thus depends upon individuals and not upon the masses. The weapons also conform to these altered conditions. In earlier times, practically none but long-distance weapons were used—the sling, the hurled spear, or the bow and arrow, weapons similar to those employed in the chase. Single combat necessitated weapons of close range—the axe, held fast in the hand, the lance, used as a thrusting weapon, and the sword. Instead of the long shield, covering almost the entire body—shields such as even the Australians and also the earliest Greeks carried—a small round shield was demanded by reason of the use of swords in fighting. Of the various weapons found at the zenith of the heroic age, therefore, the sword is the most characteristic. It is also the most typical creation of this period. It obviously originated through a gradual shortening of the lance, thus becoming a weapon specifically adapted for individual combat at close range. Thus, the tendency toward the assertion of individual personality made itself felt in warfare and in weapons, just as it did in the State, in agriculture, and in the cult of personal gods.

Similar fundamental factors underlie the last great cultural change. This we have already touched upon in our discussion of agriculture, namely, the *rise of private property*. Following inevitably upon the appearance of private property are distinctions in wealth; these lead to differences in social position. In the totemic age, the contrasting conditions of rich and poor are, on the whole, not in particular evidence; even towards the decline of the period, indeed, they are only beginning to arise. Every man is the equal of the other. Only the chiefs and a small number of the older men have a superior rank. This rank, moreover, is not due to property but to the services which ability and experience enable them to render, or to the reverence which custom metes out to them. It is not until the heroic age that a propertied class becomes differentiated from a class owning little or nothing. This change is due in an important measure to the folk migrations that inaugurate the beginning of the new age. The propertied class derives from the victorious conquerors; the original inhabitants are without property. In the warfare connected with these migrations, slaves are captured; these are employed particularly in the cultivation of the soil. Thus, the more aristocratic are exalted by their greater possessions above those who have less property. As free individuals, however, both of these classes are superior to the slaves, who, similarly to the animals used in agriculture, are themselves regarded as the possession of the free and the rich.

Bound up with these social distinctions is the *division of labour* which now arises. The landowner no longer himself manufactures the tools which he needs or the weapons with which he goes to war. A class of artisans is formed, consisting partly of those who have little property, and partly of slaves. This differentiation of labour leads to *two* phenomena which long continue to influence the development of culture. I refer to *trade* and *colonization*. The former consists in the transmission of the products of labour; the latter, in the migration of a part of the people itself into distant places, where the same conditions that led to the founding of the mother State result in daughter States. In the totemic age, there were no colonies. Extensive as were the wanderings of the Papuans, the Malays, the Polynesians, and of some of the American and African tribes, these peoples never established colonies; moreover, the group which settled in distant places always lost its connection with the mother group. True, new living conditions were sought and found, and, through mixture with the native populations, new races were produced. Nevertheless, it was not until the political age that those parts of a particular people which settled down in foreign lands continued to retain a consciousness of connection with the mother race.

Of the two above-mentioned elements of the newer culture, commerce naturally preceded colonization. Of all civilized peoples, the Semitic race was the first to open up great channels of trade. Phœnician commerce dates back to the earliest records of history. Even the Mycenian graves of Greece contain gold jewelry of Phœnician workmanship. Spacially, the trade relations of the ancient Phœnicians extended over the whole of the known Occident. It is characteristic of the Semitic race, however, that they rarely undertook actual colonization. Trade and all that is connected with it, the industrial ardour necessary to supply the objects of trade and to exchange them for grain and other natural products, has always been their chosen sphere. The Indo-Germanic races, on the other hand, have naturally inclined to colonization from early times on. In the foremost rank were the Greeks, with their colonies in Thrace, Asia Minor, Southern Italy, and Sicily. These colonial groups, moreover, always retained their connection with the mother people. Thus, the earliest culture of the Greeks was that of the colonies in Asia Minor. Later, the colonies of southern Italy exercised a strong reaction on the mother country in science and art. It was not until relatively late that the highest cultural development of the mother country followed upon that of these outposts of Greek culture.

3. The Development of Political Society

The fundamental characteristics of totemic society appear to be purely a product of nature. This is especially true of totemic tribal organization. Its simple regularity and the constant recurrence of essentially the same characteristics are the natural result of original conditions of life that were universally prevalent. A horde split up into two halves. In the simplest cases, such as we have noticed in our account of the Australians, tribal organization remained limited to this dual division. The condition that brought about this organization arose as soon as a horde that spoke the same language spread out over a fairly broad territory. The same process of division might then repeat itself in the case of each of the two halves. This gave rise to a clan organization of four or eight divisions, as found among most of the Australian tribes, and frequently also in Melanesia. Such an organization was developed also by the original inhabitants of North America, although the totemic basis here degenerated and became essentially an external form. Totemic tribal organization is unquestionably a phenomenon that arises with immanent necessity; indeed, one might almost say that its appearance involves no co-operation on the part of man himself. The division takes place of itself; it is a result of the natural conditions underlying the propagation and growth of society.

From the very beginning of the heroic age on, the development of political society gave rise to phenomena that were fundamentally different from those of earlier times. The irreconcilability of this fact with the view, still held by historians and philosophers, that the State represents the earliest form of an ordered community life, is evident. Such theories were possible only when the whole of totemic culture was as yet a *terra incognita*. Totemic tribal organization cannot possibly be interpreted as an incomplete and undeveloped form of the State. Rather is it true that totemic and political societies are completely different in kind. Essentially different characteristics and conditions of origin demarcate them from one another, even though there are certain hybrid forms, representing primarily a partial survival of older tribal customs within the newly established political society. Now, in so far as mental history always involves a regular order of development, one would, of course, be justified in maintaining that human society also necessarily eventuates in the State—that is, in a political society. Indeed, this may perhaps be the meaning of Aristotle's statement that man is a "political animal." This statement may be interpreted to refer to a *predisposition* rather than to an inherited characteristic. Nevertheless, Aristotle's view that the State gradually developed out of the family and the village community is in contradiction with the actual facts. To read back a tendency toward political development into the very beginnings of human society, moreover, results in a failure to give proper emphasis to those essential differences which distinguish the great periods of this development—differences which at the crucial points assume the form of antitheses. Furthermore, we must not overlook the fact that there are peoples who have even as yet not progressed beyond totemic tribal organization and who will very possibly never advance to the formation of a State, particularly in case this depends upon their own initiative. On the other hand, it is doubtless to be assumed that those peoples who later acquired a political organization at one time possessed a totemic tribal structure. The higher stage of political organization, however, obviously differs fundamentally from that which preceded it. The older motives have been superseded by such as are connected with the great folk migrations and tribal fusions, and with the changes consequent upon them. True, when the time was ripe, these migrations and fusions of peoples came to pass with the same necessity as did the original division of the primitive horde into two halves. Nevertheless, a new set of conditions became operative. These, of course, arose in a regular course of development out of the most primitive modes of life, and yet they were not directly derived from them. The creative power characteristic of all mental activity here manifested itself, not in the performance of miracles, but in a constant engenderment of new motives out of the interaction of existing motives with changing external conditions of life. In consequence of this constant change of motives and of existing conditions, even totemic culture made numerous attempts in the direction of political organization. Such steps were taken particularly by the semi-cultural peoples of America, who possess a relatively high civilization. It is precisely in the case of these peoples that it is instructive to notice the contrast between this political tendency and the original tribal organization.

The difference between the two fundamental forms of society, the totemic and the political, is most strikingly evident in the case of their most external characteristic—namely, in the *numbers* according to which society as a whole, as well as in its parts, is organized and divided. These numbers are the expression of inner motives ; hence they form a basis from which we may draw conclusions concerning the latter. In the case of totemic tribal organization, these motives are apparently very simple ; natural expansion over a broader territory leads to separation into groups, and this of itself gives rise to the customary division into two, four, and eight parts. How different and more complicated from its very beginnings is the organization of political society ! Here also the development proceeds according to law, and yet there is not a constant recurrence of the same motive as is in the case of totemic tribal organization. On the contrary, we find a continuous fluctation between contradictory phenomena, and the frequent appearance of new motives. Early, and still partly legendary, tradition tells us of an organization of society on the basis of the number *twelve*. This mode of organization seems to have emanated from the Babylonians. They were the people who first attempted to govern human affairs in accordance with celestial phenomena. These they observed, not in the unsystematic, imaginative, mythological manner of the natural peoples of Polynesia and America, but with the aid of astronomical instruments. True, the science of the Babylonians was also still based on mythological foundations. These mythological features, however, were combined with the idea of an all-embracing, divine rule of law. The endeavour to find this law and order in the starry sky, the greatest and most sublime sight that the human eye may behold, resulted in observations that were scientific and exact. Thus, the union of the two ideas led with a sort of inner necessity to the acceptance of the number twelve as a norm. The application of this norm to human relations was a direct result of the belief that it was of divine origin. The Babylonian calendar, whose fundamental principles, in spite of numerous reforms, have retained their authority even down to the present, was the first to emphasize the principle of bringing the courses of the sun and moon into an ordered numerical relation for the purpose of reckoning time. Taking as their point of departure the position of the sun at the vernal equinox, and following the movements of the moon until the sun returned to the same position, the Babylonians found that twelve revolutions of the moon were equivalent to one of the sun. While this observation is in reality, of course, only approximately true, to the first astronomers it might have appeared sufficiently exact to be regarded as the law of a divine world order. Thus, the year came to be divided into twelve months; and, since the moon presents four phases in each month, first quarter, full moon, last quarter, and new moon—an observation which long antedates astronomical calculation—the month was at once divided into four parts. Since the month has approximately twenty-eight days, the result was a *week*, comprising *seven days*. This number, therefore, was not, as has sometimes been erroneously assumed, derived from the seven planets. Rather is it true, conversely, that the number of the planets was, with a certain arbitrariness, first fixed at seven after this number, as well as twelve, had come to be regarded as *sacred*, because of its relation to the movements of the sun and moon. These numbers were believed to be written by the gods themselves in flaming letters on the sky. To the Babylonian, the sky furnished a revelation of the laws that should govern terrestrial life. The number twelve, especially, was adopted as the basis of the organization of human society. Of this oldest form of division, however, only meagre and occasional survivals have remained. We may refer to the legendary twelve tribes of pre-exilic Israel—later a source of much difficulty to Talmudic scholars, inasmuch as these tribes are not to be found in history—and also to the twelve gods of Greece, the twelve Apostles, etc. But the number twelve has not merely left its traces in legend ; it has also inscribed itself in the records of history. Thus, the Athenian population originally comprised twelve divisions, there being four clans (*phyles*), each of which was composed of three *phratries*. Similarly, the colonial territory of the Greeks in Asia Minor is said to have included twelve Ionic cities. Moreover, even in later times, the Amphictyonic League, which undertook the protection of the Delphic oracle, consisted of twelve amphictyons, though this, it is true, was also connected with the division of time, each of the twelve tribal groups being entrusted with the guardianship of the shrine for one month in the year. With few unimportant exceptions, however, the number twelve, which was at one time probably very widely regnant, has lost its influence. Its place in the organization of society as well as in the regulation of other aspects of human life has been taken by a numerical system that still dominates our entire culture—the *decimal* system. Even prior to the age of Columbus, the decimal system made its appearance in certain more civilized parts of the Western world where the duodecimal system was never known. That the former originated independently in different places, is rendered all the more likely by the fact that even primitive man used his ten fingers as an aid in counting, in spite of the fact that he had not as yet formed words for numbers greater than three or four. But, however natural this method of counting may be, its application to the organization of the group and the division of peoples nevertheless represents a *deliberately adopted* plan. If possible, this is even more true here than in the case of the duodecimal system. We are now face to face with the wide difference that separates political society from totemic tribal organization. In developing on the principle of dual division, the latter resembles a natural process which runs its own course apart from any operation of conscious intention, even though directly influenced, of course, by the general conditions of human life. The organization of society according to the number ten, on the other hand, can be interpreted only as an intentional act. Hence history not infrequently brings this form of organization into direct association with the names of individual lawgivers, with Clisthenes of Athens or Servius Tullius of Rome. No doubt, a basis for this new order had been prepared by the general conditions of a society which had progressed beyond the totemic stage. Its systematic introduction, however, and the series of decimal subdivisions that ensued, are only conceivable as a legislative act emanating from a personal will. In the formation of social groups, no less than in the classification and enumeration of external objects of nature, there may at times have been some vacillation of choice between the duodecimal and the decimal systems. In its application to human society, however, the decimal system finally prevailed. Indeed, the simple means of counting afforded by our ten fingers supplanted the system suggested by the firmament in every field of use, except in connection with celestial phenomena themselves and with the reckoning of time, which was directly based on the observation of these phenomena. That the victory of the decimal principle was due merely to the practical necessity of choosing the principle that was simplest and most convenient, is shown by the fact that ten was never a sacred number, as was twelve. It has a purely terrestrial and human origin. In the field of the practical necessities of life, man was victorious over the gods. Perhaps, therefore, the organization of society on the decimal principle reflects also the triumph of the secular State over theocracy. The decimal principle likewise exercised a certain influence upon the division of time, and it is surely not accidental that such influence coincides with epochs that are strongly characterized by a secularization of human interests. As early as the sixth century B.C., the great political organizer of Athens, Clisthenes, made an attempt to divide the year into ten months instead of twelve. The attempt miscarried, just as did the analogous one on the part of the first French Republic to introduce a week of ten days. As a matter of fact, objective measurements of time are derived from the heavens and not from man. On the other hand, our measurement of terrestrial spaces and our grouping of populations depend entirely upon ourselves, and therefore naturally conform to human characteristics. In these cases, it is the decimal system that is used. In view of the fact that the number ten was deliberately adopted, this number has been thought to represent an idea that emanated from a single source. Since the organization effected by Clisthenes and that of Servius Tullius in Rome fall approximately within the same century, it has been believed that in these cases, especially, we may assume this fundamental idea of division to have been borrowed. The very extensive distribution of the decimal system, however, militates against the probability of this supposition. Thus, the Book of Exodus no longer speaks of the legendary twelve tribes of Israel but tells of only *ten* tribes. We likewise hear of groups of one hundred, and of more extensive groups consisting of one thousand. These divisions also recur among the Germanic peoples, and in the far-distant realm of the Peruvian Incas. Among the latter, however, there are also distinct traces of a totemic tribal organization that antedated the invasion of the Incas. This was the foundation upon which the Inca kings and their officials finally reared an organization consisting of groups of ten, one hundred, and one thousand—indeed, the latter were even brought together to form groups of ten thousand. In certain cases, such systems may perhaps have been introduced from without or may, in part, have been acquired through imitation. Nevertheless, the supposition that they all emanated from a single region is doubtless just as improbable as is the view that the decimal system in general had but a single origin. This new grouping of the population is closely bound up with the conditions of political society. It is dependent upon *two* motives, which, though not universally operative at first, became so the very moment that political society took its rise. The first motive is of a subjective nature. It consists in an increased facility in the use of the decimal mode of counting, as a result of which larger groups, consisting of multiples of ten, are formed: besides the single group of ten, it must have become possible to conceive of groups of one hundred, one thousand, and, in rare cases, even of one hundred thousand. The other motive is objective in character. There are changes in the external conditions of life such as to demand more comprehensive and at the same time more highly organized divisions than prevailed in the natural tribal organization of the preceding age. In two distinct directions does the decimal system prove readily applicable. One is in the distribution of landed property. With the appearance of plough-culture, land gradually came to be largely converted into personal property. It was all the more necessary, therefore, for the individual to unite with others for the sake of protection and aid. Thus arose the mark-community. This naturally centred about that part of the territory which, because it was not put under the plough but was reserved for common use as well as common care, temporarily remained common property—namely, the pasture and woodland. Thus, the *mark-community* was inevitable: it resulted from the new method of cultivating the soil which brought with it a combination of personal property with common ownership. The size of the community was, of course, determined by the relation which these two forms of ownership sustained to each other, being dependent upon the fact that the amount of common property had to correspond with the number of individual owners who shared its use. The right proportion of these two sorts of property could be determined only by experience and reflection. Once ascertained, it was but natural to adopt this proportion more generally, in connection with more extensive groups of people. Here the decimal organization into groups of tens and hundreds, to which subjective influences naturally tended, promised to be convenient also from the standpoint of objective conditions.

Independently of other factors the mark-community might have permitted certain diversities in size. The groups were rendered uniform, however, through the influence of another organization, whose divisions, on the one hand, were necessarily identical with the mark-communities but, on the other hand, possessed by their very nature a strong inherent tendency toward regularity of size. I refer to the *military organization*, which was created by the political society in the interest of self-protection. In the early part of the heroic period, the individual champion was doubtless of such pre-eminent importance that the masses formed but a somewhat unorganized background. Homer presents such a picture, though his account is perhaps not so much a faithful representation of actual conditions as the result of the individualizing tendency of poetic narrative. But just as the masses very soon gain greater prominence in political life, so also do they in warfare. This encourages tactical organization. At this stage of political and military development, therefore, companies of one hundred, and soon afterwards groups of one thousand, are formed, and are organized as the chief divisions of the army. That these groups be always of approximately equal size is required by military tactics ; that the group of one hundred is the tactical unit of which the other divisions are composed, is due to the circumstance that such a group is not too large to permit of being directed by a single leader ; that the number is an even one hundred results solely from the tendency toward decimal enumeration. Since the political society is composed of individuals who are, as a rule, both mark-associates and companions in war, the two groups coalesce. The distribution of property and territorial and military organization are the determining factors in political society

Political society thus acquires a new basis. The conditions determining its character are very different from those that underlie totemic tribal organization. Quite naturally, therefore, the tribal system disappears with the rise of the State ; it is at best but fragments of it that survive in names, cult-alliances, or in bits of custom. On the other hand, the new organization exercises an influence upon all the relations of life. In part, it effects changes in existing institutions ; in part, it creates new institutions, which unite to give the political age its characteristic stamp. We have spoken of the peaceful arts of agriculture, which provide for the maintenance of society, and of the military organization, reared upon agriculture to assure safety and protection from without. There are primarily *three* additional features that characterize political society, especially at its inception. The first of these is a *reorganization of the family*. The other two are genuinely new creations, if we except certain sporadic beginnings that occur in the transitional culture. They consist, on the one hand, in the *differentiation of classes and of occupations*—both of which arise in one and the same course of development—and, on the other, in the *foundation of cities*. Doubtless this order of sequence also approximately indicates the successive steps in the establishment of the new political organization. The reorganization of the family inaugurates this development ; it is terminated by the founding of cities, for cities are the centres from which the management of the State is conducted and which mediate intercourse between the separate regions ; following upon the former and preceding the latter, is the differentiation of classes and of occupations—a result of property conditions and of military organization.

4. Family Organization within Political Society.

Wherever primitive man has been protected against foreign influences, as we have seen, he apparently always lives in monogamy. This mode of marriage is continued in the totemic age, and is the fundamental mode from which all others are deviations. These deviations we found to be the two forms of polygamy—polyandry and polygyny. In the presence of these various marriage practices, firmly established family bonds are impossible. Striking evidence of the recedence of the family as compared with the social bond, is offered by the men's club, that widely prevalent institution of the totemic age. True, the individual member of the men's club may have his own wife who lives in her particular hut, but there is no common life of husband and wife such as is essential for a true family. In certain cases, of course, marriage conditions approximate somewhat more closely to a true family life, yet the development is hindered by the overshadowing polygyny. But the beginning of the political age marks the rise of a new form of monogamy. The *enlarged monogamous family*, the so-called ancient or joint family, makes its appearance. The joint family, which is characteristic of the heroic era, takes the place of the clan. Though the latter also survives for a time, it more and more loses its importance and finally disappears altogether. Now the clan, as well as the joint family, is composed of individuals of the same ancestry—that is, of blood relations, in the wider sense—even though, in exceptional cases, it also includes members of other clans or even tribal strangers. The recedence of the clan in favour of the joint family must therefore be regarded as a process in which a limited number of closer blood relatives separate from the clan and gradually attain the dominant influence within society. Such a development presupposes first of all a sharper demarcation of the individual family. Hence the joint family directly impresses one as being an extension of the individual family. As a rule, for example, a joint family includes *three* generations: father, son, and grandchild. This series of generations terminates with the third, because the oldest male member retains the authority over the joint family only so long as there is no generation younger than grandchildren. Though a great-grandfather is honoured as the oldest member of the family, the authority over the joint family passes down to the son who has become a grandfather. Moreover, nature allows such cases as this but rarely. The life-span of three generations is approximately a century; and the average life of man is such that it happens but seldom that those who are living at any one time will outspan a century. Thus, the fact that the ancient family comprised three generations may be due to the natural limit of life, which does not seem to have changed essentially since the beginnings of civilization. The family organization under discussion, therefore, is characterized, in the first place, by monogamy; secondly, by the dominance of the man within the single family; and thirdly, by the inclusion of three generations under the authority of the oldest member of the family. This third characteristic has frequently caused the typical joint family to be called the '*patriarchal* family.' Since it was true even of the clan that the older men exercised the decisive influence, the clan may be regarded as preparing the way for a patriarchal order. Such clan alliances, for example, as the Germanic kinship groups, in which the fact of the blood relationship of the members receives particularly strong emphasis, form a sort of transition between the clan and the joint family. In the joint family, it is no longer the older generation as such that is dominant, but the *oldest individual*. This change, as a result of which authority becomes vested in an individual, is paralleled by that which leads to individual rulership within the State. Thus, totemic tribal organization is doubly exposed to disintegration, from below and from above. On the one hand, the patriarchal joint family undermines the leadership of the clan-elders. On the other hand, the clans, together with the tribes whose divisions they form, are shorn of their power; they become fused into one group which, with the rise of political society, passes under the rulership of a single chieftain. It is particularly important to notice that, when the joint family emerges and clan organization is consequently dissolved, one of the most important functions of the more restricted clan alliances, so far as concerns the inner life of society, passes from the clan to the joint family. I refer to *blood-revenge.* Not until it underwent many changes did retribution come to be an affair of the State. Thus, the patriarchal family brings to completion a twofold series of changes, whose gradual beginnings may be discerned as early as the previous age. These are, in the first place, the displacement of maternal descent by *paternal descent,* and, secondly, the development of *chieftainship.* The latter at once concludes and annuls totemic tribal organization. The motives to the former show how untrue to the real nature of the difference between the two social institutions it is to speak of the contrast between mother-*right* and father-*right,* or even between maternal *rule* and paternal *rule,* instead of referring to the transition as one from maternal *descent* to paternal *descent.* Mother-right is to be found at most in a limited sense, as applying to certain rights of the kinship community and, connected with these, at a later time, to the inheritance of property ; mother-*rule* never occurs, or at most is an abnormal and exceptional phenomenon having scarcely any connection with maternal descent as such. The motives to maternal descent, as we have seen, are totally unrelated to the question of dominance within the family ; they are the direct result of a separation of the sexes, which manifests itself likewise in the men's clubs. Paternal descent, on the other hand, is from the very outset based on paternal rule. In the form of father-right, paternal rule prevails even in the case of the primitive monogamous family. Its original source is the natural physical superiority of man ; later, it derives its main strength from the fact—reflected also in the origin of chieftainship—that the general affairs of peace, as well as of war with hostile tribes, become subject to the authority of leaders. This latter factor comes to reinforce the former at that stage of development, particularly, which is characterized by the dissolution of totemic institutions and the re-emergence of the monogamous family. It is this change, together with the growing influence of chieftainship, that marks the beginning of the political age.

Thus, the restoration of the monogamous family came as a result of political organization. The general course of development was the same everywhere, though the particular steps varied greatly. It was especially in connection with the rise of the patriarchal joint family, which is intermediate between the kinship group and the individual family, that obstructing influences sometimes manifested themselves. In such cases, the course of development was at once deflected directly towards the individual family. A patriarchal family organization of a sharply defined character appeared very early among many of the Semitic tribes, particularly among the Israelites. Of the Indo-Germanic peoples, it was especially the Romans who long preserved the patriarchal system ; among the Greeks and the Germanic peoples, it had already disappeared in early times in favour of the single family. That which preserved the joint family was probably the force of tradition, coupled with reverence of age ; the single family reflects a sense of freedom on the part of individuals. This brings out clearly the essential difference between the original monogamy, which was due to natural instinct and the simple conditions of primitive life, and the monogamy that was reinstituted as a result of the new tendencies of political society. In the former case, no progress was made beyond the natural starting-point, namely, the single family ; in the latter case, the joint family mediated the transition between the dissolution of clans and the establishment of political society. Inasmuch as the acts of primitive man were largely determined by instincts, the original monogamy is not to be interpreted as conformity to a norm. The reason for the almost universal occurrence of monogamous marriage is to be found in the uniformity of the conditions of life and of the social impulses. The monogamy of the political age, on the other hand, is confronted by all those conflicting tendencies which had previously given rise to the various polygamous marriage-unions of totemic society. *One* of these modes of marriage especially, namely, *polygyny*, finds favourable conditions of development in the new political order. It receives fresh impetus as a result of that very dominance of man which brought about the transition from the maternal descent of earlier times to paternal descent. Polyandry and group-marriage, on the other hand, have by this time disappeared, either entirely or, at least, with rare exceptions. Moreover, the character of polygyny has changed. This is apparent from the distinction between *chief wife* and *secondary wife*—a distinction which has, indeed, an analogy in certain phenomena of the totemic period, but which, as a result of the conditions of public life, now rests upon an entirely different basis. The chief wife is taken from one's own tribe ; the secondary wife belongs to a strange tribe, being, in many cases, a slave captured in war. Thus, these changes in polygyny reflect the warlike character of the age, as well as a growing tendency toward a return to monogamy. On the other hand, however, we also discern certain tendencies of a retrogressive nature. These occur particularly within Islamitic culture, whenever the difference between chief and secondary wives is either annulled or is subordinated to the will of the husband. Such deviations from the general trend of development are usually attributed to the influence of personalities. It is not impossible, however, that they are due in this case to the fact that Islamism spread to peoples of totemic culture. But in other departments of life also, remnants and traces of totemic culture have passed down to the heroic era. A striking example appears in the case of the Spartan State. The fact that the men lived in the city, engaged in military drill and political affairs, while the women, together with the slaves, cultivated the fields outside of the city, clearly betrays the influence of the ancient institution of the men's club.

5. The Differentiation of Classes.

We have seen that the family assumes a new status within political society. It comes to be a compact unit, contrasting markedly with the groups composed of the same sex—in particular, the men's clubs—that dominated the preceding period. The *differentiation of classes* was a no less potent factor in the development of political society. Its beginnings, no doubt, go back to the declining period of totemic tribal institutions, but only in the political age does it become an important influence in social organization. This is due to *two* conditions, which are themselves the direct result of the folk migrations that mark the beginning of the political age. The first of these conditions consists in changes affecting property rights; the other, in the subjection of the native populations by the more energetic immigrants. The origin of property, as is well known, is even to-day generally traced, from an abstract juristic point of view, to the occupancy of an ownerless piece of land. This theory, however, is too abstract to be generally true. Above all, it presupposes the existence of ownerless land. But this is seldom to be found. Even when a migrating people occupies new lands, it, as a rule, conquers a territory that was previously in the possession of other tribes. If, therefore, we have in mind the sort of property that was most significant for the development of political culture, we should trace its origin to an *expropriation of earlier owners* rather than to an occupation of ownerless land. Contradicting the abstract theory, moreover, is the fact that it is not the individual who becomes the owner of property through such occupation, but the *entire tribe*, the people that has immigrated and has dispossessed the original inhabitants. Property, therefore, was originally *common property*. True, even in early times, it was no longer all of the land that was held in common ownership. Nevertheless, the conditions of ownership that have emerged in the course of the development of political society give unmistakable evidence of having originated in common ownership. Even up to fairly recent times, woodland and meadow have remained, either entirely or in part, common property; usually there is also a special temple-property set apart for purposes of cult. Everything goes to show that these cases are to be regarded as remnants of a common property that was at one time more comprehensive, and not as the result of joining pieces of property that were at one time owned by individuals. The latter hypothesis is contradicted by the whole direction of development of private property. Interacting with changes in property rights are racial differences. The conquering immigrant peoples subjugate the native races or crowd them back. All the cultural peoples that possess a political organization are the product of folk mixtures. The subjugation of an original population may lead to varying results, depending on the racial difference between the peoples involved. If this difference is very great and the numerical relation makes the absorption of the one by the other impossible, there develops a distinction of castes, as in India, where the lower castes are clearly distinguishable from the higher, even as to physical characteristics. The situation is radically different where there is less divergence between the two populations. In such cases, racial distinctions do not occur, or at least only to a small extent ; in their stead, we find differences with respect to property and power. The conquering race becomes a privileged class ; those who are subjugated form a class of dependents who possess fewer rights. There is no impassable barrier between the two classes, however, as there is in the caste system. The more a fairly unitary folk-type emerges from the racial fusions, and the more other factors than descent come into prominence—such as common interest in internal order and external defence, or a remarkable personal ability on the part of individual leaders of the lower classes—the greater the tendency, on the one hand, towards the abolition of traditional differences, and, on the other, towards an increased recognition of personal achievement as the basis of social standing. Such social struggles as occurred in the history of Greece and Rome from their early days on, are particularly illuminating as regards this point, for they exhibit clearly the motives that were originally involved —motives that later everywhere become more complicated.

From the very outset these motives exert a potent influence on property relations. The occupied territory first becomes the common property of the separate divisions of the immigrant tribe. The individual, however, vies with his tribal associates for the possession of the territory, and the new agricultural conditions connected with the introduction of cattle and of the plough favour division of the land. In addition to the superior ability of an immigrant race, it is its superior civilization that assures to it the supremacy over the native races. This superior civilization, however, involves a strong tendency toward individual industry, and thus toward the differentiation of personal property from common property. The success which the individual owner enjoys in his labour develops in him a consciousness of freedom, and this leads him to compete with his tribal associates both in the acquisition of property and in the attainment of power over the native population. Thus, the division of common property is succeeded by an inequality of personal property—an inequality which, from the very beginning, shows an unconquerable tendency to increase. This tendency is fostered by the fact that political organization makes it possible for individuals to exercise a certain control over common affairs. Property considerations become more and more decisive as regards class distinctions. In addition to descent from privileged ancestors, it is property that gives the individual his social position. An individual belonging to a people that at one time formed a class without rights, may rise to the ranks of the privileged classes, or, if the significance attached to birth continues to be maintained, he, together with those like him, may at any rate attain to an independent influence in public life. Property, however, not only affords increased rights ; it also entails greater obligations. The wealthy possess a better military equipment, and are therefore enlisted in the more efficient, but also the more dangerous, divisions of the army. They are entrusted with leadership in war as well as with authority in times of peace. Individual initiative makes itself felt, and this, coupled with the opportunity for the exercise of such initiative, causes political development to appear, from an external point of view, as a series of separate voluntary acts on the part of individual personal leaders. This, however, is not the real truth of the situation so far as its inner motives are concerned. The heroic age is the epoch in which the action of the masses, impulsive and under the sway of environmental conditions, is more and more subjected to the direction of individual leaders who have become clearly conscious of the tendencies inherent in the social body. For this reason the heroic age is pre-eminently the *era of personalities.* Just as the personal god is dominant in mythology and religious cult, so the human personality plays the leading rôle in the State, and particular, outstanding individuals determine the conditions that regulate external life.

As personality comes into prominence, however, conflicts inevitably arise between individuals who feel themselves called to be the vehicles of this personal power. Political society was not only created by war, but it also continues to remain a theatre where conflicts are fought with changing fortunes. Together with the effort to abolish class distinctions, moreover, there gradually comes a demand for equality of rights. As a result, the influence of dominating personalities, even though never eliminated, is more and more subject to changing conditions. Thus regarded, the general course of events is indicated by reference to *two* phenomena: firstly, by the development of the State and of the judicial system, and, secondly, by the transformations which the character of the hero undergoes in the course of history. The first of these phenomena will presently be discussed in some detail; the second, which puts its stamp upon the particular periods of history in question, consists in the gradual displacement of the warrior-hero by the hero of peace. Even legend indicates that this is the sequence of the qualities that are supremely prized in personality. Thus, in the legend of the kings of Rome, the warlike Romulus, founder of the city, is followed by Numa Pompilius, the organizer of religious cult, who is succeeded in due time by the secular lawgiver, Servius Tullius. The warrior-hero appears first; he suggests the origin of political society in warfare. The founder of deity cults is his immediate successor. The law-giver, or the political hero in the true sense of the word, stands at the zenith of the age. The warrior initiates, whereas the legislator completes the organization of society. Then commences the age of citizenship, which no longer entertains a hero-ideal as such but, instead, prizes civic virtues. On this plane of culture, the general demands of political life and of cult are augmented by the particular duties which grow out of the position which the individual occupies within society. The position itself is conditioned primarily by the rise of *differences of vocation*.

6. The Differentiation of Vocations.

The above discussion will already have indicated the general significance of the differentiation of vocations in the development of political society. While the origin of classes is coincident with the rise of the State, separate vocations appear only at its zenith. At first there were no distinctions of vocation. The pursuits of war and politics were common to all free men ; and, while admitting of class distinctions, they allowed no vocational differences. The priesthood alone represented a class which followed a specific vocation, while also engaging in other occupations, particularly in politics. The earliest forms of specialized vocations were foreshadowed even in the totemic age. In the heroic period, they merely adapt themselves to the new social order resulting from the rise of a ruling class and the consequent class distinctions. Under the influence of deity cults, moreover, the social position of the priesthood changes, as do also its vocational practices. The transformations in cult are an important factor in elevating the class and the profession concerned in its administration, securing for them a more or less important, and in some cases a dominant, influence upon political life. In contrast with this, all forms of human labour not connected with politics and warfare are *degraded*. This results in occupational differences, which are henceforth closely bound up with class distinctions. The depreciation of which we speak, however, is not of sudden occurrence, nor does it appear everywhere to the same extent. The conditions that give rise to political society also involve a participation in the pursuits of politics and warfare on the part of the freeman, who, as an agriculturist, breeds his own domestic animals and guides his plough over the fields. Due to these same conditions, moreover, agriculture maintains a respected position even in later times, partly, no doubt, as a result of the fact that the free farmer continues to enjoy the privilege of participating in political and military affairs. Various accessory vocations come to be sundered out from the tasks of the early agriculturist, who, originally, himself manufactured the implements required for his work and was thus the primitive artisan. Political activity and the equally esteemed military vocation come more and more to be given the place of highest honour. The occupation of the farmer and that of the wealth-accumulating merchant, however, are also held in high regard, doubtless because of the growing desire for property. The independent task of the artisan, as well as art—the latter at first scarcely distinguishable from artisanship—are either left to the dependent population and slaves or, after class distinctions are well developed, are given over to the lower class of citizens as occupations of less esteem.

But in the case of vocational distinctions, just as in that of class differentiation, the process of depreciation is succeeded by a tendency toward *equalization*. This is due to a general shift in values. The rhapsodist of Homeric times, though welcomed as a guest by the superior classes, was not himself regarded by them as a companion of equal rank. It is only gradually that the value placed on an art becomes transferred to the artist himself. That this occurs is due in an important measure to the fact that the arts of outstanding significance—gymnastics, poetry, and music—are not practised merely by a specific profession, but are also favourite occupations of the warrior or the statesman in his hours of leisure. The respect accorded the artist is gradually extended to such other arts as already constitute vocational labour; as external culture becomes more refined, even the artisan wins a growing esteem, through his decoration of weapons, implements, and clothing. In the case of the arts that require a particularly high degree of vocational training, it is significant to note that, in spite of the high estimate placed on his product, the artist himself is able to rise but slowly above the plane of the mere artisan. Thus, the measure of esteem accorded to the arts gradually diminishes, according as we pass from those that spring up spontaneously, solely from inner impulse, to those that minister to the satisfaction of needs. The immediate cause for this gradation of values probably lies in the fact that political activity, which here forms the mediating link, is itself of the nature of a free vocation, requiring the exercise particularly of mental capacities. For this reason, however, the regard in which the various occupations are held tends to be equalized according as class distinctions disappear. The latter, however, occurs in proportion as all citizens come to acquire equal privileges in the exercise of political rights. To the majority, indeed, political activity remains but a secondary vocation, being overshadowed by the main occupation, which requires the greater amount of attention. Because of its political character, however, it is the secondary vocation that primarily determines the social position of the individual. The fact that all citizens come to participate in political activity, therefore, even though failing to equalize the esteem in which the various occupations were held, nevertheless caused the disappearance of the distinctions in personal status which occupational differences originally involved.

7. The Origin of Cities.

The differentiation of classes and vocations is conditioned, in a large measure, by a change in the spacial distribution of the population. This change is a result of the rise of political society, and comes to be the outstanding external characteristic of the State as soon as the latter begins to assume definite form. I have in mind the *foundation of cities*. In the totemic age, there were no cities, but at most fair-sized groups of huts or houses, forming villages. These village settlements were all equally independent; they differed at most as regards spacial extent. But the city, in its *original* form, always exercised control over a smaller or larger stretch of territory, consisting either of separate farms or of villages with the territory belonging to them. As the seat of political power, the city was an infallible indication of the existence of the State. Hence it is that those who discuss the original forms of political society are not infrequently led to regard State and city as identical. Such an identification, however, is not at all justifiable. Even in their beginnings the Greek States and the Roman State were not mere city States; all that may be said is that the political power was centred in the city. This is true, also, of the original city as it existed in the Orient and in the ancient civilizations of Mexico and Peru. The same characteristic distinguishes the early city from the many later sorts of cities that arose in response to the needs of intercourse and trade. The original city was the abode of the political and military leaders of the people who occupied the new territory and thus formed a State. This appears most strikingly in the case of Sparta—the State which preserved most fully the features of an earlier form of social organization. One might almost be inclined to say that the men's club developed by totemic tribal organization was here present in the form of a city of men established within a political order. But even in Athens and in the other Greek States the city was only the seat of the political power, whereas the State embraced the adjacent territory as well. The centre of the city, therefore, was the castle. This constituted the military defence of the State, and was the dwelling of the king or, in republican forms of government, of the highest officials. Connected with the castle was the temple of the guardian deity of the city. The immediate environment of the temple was the meeting-place of those who inhabited the territory protected by the castle and its temple. Here they assembled, partly for trade and partly for deliberative or popular gatherings. The economic and political intercourse which centred about the castle fostered the growth of a larger city, inasmuch as numbers of the rural inhabitants gradually settled down under the close protection of the castle. Directly connected with this development was the separation from agriculture of the occupations of art, handicraft, trade, and eventually of political office. Because of their enormous extent, the great Oriental realms included a number of city centres. Yet even here the original conditions maintained themselves, inasmuch as *one* of these cities continued to be not only the political seat of the State but also the chief centre of cult. The guardian deity of the leading city was likewise the guardian deity of the State, and, as such, was supreme among the gods. Cult was thus patterned after the political order. This influence of the city upon cult was reflected in temple construction. The totemic age possessed no cities, and it likewise lacked temples. Temples, therefore, are not only indicative of deity cult, whose development is bound up with political society, but they also signalize the existence of cities. The temple itself was characterized by a very rich architecture. In Babylonia it was the mighty tower, in Egypt the pair of obelisks at the entrance, which proclaimed to the surrounding neighbourhood the dwelling-place of the deity and the seat of political power. The two were identical, for it was in the name of the guardian deity of the city that the State was originally governed and that justice was meted out. In Oriental realms, the ruler was the representative of the deity, and the priests were the State officials, as well as the devotees of science and art. Tradition, together with numerous usages preserved in custom and laws, testify to the same original unification of religious and political authority in Greece and Rome. Although the State here became secularized at a comparatively early time, and art and science likewise freed themselves from theocratic dominance, the idea of a guardian deity of the city and State was long maintained. It was this that invested the secularized legal system with a halo of sanctity. If the course of development in Greece and Rome differed from that of the Oriental realms, this may be due, in an important measure, to the fact that they very early broke up into a considerable number of independent city States. Herein, of course, is expressed the character of Indo-Germanic peoples. Even in very ancient times they manifested a disposition to allow free play to the assertion of the individual personality ; this differentiates them from the Semitic race, with its strong inclination to hold fast to traditional norms. Hence it is that, while the cult of the various Greek cities remained practically the same, the cities themselves became distinct political communities. The status of the Delphic priesthood, in whom this unity of cult very early found its expression, was therefore naturally reduced to that of an advisory council. In the individual States, the dominance of political interests and the struggle for power, which was heightened by the personal inter-relationships within the narrow circle of the city, deprived the priesthood of all authority except over cult. True, in the case of Rome, the original union of political order and religious cult was firmer and more permanent, due to the fact that *one* city early gained the supremacy over the other Italian cities and States. And yet, hand in hand with the extension of political dominance, went the adoption of cults that were previously strange. This led to a number of competing priest-associations, none of which could gain the leadership, since all alike were but servants of the political power.

Thus, in spite of considerable diversity as to incidental conditions, city and State were closely bound up with each other in the development of political society. We find no city apart from a State, and it is doubtful whether there was a State without a city as the seat and centre of its political power. But this correlation obtained only during the period of the genesis of States and of the attendant rise of the *original* city. Once States have come into existence, many other conditions may lead to the establishment of a community which, as regards extent and relative political independence, is of the nature of a city. Such phenomena may be referred to as the *secondary* foundation of cities ; they are possible only on the basis of a previously existing political society. An approximation to original conditions occurs when a victorious State either establishes cities in the conquered provinces, centralizing in them the power over the respective territories, or transforms cities that already exist into political centres. Occurrences of this sort were frequent during the extension of Alexander's world-dominion and at the time of the Roman Empire. The same fact may be observed at a later period, in connection with the occupation of the Italian cities by the Goths and Lombards. The German cities founded during the Middle Ages differ still more widely from the original type. These cities first arose as market centres, and then gradually acquired political privileges. Thus, the process of the original foundation of cities was, as it were, reversed. In the latter case, the castle came first and the market followed ; the mediæval city began as a market and reached its completion with the building of a castle. In mediæval times, however, leadership was not originally vested in the city but in rulers who occupied isolated estates scattered here and there throughout the country. Yet these secondary phenomena and their further development do not belong to our present problem of the origin of political society.

8. The Beginnings of the Legal System.

The social regulations which we have thus far considered find their consummation in the *legal system*. This possesses no content independent of the various social institutions, but merely provides certain norms of action with a social sanction. As a result, these norms are protected against violation or are designated as regulations which, whenever necessary, are defended against violators by the use of external force. Thus, the legal system does not involve the outright creation of a social order. It consists primarily in the singling out, as definite prescriptions, of certain regulations that have already arisen in the course of social life, and that are for the most part already maintained by custom. The enforcement of these regulations is expressly guaranteed by society, and means are established whereby this pledge is to be redeemed. Thus, the most important social institutions—the family, the classes, the vocations, village settlements and cities, and also the relations of property, intercourse, and contract, which these involve—were already in existence before becoming constituent parts of a legal system. Moreover, the advance beyond custom and the settlement of difficulties case by case was not made suddenly or, much less, at the same time in all regions, but came only very gradually. The formulation of laws did not, as a rule, begin in connection with the political community and then pass down to the more restricted groups, ending with the single individual. On the contrary, law began by regulating the intercourse of individuals; later, it acquired authority over family relations which had remained under the shelter of custom for a relatively long period; last of all, it asserted itself also over the political order. That is to say, the State, which is the social organization from which the legal system took its rise, was the very last institution in connection with which objective legal forms were developed. We may account for this by reference to a factor which played an important rôle from the very outset. After the legal system had once grown up out of custom and had subjected many of the important fields of the latter to its authority, it was able of itself to create regulations, which were thus from the very beginning legal prescriptions. Such primarily legal regulations arose in connection with conditions in which, frequently, the fact that there be some law was of more importance than the precise character of the law. But even in these cases the regulations were always connected with the larger body of law that was rooted in custom. This larger body of law was but supplemented by ordinances that were called into being by temporal and cultural conditions.

The transition from custom to law reflects the joint influence of *two* factors, which, particularly at the outset, were themselves closely connected. The first of these factors consists in the rise of firmly established forms of rulership, which are indicative also of the transition leading to *States* ; the other is the *religious* sanction which was attached to those regulations that were singled out by the law from the broader field of custom. Both factors indicate that the heroic age properly marks the origin of the legal system, even though it be true that all such changes are gradual and that occasional beginnings of the legal system, therefore, may be found at an earlier period, in connection with the very ancient institution of chieftainship. As regards the external social organization and the religious life of the heroic age, these are characterized, respectively, by the development of strict forms of rulership and by the origin of a deity cult. Each of these social phenomena reinforces the other. The kingdom of the gods was but the terrestrial State projected into an ideal sphere. No less was the development of the legal system dependent upon the union of the two factors. Neither the external force of the political authority governing the individual nor the inner constraint of religious duty sufficed in itself to establish the tremendous power characteristic of the legal system from early times on. It is true that, at a later period, the feeling that law represents a religious duty gave way to the moral law of conscience. The latter, however, itself owes its origin to the increasing influence of the political authority which is at the basis of the legal system ; moreover, as an inner motive reinforcing the external compulsion of the law, it continued to preserve a similarity to the religious source from which it sprang. True, a significant change occurred. During the early stages of legal development, the weight of emphasis fell on the religious aspect of law, whereas it later more and more shifted to the political side. At first, the entire body of law was regarded as having been given directly by the deity, as was the case, for example, with the Ten Commandments of Moses and with the Israelitic Priests' Code, which clothes even the most external modes of life in the garb of religious commands. Sometimes a twofold credit is given for the introduction of the legal system, in that the one who wields the power is regarded as administering justice both in his own name and as commissioned by the gods. An illustration of this is the Babylonian code of Hammurabi. It is, naturally, when the priests wield the authority that the laws are most apt to be ascribed exclusively to the gods. The tendency, on the other hand, to give the ruler a certain amount of credit for legislative enactments, is greatest whenever the ruler occupies also the position of chief priest. The direct impetus to such a union of priesthood and political authority is to be found in the rise of the legal system itself, for this resulted from a fusion of religious and political motives. The idea that the earthly ruler is the terrestrial representative of a world-governing deity, or, as occurs in extreme cases, that he is the world-governing deity himself, is, therefore, a conception that is closely bound up with the rise of political society and that receives pregnant expression in the earliest forms of the legal system. No trace of such a conception was associated with the chiefs of the totemic period. Their position was entirely distinct from that of the magicians, the shamans, and the medicine-men, who were the original representatives of the priestly class that later arose in the age of deity cults. But it is for this very reason that the mandates of the totemic chief cannot be said as yet to have constituted a legal system; they were commands which were given as occasion demanded, and which were determined partly by the will of the chief and partly by transmitted customs. Secular and religious motives are to be found in similar combination elsewhere, even among tribes that are usually regarded as peoples of nature, as, for example, particularly those of Polynesia. In cases such as these, however, there are present also the beginnings of a legal system, as well as its correlates, the fundamentals of a political organization and of a deity cult. Whether these are the remnants of a culture brought by these migratory peoples from their original Asiatic home, or whether they represent an independently achieved culture that has fallen into decay, we need not here inquire.

That the development of the legal system is dependent upon the first of these phenomena—that is, upon political organization—is directly apparent from the fact that the administration of justice in general presupposes two sources of authority. Here again the beginnings are to be found in the totemic age. During this period, the administration of justice was vested, in the first place, in a relatively restricted group of the older and experienced men, such as exercised authority over the older members of the horde even in pretotemic times. Judicial powers were assumed, in the second place, by individual leaders in the chase or in war. The authority of the latter, it is true, was temporary, frequently shifting with changing circumstances; it was all the more effective, however, for the very reason that it was centred in single individuals. Now, the initial step in the formation of a legal system—which, as already remarked, was at first concerned merely with what we would call civil justice—was taken when the quarrels of individuals came to be settled in the same way as were matters of common concern to the clan or tribe—namely, by the decisions of the two long-established authorities, the 'council of elders,' as they later continued to be called among many civilized peoples, and the individual leader or chieftain. Even in relatively primitive times, fellow-tribesmen or clansmen who disagreed as to the ownership of an object or perhaps as to whether or not some mutual agreement had been kept, and who preferred a peaceful decision to settlement by combat, were accustomed to seek the decision of the elders or of a man of commanding respect. Thus, these initial stages of legal procedure indicate that the earliest judge was an *arbitrator*; he was freely selected by the disputants, though he constantly became more firmly established in his position as a result both of his authority in the general affairs of the tribe and of tradition. We next find the *appointed* judge, who owes his office to political authority, and who decides particular controversies, not because he has been asked to do so by the parties themselves but 'of right' and as commissioned by the State; supported as he is by the political power. his decision has compelling force. As soon as the State assumes the function of deciding the controversies of individuals, the judge becomes an *official*. Indeed, he is one of the first representatives of officialdom. For, in the early stages of political organization, all matters other than the quarrels of individuals are regulated by ancient customs, except in so far as war and the preparation for war involve conditions that necessarily place authority of an entirely different sort in the hands of particular individuals. Thus, together with the offices of those who, though only gradually, come to have charge of the maintenance of the military organization even in times of peace, the office of the judiciary represents one of the earliest of political creations. In it, we find a parallel to the division of power between the ruler and a separate council of experienced men, an arrangement that represents a legacy from the period of tribal organization, but that only now becomes firmly established. The individual judge and the college of judges both occur so early that it is scarcely possible to say whether either antedated the other. Affecting the development just described are two other conditions, capable of bringing about a division of judicial authority at an early time. One of these conditions is the connection of the state with deity cult, as a result of which the secular power is limited by the authority of the priesthood, whose chief prerogative comes to be penal justice. The second factor in the differentiation of judicial functions consists in the institution of chieftainship, one of the two characteristic features of political society. Chieftainship involves a tendency towards a delegation of the supreme judicial authority to the ruler. This is particularly the case during the first stages of political organization, which still reflect the fact that the external political power of the chieftain grew up out of the conditions attendant upon war. Even though the secular judiciary, which originated in the council of elders, or, in certain cases, the judicial office of the priest, also continues to be maintained, the ruler nevertheless reserves for himself the authority over the most important issues. Particularly in doubtful cases, in which the ordinary judge has no traditional norms to guide his decision, the 'king's court' intervenes in order, if necessary, to secure a recognition of the claim of reasonableness. This is especially apt to occur in connection with capital crimes. Hence it is that, even after penal law has once become a matter of general governmental control—which, as a rule, occurs only at a later stage of legal development—the final decision in criminal cases usually rests with the ruler. Generally, moreover, it is the ruler alone who has sufficient power to put an end to the blood-revenge demanded by kinship groups. Owing to the fact that, in his capacity of military leader, the ruler possesses power over life and death during war with hostile tribes, he comes to exercise the same authority in connection also with the feuds of his fellow-tribesmen. Modern States have retained a last remnant of this power in the monarch's right to pardon, an erratic phenomenon of a culture that has long since disappeared.

Thus, the State, as such, possesses an external power which finds its most direct expression—just as does the unity of the State—in the exercise of judicial authority on the part of the ruler. In the beginnings of legal development, however, law always possesses also a *religious sanction*. True, the above-mentioned unification of the offices of priest and judge or of the authority of priest and ruler—the latter of which sometimes occurs in connection with the former—may be the result of particular cultural conditions. This, however, but indicates all the more forcibly how permanent has been the religious sanction of law. Such a sanction is evidenced by the words and symbolisms that accompany legal procedure even in the case of secular judges and of the relations of individuals themselves. Not without significance, for example, is the solemnity manifested in the tones of those who are party to a barter, a contract, or an assignment of property. Indeed, their words are usually accompanied by express confirmations resembling the formulas of prayer and imprecation ; the gods are invoked as witnesses of the transaction or as avengers of broken pledges. Because of the solemnity of the spoken word, speech was displaced but slowly by writing. Long after the latter art had been acquired, its use continued to be avoided, not only in the case of legal formulas, such as the above, but occasionally even in connection with more general legal declarations. In the Brahman schools of India, for example, the rules of legal procedure, as well as the hymns and prayers, were for centuries transmitted purely through memory ; we are told, moreover, that in ancient Sparta it was forbidden to put the laws in writing. To an age, however, which is incapable of conceiving even a legal transaction except as a perceptual act, the spoken word by itself is inadequate to give the impression of reality. As an indication that he has acquired a piece of land, the purchaser lifts a bit of soil from the earth, or the vendor tosses a stalk of grain to him—a ceremony which is imitated in the case of other objects of exchange and which has led to the word 'stipulation' (from the Latin *stipulatio*, throwing of a stalk). Another symbol of acquisition is the laying on of the hand. Similar to it is the clasp of right hands as a sign of mutual agreement. By this act the contracting parties pledge their freedom in case they break the promise which they are giving. When the fact that the two parties lived at some distance from each other rendered the hand clasp impossible, the Germans were accustomed to exchange gloves. One who challenged another to a duel likewise did so by the use of a glove, even though his opponent was present. By throwing his glove before his opponent the challenger gave expression to the distance which separated him in feeling from his enemy. In this case, the symbol has changed from a sign of agreement to the opposite. All the symbols of which we have been speaking agree in having originally been regarded, not as symbols, but as real acts possessing certain magical potencies. When an individual, who is acquiring a piece of land, picks up a bit of soil while speaking the appropriate words, he intends to produce a magical effect upon the land, such that disaster will come to any one who may seek to deprive him of it. He who offers his hand in sealing a compact signifies that he is prepared to lose his freedom in case he fails to keep his word. For this reason the shaking of hands is sometimes supplemented by the extension of a staff—a special use of the magical wand which occurs particularly when the pledge is administered by a judge. In a second stage of development, the act loses the status of reality, but it remains associated with religious feelings. At a third stage, it becomes a mere matter of form, though the solemnity with which it envelops the transaction adds to the impressiveness of the latter and fixes it more firmly in memory.

Combined with the word, thus, is a gesture that faithfully reflects its meaning. Moreover, other individuals are summoned to witness the legal transaction. This is done, not so much that these persons may later be able to give definite testimony, as that they, too, shall hear the word and see the gesture, and so, in a sense, enhance the reality of that which is transpiring. Besides this oldest form of witness, who is not to testify regarding that which he has experienced, as occurs in later times, but who is merely present on the occasion of the legal transaction, there is the *compurgator*, who substantiates the oath of the man involved. The latter fortifies his statements by invoking the gods as witnesses. Now, the oath of the compurgator does not relate to the testimony of his companion, but merely to the companion himself ; it is a pledge to share the punishment of the latter in case he swears falsely. As in battle, so also in calling upon the terrible powers whose vengeance is to fall upon the perjurer, companion stands protectingly by the side of companion. Thus, the oath itself is a ceremony both of cult and of magic. As a cult activity, the oath was originally given at the place where the cult was administered—that is, in the immediate presence of the gods ; the method of procedure was to raise the fingers and to point them directly to the gods, who were regarded as witnesses of the act. The magical nature of the oath appears in the fact that the latter involved the conjuration of an object, which was to bring disaster upon him who took the oath in case he swore falsely. Thus, the Germans swore by their battle-steeds or their weapons, and, in so doing, they laid their hands upon these objects; or, instead of the latter, they used an oath-staff—one of the numerous metamorphoses of the magical wand—which was extended toward him who received the oath, whether the opposing party or the judge. This oath signified that the object by which the individual swore would bring ruin upon him in case he committed perjury. The oath, therefore, came to be a fixed and definitely prescribed means of judicial procedure, though this occurred only after deity cult effected a union of the two factors, cult and magic. Nevertheless, the beginnings of this development are to be found as early as the totemic age, and they approximate to the cult-oath particularly in those regions that practise ancestor worship. The Bantu, for example, swears by the head of his father or the cap of his mother, as well as by the colour of his ox. In all these cases, the intention is that the perjurer shall suffer the vengeance which the demon of the deceased or of the animal visits upon him who swears falsely.

Closely related in its motives to the oath is another legal institution, the *ordeal*. In the earliest form of the ordeal, the strife of individuals was settled by a duel. Such an ordeal was very similar to the sword-oath, at least among Indo-Germanic peoples. Just as the man who swore by his weapons invoked death by their agency in the indefinite future, so each of the participants in the duel sought to bring these magical powers into immediate effect in the case of his opponent. Not to him whose arm is the stronger, but to him who has the stronger cause, will the gods grant victory through the magic of his weapon. Like the oath, therefore, the ordeal was originally a method of legal procedure in civil cases. Like the oath, furthermore, it was, in its beginnings, a means whereby individuals settled their controversies independently of a judge. It is at this point that the punitive action of individuals gives way to public legal procedure. Originally, crimes against life and property were dealt with by individuals; the endeavour to secure the judgment of the gods by means of the duel was doubtless one of the earliest steps by which the penal process became a public procedure, and the punishment itself, therefore, became raised above the plane of mere revenge. Blood revenge involved an unexpected attack in the open or from ambush. To renounce this custom in favour of the duel, therefore, was in harmony with the character of the heroic age. For this was the period in which the ideal of manly honour was rapidly gaining strength, and in which, therefore, it was regarded as unworthy under any circumstances to take the life of a defenceless man. The principle accepted as self-evident in war, namely, that the person attacked have an opportunity to defend himself, became, in a warlike age, a maxim applying also to times of peace. Moreover, even though it be true of the ordeal as of the oath that, at the outset, cult was secondary to magical conjuration, nevertheless, the dominance of the latter varied with the degree in which the State freed penal justice from the passion for revenge on the part of individuals. The ordeal thus came to be more than merely a combat between the accuser and the accused. The judge in charge of the combat acquired the duty of determining guilt or innocence, and, as a result, the ordeal assumed other forms. Only the one who was accused was now involved. The ordeal changed from a magic combat into a *magic test*, which came to be regarded as a direct revelation of the decision of the deity. This led to the adoption of means of proof other than combat. It was obviously cult that caused penal justice as such to be taken out of the hands of private individuals. For this reason it was particularly sacrilege that demanded a magical judgment independent of the combat of individuals. In cases of sacrilege, the deity himself tested the assertions of the one who endeavoured to free himself from the charges of religious crime. The means for determining guilt or innocence were fire and water—the same agencies that had long been employed by religious cult for purposes of lustration. That the tests by water and by fire used in connection with the witchcraft cases of mediæval times still possessed a magical significance is unmistakable. If the witch sank in the water—that is, if she was received by the purifying element—she was guiltless. If the accused was not injured by holding a glowing iron in his hand or by walking barefooted over coals, this also was regarded as indicative of innocence. Apparently the underlying conception was that the deity who gave to water and fire the power of purifying a sinner from his guilt also communicated to them the power of freeing the innocent from an accusation and of withholding assistance from the guilty. Hence it is that while these modes of divine judgment were not, indeed, as common as was purification by means of water and fire, they nevertheless appeared again and again, so far as their fundamental characteristics are concerned. They were resorted to by the Germanic peoples, and were prevalent also in Græco-Roman antiquity, and in India; trial by water was likewise a custom in Babylonia, where it was prescribed by Hammurabi as a means by which a suspected person might free himself. We have noticed how, in the case of the ordeal and particularly of its earliest form, judicial combat, the legal controversies of individuals concerning rights relating to property, buying and selling and other agreements, came to be considered from the standpoint of *punishment*. This process is characteristic of the development of penal law in general.

9. THE DEVELOPMENT OF PENAL LAW.

As an institution protected by the State, the administration of penal law everywhere grew up out of civil law. The judge who was appointed by the State to arbitrate personal controversies developed into a criminal judge. Still later these two judicial offices became distinct. This separation began in connection with the most serious offences, such as seemed to demand a separate tribunal. The determining feature, in this instance, was, at the outset, not any qualitative characteristic of the offence but its gravity. Now, at the time when deity cults were at their zenith, the most serious crimes were held to be those connected with religion, namely, temple sacrilege and blasphemy. Only at a relatively late period were crimes against life and limb classed along with those affecting religion; to these were added, shortly afterwards, violations of property rights. That murder, though the most frequent crime of early culture, should not be penalized by political authority until so late a period, is directly due to the fact that it has its origin in the strife of individuals. In such a strife, each man personally assumes all consequences, even though these consist in the loss of his life. Even to slay a man from ambush is regarded as justifiable by primitive society if an individual is avenging a crime from which he has suffered. As family and kinship ties become stronger, the family or kin participates as a group in the quarrels of its individual members, just as it does in war against hostile tribes. A murder, whether or not it be an act of vengeance, is avenged by a fellow-member of the victim, either upon the murderer or upon some one of his kin, inasmuch as in this case also the group is regarded as taking the part of the individual This is the practice of *blood-revenge*, a practice which antedates the heroic age but which nevertheless continues to exercise a powerful influence upon it. Blood-revenge is so closely bound up with totemic tribal organization that it was probably never lacking wherever any such system arose. Its status, however, was purely that of a custom, not that of a legal requirement. It was custom alone, and not political authority, that compelled one kinsman to avenge the death of another. It was custom also that sought to do away with the disastrous results of a continuous blood-feud by means of an arrangement that came to take the place of blood-revenge. This substitute was the 'wergild,' which was paid as an indemnity by the malefactor to the family of the one who had been murdered, and which thus maintained precisely the same relation to blood-revenge as did marriage by purchase to marriage by capture. In the former case, however, the substitution of a peaceful agreement for an act of violence gave the political authority its first occasion to exercise its regulative power. This first manifestation of power consisted in the fact that the political authority determined the amount which must be paid in lieu of the blood-guilt. With the institution of wergild the entire matter becomes one of civil law. Only one further step is necessary, and the law of contract will indirectly have established the penal authority of the State. This step is taken when the State *compels* the parties to enter into an agreement on the basis of the wergild. The advance, however, was not made at a single bound, but came only through the influence of a number of intermediate factors. That which first demanded a legal determination of the amount of expiation money was the necessity of estimating the personal value of the one who had been murdered, according as the individual was free-born or dependent, of a high or of a low class, an able-bodied man or a woman. Such a gradation in terms of general social status suggested the propriety of allowing temporary and less serious injuries to life and limb to be compensated for on the basis of their magnitude. But the estimation of damages in such cases again made civil jurisdiction absolutely necessary.

Closely interconnected with this complex of social factors, and imposing a check upon the impulse for vengeance that flames up in blood-revenge, was a religious influence—the fear of contaminating by a deed of violence a spot that was sanctified by the presence of invisible gods. No violence of any kind was allowed within sacred precincts, particularly in places set apart for sacrifice or for other cult ceremonies ; least of all was violence tolerated in the temple, for the temple was regarded as the dwelling of a deity. Such places, therefore, afforded protection to all who fled to them from impending blood-revenge or other sources of danger. The sacred place also stood under the protection of the community ; any violation of it brought down upon the offender the vengeance of the entire group, for the latter regarded such sacrilege as a source of common danger. Thus, the protection of the *sanctuary* came to be a legal right even at a time when retribution for the crime itself was left to the vengeance of individuals. The right of protection afforded by the temple, however, was sometimes held to exist also in the case of the dwellings of persons of distinguished power and esteem, particularly the dwellings of the chief and of the priest. Indeed, prior to the existence of public temples, the latter were doubtless the only places of refuge. In this form, the beginnings of a right of refuge date back even into the totemic age. At that early time, however, the protection was apparently due, not so much to directly religious factors, as to the personal power of the individual who afforded the refuge, or also, particularly in Polynesia, to the 'taboo' with which the upper classes were privileged to guard their property. But, since the taboo was probably itself of religious origin, and since the medicine-man, and occasionally also the chief, could utilize demoniacal agencies as well as his own external power, even the very earliest forms of refuge were of the general nature of religious protection. In some cases, the right of refuge eventually became extended so as to be connected not only with the property set apart for the chief or the priest but also with the homes of inferior men. This, however, was a relatively late phenomenon. Its origin is traceable to the cult of household deities, first of the ancestral spirits who guard domestic peace, and then of the specific protective deities of the hearth by whom the ancestral spirits were supplanted. As a rule, it was not the criminal but the visiting stranger who sought the protection of the house. The right to hospitality thus became also a religiously sanctioned right to protection. The guest was no less secure against the host himself than against all others. The right of protection afforded by the house, therefore, should probably be interpreted as a transference of the right of refuge inherent in sacred precincts. The protective right of the chief was doubtless the beginning of what in its complete development came to be household right in general.

The divine protection afforded by the sanctuary obviously offers but a temporary refuge from the avenger. The fugitive again encounters the dangers of blood-revenge as soon as he leaves the sacred precincts. Nevertheless, the time that is thus made to elapse between the act and its reprisal tempers the passion of the avenger, and affords an opportunity for negotiations in which the hostile families or clans may arrange that a ransom be paid in satisfaction of the crime that was committed. Moreover, the chief or the temple priest under whose protection the fugitive places himself, is given a direct opportunity for mediating in the capacity of an arbitrating judge, and later, as the political power gradually acquires greater strength, for taking the measures of retribution into his own hands. Revenge, thus, is changed into punishment, and custom is displaced by the norm of law, which grows up out of repeated decisions in the adjudication of similar cases.

Sojourn in a place of refuge resembles imprisonment in that it limits personal freedom. One might, therefore, be inclined to suppose that, through a further development other than that described above, the sanctuary led to a gradual moderation of punishment by introducing the practice of *imprisonment*. Such a supposition, however, is not borne out by the facts. At the time when the transition from the place of refuge into the prison might have taken place, the idea of reducing the death penalty to the deprivation of freedom was still remote. The value which the heroic age placed on the life of the individual was not sufficiently high to induce such a change, and the enforcement of prison penalties would, under the existing conditions, have appeared difficult and uncertain. Hence imprisonment was as yet entirely unknown as a form of punishment. Though the State had suppressed blood-revenge, it showed no less an inclination than did ancient custom to requite not only murder but even milder crimes with death. Indeed, inasmuch as the peaceful mode of settlement by ransom gradually disappeared, it might be truer to say that the relentlessness of the State was even greater than that of blood-revenge. The oldest penal codes were very strongly inclined to impose death penalties. That the famous Draconian laws of Athens became proverbial in this respect was due merely to the fact that other ancient legal codes, though not infrequently more severe, were still unknown. The law of King Hammurabi punished by death any one who stole property belonging to the court or the temple, or even to one of the king's captains; the innkeeper who charged her guests extortionate prices was thrown into the water, and the temple maiden who opened a wine-shop was burned to death. Whoever acquired possession of stolen goods, or sheltered a runaway slave, was put to death, etc. For every crime that was judged to be in any way serious, and for whose expiation a money ransom was not adequate, the law knew only the one penalty, death. The earliest law made no use of custody except in connection with civil justice. The debtor was confined in the house of the creditor. This simply enforced the pledge involved in the shaking of hands at the time when the debt was contracted—an act by which the debtor vowed to be responsible for his debt with his own person.

The confinement of the debtor was at first a matter that was left to individuals, and its original sanction was custom; later, however, it came under the supervision of the legal system of the State. This suggested the adoption of confinement in connection with other crimes, in which the death penalty appeared too severe a punishment and the exaction of money one that was too light, as well, primarily, as too dependent upon the wealth of the guilty individual. Contributory to this change, was a practice which, similarly to confinement, was also originally an arrangement between individuals, and was rooted in custom. I refer to the holding of individuals as pledges, to the hostage, who gave security with his own person for the promise of another. The hostage is of the nature of a forfeit, guaranteeing in advance the fulfilment of the obligation. For this reason the holding of hostages came to be practised not merely in the case of property contracts but in connection with every possible obligation of a private or a public nature. This development was furthered by the fact that hostages came to be held in times of war, and, as a result, were given also upon the assumption of public duties. In both cases, custody changed from a private arrangement into a public concern. This change made it possible for a judge to impose the penalty of imprisonment whenever the transgression did not appear to warrant death. Imprisonment is a penalty that admits of no fewer degrees than does a fine, and has the advantage of being independent of the irrelevant circumstance of the wealth of the one who is condemned. Moreover, the restriction of arbitrary deprivations of freedom in favour of custody on the part of the political power, makes it possible to hold a suspect whose case requires examination before a judicial verdict can be given. Thus arises the practice of confinement during investigation, an incidental form of legal procedure which is influenced by, and in turn reacts upon, the penalty of imprisonment. Such confinement makes it possible to execute the penalty of imprisonment in the case of those whom investigation shows to be guilty. But this is not its only important result. It also leads to those barbarous methods which, particularly during the early stages of this development, are connected with the infliction of the punishment itself as well as with the preceding inquisitorial activities. The public administration of justice is still affected by the passion for vengeance which comes down from the earlier period of blood-revenge. To this coarser sense of justice a merely quantitative gradation of punishment is not satisfactory; the punishment must rather be made to correspond qualitatively with the crime that has been committed. Hence the many different modes of prison punishment—more numerous even than the modes of inflicting the death penalty—and of the means of torture, which are often conceived with devilish cunning. These means of torture come to be used also in the inquisitional procedure; the endeavour to force a confession causes them to become more severe, and this in turn reacts upon the punishment itself. On the whole, the ultimate tendency of imprisonment was greatly to restrict the death penalty and thus to contribute to more humane methods of punishment. Nevertheless, it is impossible not to recognize that this result was preceded by an increasing cruelty. The fact that the prisoner was under the control of the punitive authority for a longer period of time led to a multiplication of the means of punishment. How simple, and, one might say, how relatively humane, was blood-revenge, satisfied as it was to demand life for life, in comparison with the penal law of the Middle Ages, with its methods of forcing confession by means of the rack and of various forms of physical suffering and of death penalties!

The same is true of a further change inaugurated by the passing of blood-revenge into punishment. This change likewise led to a decided restriction of the death penalty, yet it also, no less than the forcing of confession, brought upon penal justice the stigma of systematic cruelty. The assumption of penal power on the part of the public judiciary, in conjunction with the possession of unlimited control over the person and life of the malefactor, led to the adoption of a principle which long continued to dominate penal justice. This principle was drastically expressed in the Priests' Code of the Israelites, "Eye for eye, tooth for tooth." True, this *jus talionis* was already foreshadowed in the custom of blood-revenge, and yet the simple form which it here possessed, 'a life for a life,' made it a principle of just retribution, and not a demand sharpened by hate and cruelty. In the case of blood-revenge, moreover, the emotions of revenge were moderated by virtue of the fact that considerations of property played a rôle. Requital was sought for the loss which the clan sustained through the death of one of its members. Hence the clan might be satisfied with a money compensation, or, occasionally, with the adoption either of a fellow-tribesman of the murderer, or, indeed, even of the murderer himself. In contrast with this, even the most severe physical injuries, so long as they did not result in death, were originally always left to the retaliation of the individual. This retaliation was sought either in direct combat, or, in the heroic age proper, in a duel conducted in accordance with regulations of custom. All this is changed as soon as the State abolishes blood-revenge and assumes jurisdiction over cases of murder. In the event of personal injuries, the judge determines the sentence, particularly if the individual is unable for any reason to secure retaliation—having been rendered helpless, for example, through his injury, or being prevented by the fact of class differences. Under such circumstances it is but natural that the principle, 'a life for a life,' which has been borrowed from the institution of blood-revenge and has been applied to the punishment for murder, should be developed into a scale of physical punishment representing the more general principle 'like for like.' He who has destroyed the eye of another, must lose his own eye; whoever has disabled another's arm, must have his arm cut off, etc. Other injuries then came to be similarly punished, even those of a moral character to which the principle "eye for eye, tooth for tooth" is not directly applicable. The hand which has been implicated in an act of sacrilege, such as the commission of perjury, is to be cut off; the tongue which has slandered, must be torn out. Originally, the death penalty was employed all too freely. Hence this substitution of a physical punishment which spared the life of the offender was doubtless in the direction of moderation. But, since this substitution gave rise to cruelties that resulted in the infliction of various sorts of death penalties, preceded and accompanied by tortures, its original effect became reversed, just as in the case of imprisonment. Moreover, the two forms of punishment—imprisonment and death—and the degree to which these were carried to excess differed according to civilization and race. The *jus talionis* was the older principle of punishment. It is more closely bound up with man's natural impulse for retaliation, and therefore recurs even within humane civilizations, sometimes merely in suggestions but sometimes in occasional relapses which are of a more serious sort and are due to the passion for revenge. In fundamental contrast with the Mosaic law, Christianity repudiated the requital of like with like. Perhaps it was the fear of violating its own principle that led it, in its later development, to seek in the cruelties of severe prison penalties a substitute for the repressed impulse to revenge which comes to expression in coarser conceptions of justice. Nevertheless, this substitution was superior to the inflexible severity of the *jus talionis* in that it more effectively enabled milder customs to influence the judicial conscience.

But there is still another respect in which the recedence of the principle of retaliation gradually led to an advance beyond the legal conceptions characteristic of the heroic age. The command for strict retribution takes into consideration merely the *objective* injury in which a deed results; to it, it is immaterial whether a person destroys another's eye accidentally or intentionally. The same injury that he has caused must befall him. Whoever kills a man must, according to the law of Hammurabi, himself suffer death; if he kills a woman, he is to be punished by the death of his daughter. If a house collapses, the builder who constructed it must suffer death. For a successful operation, the physician receives a compensation; if the operation fails, the hand that has performed it is cut off. The same law determines both reward and punishment. Moreover, it includes within its scope even intellectual and moral transgressions. The judge who commits an error is to be dismissed from office in disgrace; the owner who neglects his field is to be deprived of it.

10. THE DIFFERENTIATION OF LEGAL FUNCTIONS.

The direct impetus to overcoming the defects that were inherent in penal justice as a result of its having originated in the conflicts of individuals, did not come from a clear recognition of differences in the character of the crimes themselves, but primarily from the fact of a gradual *division of judicial functions*. This is shown particularly by the development of Græco-Roman as well as of Germanic law. It is in the criminal court, which supersedes blood-revenge, that public authority is most directly conscious of its power over the individual. Hence the criminal court appears to be the highest of the courts, and the one that most deeply affects the natural rights of man. Its authority is vested solely in the ruler, or in a particularly sacred tribunal. This is due, not so much to the specific character of the crimes over which it has jurisdiction, as to the respect which it receives because it assumes both the ancient duty of blood-revenge and the function of exacting a requital for religious guilt. Similarly, other offences also gradually pass from the sphere of personally executed revenge or from that of the strife of individuals, and become subject to the penal authority of the State. The division of judicial authority, to which these tendencies lead, is promoted by the differentiation of public power, as a result of which the administration of justice is apportioned to various officials and magistrates, as well as are the other tasks of the State. It is for this reason that, if we consider their civilization as a whole, the constitutional States of the Occidental world were led to differentiate judicial functions much earlier than were the great despotic monarchies of the Orient. These monarchies, as the code of Hammurabi shows, possessed a highly developed husbandry and a correspondingly advanced commercial and monetary system, whereas they centralized all judicial functions in the ruler.

Thus, the State gains a twofold power, manifested, in the first place, in the very establishment of a judicial order, and, secondly, in the differentiation of the spheres of justice in which the authority of the State over the individual is exercised. This finally prepares the way for the last stage of development. The state itself becomes subject to an established legal order which determines its various functions and the duties of its members. There thus originates an officialdom, organized on fixed principles and possessing carefully defined public privileges. The people of the State, on the other hand, are divided into definite classes on the basis of the duties demanded of them as well as of the rights connected with these duties. These articulations of political society, which determine the organization of the army, the mode of taxation, and the right of participation in the government of the State, develop, as we have already seen, out of totemic tribal organization, as a result of the external conditions attendant upon the migrations and wars connected with the rise of States. But they also exhibit throughout the traces of statutes expressing the will and recording the decisions of individual rulers, though even here, of course, universal human motives are decisive. After the political powers of the State have been divided and have been delegated to particular officials and official colleges, and after political rights have been apportioned to the various classes of society, the next step consists in rendering the organization of the State secure by means of a *Constitution* regulating the entire political system. In the shaping of the Constitution, it cannot be denied that individual legislators or legislative assemblies played a significant rôle. Nevertheless, it must be remembered that it is solely as respects the *form* of State organization that the final and most comprehensive legal creation appears to be predominantly the result of the will acts of individuals. The *content* of the Constitution is in every respect a product of history; it is determined by conditions which, in the last analysis, depend upon the general culture of a nation and upon its relations with other peoples. These conditions, however, are so complex that, though every form of Constitution and all its modifications may be regarded as absolutely involved in the causal nexus of historical life, the endless diversity of particular conditions precludes Constitutions from being classifiable according to any universal principle. Constitutions can at most be classified on the basis of certain analogies. The most influential attempt at a genetic classification of the various historical forms of government was that of Aristotle. But his classification, based on the number of rulers (one, a few, many, all) and on the moral predicates of good and evil (monarchy and tyranny, aristocracy and oligarchy, etc.), offers a purely logical schema which corresponds but partially with facts. True, it not infrequently happens that the rule of all—that is, democracy—gives way to the evil form of individual rulership—namely, tyranny. An aristocracy, however, or even a monarchy, may likewise develop into a tyranny. What the change is to be, depends upon historical conditions. Nor are monarchy, aristocracy, or the rule of the middle class forms of government that are ever actually to be found in the purity which logical schematization demands. Even in the Homeric State there was a council of elders and an assembly of freemen——an agora—in addition to the king. Indeed, if we go back still farther and inquire concerning those more primitive peoples of nature who are merely on the point of passing from tribal organization to a political Constitution, it might perhaps be nearer the truth to assert that democracy, and not monarchy, was the form of the early State. The fact is that the organization characteristic of the State as a whole is the product of historical factors of an exceedingly variable nature, and that it never adequately fits into any logical system that is based on merely a few political features. Even less may a logical schema of this sort be regarded as representing a universal law of development.

Thus, the State is indeed the ultimate source of all the various branches of the legal system. So far as the fundamental elements of its own Constitution are concerned, however, it is really itself a product of *custom*, if we take this term in its broadest sense, as signifying an historically developed order of social life which has not yet come under the control of political authority. The course of development is the very opposite of that which rationalistic theories have taught, ever since the time of the Sophists, concerning the origin of the State. These theories maintain that the legal system originated in connection with the State, and that it then acquired an application to the separate departments of life. The reverse is true. It is with the determination of the rights of individuals and with the settlement of the controversies arising from these rights that the legal power of the State takes its rise. It is strengthened and extended when the custom of personal retribution comes to be superseded by penal law. Last of all comes the systematic formulation of the political Constitution itself. The latter, however, is never more than a *development*; it is not a creation in the proper sense of the word. Even such States as the United States of North America and the new German Empire were not created by lawgivers, but were only organized by them in respect to details. The State as such is always a product of history, and so it must ever remain. Every legal system presupposes the power of a State. Hence the latter can never itself originate in an act of legislation, but can only transform itself into a legal order after it has once arisen.

11. The Origin of Gods.

At first glance it may seem presumptuous even to raise the question as to how gods originated. Have they not always existed? one is inclined to ask. As a matter of fact, this is the opinion of most historians, particularly of historians of religion. They hold that the belief in gods is underived. Degenerate forms may arise, the belief may at times even disappear altogether or be displaced by a crude belief in magic and demons, but it itself can in no wise have been developed from anything else, for it was possessed by mankind from the very beginning. Were it true that the belief in gods represents an original possession of mankind, our question concerning the origin of gods would be invalidated. The assumption, however, is disproved by the facts of ethnology. There are peoples without gods. True, there are no peoples without some sort of supersensuous beings. Nevertheless, to call all such beings 'gods'—beings, for example, such as sickness-demons or the demons which leave the corpse and threaten the living—would appear to be a wholly unwarranted extension of the conception of deity. Unbiased observation goes to show that there are no peoples without certain conceptions that may be regarded as precursors of the later god-ideas. Nevertheless, there can be no doubt that there are some peoples without gods. The Veddahs of Ceylon, the so-called nature-Semangs and Senoi of Malacca, the natives of Australia, and many other peoples of nature as well, possess no gods, in our sense of the word. Because all of these primitive peoples interpret certain natural phenomena—such as clouds, winds, and stars—in an anthropomorphic fashion, it has been attempted time and again to establish the presence of the god-idea of higher religions. Such attempts, however, may be straightway characterized as a play with superficial analogies in which no thought whatsoever is taken of the real content of the god-conception.

Accepting the lead of ethnological facts, then, let us grant that there are stages in the development of the myth in which real gods are lacking. Even so, two opposing views are possible concerning the relation of such 'prereligious' conditions to the origin of the god-ideas essential to religion. Indeed, these views still actively compete with each other in the science of religion. On the one hand, it is maintained that the god-idea is original, and that belief in demons, totemism, fetishism, and ancestor worship are secondary and degenerate derivatives. On the other hand, the gods are regarded as products of a mythological development, and, in so far, as analogous to the State, which grew up in the course of political development out of the primitive forms of tribal organization. Those who defend the first of these views subscribe to a degeneration theory. If the ancestors reverenced in cult are degenerated deities, and if the same is true of demons and even of fetishes, then the main course of religious development has obviously been downward and not upward. The representatives of the second view, on the contrary, assume an upward or progressive tendency. If demons, fetishes, and the animal or human ancestors worshipped in cult antedate gods, the latter must have developed from the former. Thus, the views concerning the origin of gods may be classified as *theories of degeneration* and *theories of development*.

But the theories of degeneration themselves fall into two classes. The one upholds an original monotheism, the basis of which is claimed to be either an innate idea of God or a revelation made to all mankind. Obviously this assumption is itself more nearly a belief than a scientific hypothesis. As a belief, it may be accounted for in terms of a certain religious need. This explains how it happens that, in spite of the multiplication of contradictory facts, the theory has been repeatedly urged in comparatively recent times. Only a short time ago, even a distinguished ethnologist, Wilhelm Schmidt, attempted to prove that such an original monotheism was without doubt a dominant belief among the so-called Pygmies, who must, in general, be classed with primitive peoples. The argument adduced in support of this view, however, unquestionably lacks the critical caution otherwise characteristic of this investigator. One cannot escape the conviction that, in this case, personal religious needs influenced the ethnological views, even though one may well doubt whether the degeneration theory is a theory that is suited to satisfy such needs.[1] The second class of theories adopts the view that the basis of all religious development was not monotheism but primitive polytheism. This polytheism is supposed to have originated, at a very early age, in the impression made by the starry heavens, particularly by the great heavenly bodies, the sun and the moon. Here for the first time, it is maintained, man was confronted by a world far transcending his own realm of sense perception; because of the multiplicity of the motives that were operative, it was not the idea of one deity but the belief in many deities that was evoked. In essential contrast with the preceding view, this class of theories regards

[1] Concerning this alleged monotheism among primitive peoples, cf. supra, pp. 78 f.

all further development as upward. Monotheism is held to be a refined religious product of earlier polytheistic conceptions. In so far, the hypothesis represents a transition to developmental theories proper. It cannot be counted among the latter, however, for it holds to the originality of the god-idea, believing that this conception, which is essential to all religion, was not itself the product of development, but formed an original element of man's natural endowment. Moreover, the theory attaches a disproportionate significance to the transition from many gods to a single god. It is doubtful, to say the least, whether the intrinsic value of the god-idea may be measured merely in terms of this numerical standard. Furthermore, the fact is undeniable that philosophy alone really exhibits an absolute monotheism. A pure monotheistic belief probably never existed in the religion of any people, not even in that of the Israelites, whose national deity, Jahve, was not at all the sole god in the sense of a strict monotheism. When the Decalogue says, "Thou shalt have no other gods before me," this does not deny the existence of gods other than Jahve, but merely prohibits the Israelites from worshipping any other deity. These other gods, however, are the national gods of other peoples. Not only do these other tribal gods exist alongside of Jahve, but the patriarchal sagas centre about individuals that resemble now demonic and now divine beings. The most remarkable of these figures is Jacob. In the account of his personality there seem to be mingled legends of differing origin, dating from a time probably far earlier than the developed Jahve cult. The scene with his father-in-law, Laban, represents him as a sort of crafty märchen-hero. He cheats Laban through his knowledge of magic, gaining for himself the choicest of the young lambs by constructing the watering troughs of half-peeled rods of wood—a striking example of so-called imitative magic. On the other hand, Jacob is portrayed as the hero who rolls from the well's mouth the stone which all the servants of Laban could not move. And finally, when he wrestles with Jahve by night on the bank of the stream and is not overcome until the break of day, we are reminded either of a mighty Titan of divine lineage, or possibly of the river demon who, according to ancient folk belief, threatens to engulf every one who crosses the stream, be it even a god. But what is true of the figures of the patriarchal sagas applies also, in part, to Jahve himself. In the remarkable scene in which Jahve visits Abraham near the terebinths of Mamre, he associates with the patriarch as a *primus inter pares*. He allows Sarah to bake him a cake and to wash his feet, and he then promises Abraham a numerous posterity. He appears as a man among men, though, of course, as one who is superior and who possesses magical power. Only gradually does the god acquire the remoteness of the superhuman. Abraham is later represented as falling down before him, and as scarcely daring to approach him. Here also, however, the god still appears on earth. Finally, when he speaks to Moses from the burning bush, only his voice is perceptible. Thus, his sensuous form vanishes more and more, until we come to the Jahve who uses the prophets as his mouthpiece and is present to them only as a spiritual being. The purified Jahve cult, therefore, was not an original folk-religion. It was the product of priests and prophets, created by them out of a polytheism which contained a rich profusion of demon conceptions, and which was never entirely suppressed.

If an original monotheism is nowhere to be found, one might be tempted to believe, conversely, that *polytheism* represents the starting-point of all mythology. In fact, until very recently this was doubtless the consensus of opinion among mythologists and historians of religion, and the idea is still widely prevalent. For, if we hold in any way to the view that the god-idea is underived, there is but one recourse, once we abandon the idea of an original monotheism. The polytheistic theory is, as a rule, connected with the further contention that god-ideas are directly due to celestial phenomena. In substantiation of this view, it is pointed out that, with the exception of the gods of the underworld, the gods are usually supposed to dwell in the heavens. Accordingly, it is particularly the great heavenly bodies, the sun and the moon, or also the clouds and storms, to which—now to the one and now to the other, according to their particular tendency—these theories trace the origin of the gods. Celestial phenomena were present to man from the beginning, and it is supposed that they aroused his reflection from earliest times on. Those mythologists who champion the celestial theory of the origin of religion, therefore, regard god-ideas as in great measure the products of intellectual activity; these ideas are supposed to represent a sort of primitive explanation of nature, though an explanation, of course, which, in contrast to later science, is fantastical, arbitrary, and under the control of emotion. During the past century, moreover, this class of hypotheses has gradually placed less emphasis on emotional as compared with rational factors. In the first instance, it was the phenomena of storms, clouds, thunder, and lightning that were thought to be the basis of deity belief; later, the sun came to be regarded as the embodiment of the chief god; the present tendency is to emphasize particularly the moon, whose changing phases may easily give rise to various mythological ideas. Does not the proverbial 'man in the moon' survive even to-day as a well-known fragment of mythological conceptions of this sort? Similarly, the crescent moon suggests a sword, a club, a boat, and many other things which, though not conceived as gods, may at any rate be regarded as their weapons or implements. The gods, we are told, then gradually became distinguished from celestial objects and became independent personal beings. The heroes of the hero saga are said to be degenerated gods, as it were. When the myth attributes a divine parentage to the hero, or allows him to enter the realm of the gods upon his death, this is interpreted as indicative of a vague memory that the hero was once himself a god. The lowest place in the scale of heroes is given to the märchen-hero, though he also is supposed in the last analysis to have originated as a celestial deity. The märchen itself is thus regarded as the last stage in the decline of the myth, whose development is held to have been initiated in the distant past by the celestial myth. Accordingly, the most prevalent present-day tendency of nature mythology is to assume an orderly development of a twofold sort. On the one hand, the moon is regarded as having been the earliest object of cult, followed by the sun and the stars. Later, it is supposed, a distinction was made between gods and celestial objects, though the former were still given many celestial attributes. On the other hand, it is held that the gods were more and more anthropomorphized; their celestial origin becoming gradually obscured, they were reduced to heroes of various ranks, ranging from the heroic figures of the saga to the heroes of children's märchen. These theories of an original polytheism are rendered one-sided by the very fact that they are not based upon any investigations whatsoever concerning the gods and myths actually prevalent in folk-belief. They merely give an interpretation of hypothetical conceptions which are supposed to be original, and it is from these that the gods of actual belief are derived. Those who proceed thus believe that the task of the psychologist of religion and of the mythologist is completed with the demonstration that back of every deity of myth there lurks a celestial phenomenon. It has been maintained, for example, that every feature of the Biblical legend of Paradise had its origin in ideas connected with the moon. Paradise itself is the moon. The flaming sword of the angel who guards Paradise is the crescent moon. Adam is either the half-moon or the familiar man in the moon. Finally, Adam's rib, out of which Eve was created, is again the crescent moon.

We need not raise the question whether such a mode of treatment ever correctly interprets any actual mythological conception, or whether it represents nothing other than the creation of the mythologist's imagination. This much is clear, that it leaves out of consideration precisely those mythological ideas and religious views that really live in folk-belief. Doubtless we may assume that celestial phenomena occasionally factored as assimilative elements in the formation of mythological conceptions. But such conceptions cannot possibly have been due exclusively to celestial factors, for the very reason that, even where these are indubitably present, they are inextricably interwoven with terrestrial elements derived from man's immediate environment. Consider, for example, the figure of Helios in Greek mythology. His very name so inevitably suggests the sun that this connection remained unsevered throughout later development. Nevertheless, the Greeks no more identified the god Helios with the sun than they did Zeus himself with thunder and lightning. On the contrary, these celestial phenomena were all only attributes of deities. The god stands in the background, and, in the idea which man forms of him, the image of human heroes plays no less a part than do the impressions made by the shining heavenly bodies. These various interpretations of nature mythology, therefore, overlook an important psychological factor which is operative even in elemental experiences, but which attains increasing significance in proportion as the psychical processes become more complicated, and especially, therefore, in the formation of mythological conceptions. I refer to the *assimilative fusion of psychical elements of differing origins*. No external object is perceived precisely as it is immediately given in reality. In the experience of it, there are fused numerous elements whose source is within ourselves; these partly reinforce and partly suppress the given elements, thus producing what we call the 'perception' or the 'apprehension' of the object. The process of assimilation is greatly influenced by the emotions that may be present. To the frightened person, thunder and lightning suggest a god who hurls the lightning. Such a person believes that he really sees this god. Either the surrounding portions of the sky assume, in his imagination, the form of an immense anthropomorphic being, or the thunder and lightning lead his gaze to the canopy of clouds, hidden back of which he thinks that he discovers, at least in vague outline, the thundering Zeus. To gain some appreciation of the tremendous potency of assimilative processes, one need but recall certain situations of ordinary life, such as are experienced even apart from the influence of fear or ecstasy. Consider, for example, the vivid impression that may be aroused by theatrical scenery, which in reality consists of little more than suggestive outlines. A particularly striking illustration is offered also by the familiar puzzle pictures. In a picture of the foliage of a tree there are sketched the outlines of a human face or of the head of a cat. An uninitiated observer sees at first only the foliage. Not until his attention has been directed to it does he suddenly discover the head. Once, however, he has seen the latter, he cannot suppress it, try as he may. Here again it is sometimes but a few indistinct outlines that evoke the picture. The truth is that to a very great extent the observer reads the head into the drawing through the activity of his imagination. Now, it is but natural that such an assimilation should be immeasurably enhanced under the influence of the emotions which excite the mythological imagination. As is well known, Apollo, as well as Helios, was represented by the image of the sun. This image, however, was even less adequate to embody the idea of the Greek in the former case than it was in the latter. The Greek was able, however, to imagine the radiant sun as an attribute of the deity or as a manifestation of his activity. He could see in the sun the shield or chariot of the god; in the sun's rays, his missiles. Here again, however, he had in mind the indefinite outlines of a powerful anthropomorphic god, who could become independent of the natural phenomenon according as his name was free from connection with it.

Thus, even those nature gods who might appear to be purely celestial deities, as, for example, Helios, or the lightning-hurling Zeus, are the products of a psychological assimilation of perceptual elements, the most important of which have their ultimate source in terrestrial life. Hence it is that, wherever the nature myth has reached its complete development, the gods appear in *human form*. It is only in an age still influenced by totemic ideas that zoömorphism occurs alongside of anthropomorphism, or in combination with it. Of such figures, the one which maintained itself longest—as is shown by the history of ancient Egypt—was that of a human body with the head of an animal. After this connection of an incipient deity cult with the ideas of the preceding age had disappeared, the only remaining trace of totemism was the fact that an animal was represented as accompanying the deity. Eventually the animal became a mere symbol used by art in its pictorial representations of the god. Doubtless the lamb, as a symbol of Christ, may be regarded as a late survival of a stage of deity belief which was still semi-totemic, and under the influence of the sacred animals of older cultural religions. The expression 'sacred animals,' moreover, points to the fact that the worship and veneration paid to the god influenced also the attitude taken toward the animal. But however far this development of the god-idea may have advanced, the essential elements of the conception nevertheless remained of *terrestrial* origin. In the mythological assimilation-complexes that gave rise to gods, celestial phenomena furnished but a part of the elements. At best, they were the exciting stimuli; in many cases, it is doubtful whether they exercised any influence whatsoever upon the origin of mythological conceptions. Whether, for example, the crescent moon has actually any connection with the flaming sword of the angel of Paradise, or whether it suggested the club of Hercules, this and much else is possible, but is incapable of demonstration. Even where this influence upon mythological conceptions is incontestable, celestial phenomena are subordinate to terrestrial factors, and in most cases they have left no trace in consciousness. Proof of the dominant importance of the terrestrial environment is not far to seek. Even the celestial gods are conceived as men or as anthropomorphic beings, and it is usually the earth that is regarded as the scene of their activity.

The theories maintaining the originality of the god-idea have more and more been displaced by the contrary view, namely, that the gods developed out of lower forms of mythological thought. Here there are *two* distinct interpretations. The first and the older is the *ancestor theory*. This represents a particular form of animism, for the soul of the ancestor is thought to become a god. The worship of the god, therefore, is held to have been originally a reverence paid to the ancestor. The main evidence for this view is found in the ancestor worship which is actually being practised, among many peoples, even at the present time. Prior to the Jahve religion, such a cult is supposed to have prevailed even among the Israelites. Do not the patriarchs Abraham, Isaac, and Jacob appear as the ancestors of the later tribes of Israel? More significant still are the ancestor cults that have prevailed in China and Japan since very ancient times. It should be remembered, however, that these cults, wherever they occur, represent but more or less prominent elements of more extensive mythological and religious conceptions. Hence the ancestor theory, also, is an arbitrary construction based on a presupposition which is in itself very improbable, namely, that all mythology and religion must eventually be traceable to a single source. The contention, for example, that a Zeus or a Jahve was a human ancestor elevated into a deity is a completely arbitrary supposition, lacking the confirmation of empirical facts.

Finally, there is another theory which, like the ancestor hypothesis, seeks to derive gods, or at least the beings generally regarded as gods, from more primitive mythological ideas. This theory, which was developed by Hermann Usener, the most prominent student of the science of religion among recent classical philologists, might perhaps be referred to, in distinction from the soul and ancestor hypothesis, as the *demon theory* of the origin of gods. Usener agrees with the rival hypothesis in assuming that the exalted celestial deities were not the first of the higher beings who were feared or worshipped in a cult, but that there were other more temporary gods. Though these many temporary gods are described as demoniacal beings, they are nevertheless regarded as gods of a primitive sort. Usener distinguishes three stages in the development of gods. First, there was the 'god of the moment.' Some phenomenon—such, for example, as a flash of lightning or a clap of thunder—was felt to be divine. But, inasmuch as the impression was vanishing, the mythological idea in question was that of a 'god of the moment.' Then followed a second stage, in which a demoniacal power was associated with a particular place. Following upon these local gods came other gods, representing the guardian powers of a tribe, a vocation, or some other social group. At the third stage of development, the 'particular god' acquired a personal nature, and thus finally became a god proper. The gods of this final stage are called by Usener 'personal gods.'

Although this theory is doubtless in greater consonance with certain general characteristics of myth development than is the ancestor theory, we would urge, as one chief objection, the fact that its god-concept unites mythological-religious elements of a very different nature. In particular, the so-called 'god of a moment' is neither a god, in the proper sense of the word, nor even a demon, but either a particular impression arousing fear, or, on a higher plane, a single manifestation of the activity of a demon or god. The Greeks referred the flash of lightning to Zeus, the lightning-hurler. On a more primitive level, the North American Indian sees in the lightning and thunder the acts of a demon hidden in the clouds. In neither case are the momentary phenomena identified with gods or demons themselves. There is not a shadow of proof in the entire history of myth that such acts or attributes as these, which were attributed to gods and demons, ever existed as independent realities of even but a moment's duration. The so-called 'particular gods,' on the other hand, are in every respect demons and not gods. They are not personal in nature ; this also implies that they are not conceived as having a particular form, for somehow the latter always leads to personalization. As a matter of fact, these 'particular gods' are only objectified emotions of fear and terror. Spirits, in the sense of magical agents of disease conceived as invisible beings, or occasionally imaged in the form of fantastic though ever-changing animal shapes, are not gods, but demons. The same holds true of the multitude of nature demons that infest field and forest and the vicinity of streams and gorges. Wherever myth has given these spirits definite forms, they reveal no evidence of traits such as would constitute them individual personalities. This, of course, does not imply that there are no cases at all in which the indeterminate traits ascribed to them are so combined as to result in individual beings. When this occurs, however, we have already transcended the stage of so-called 'particular gods.' Such beings as the Greek Pan or the Germanic Hel must already be classed with gods proper, even though they exhibit traits indicative of a demoniacal past ; for the narrowness of character which they manifest results from the fact that they originated directly in a particular emotion. Surely, therefore, the decisive emphasis in the case of deity ideas in general must be placed on the attribute of personality. Gods are personal beings, whose characters reflect the peculiarity of the people who have created them. We see in the god Jahve of the Israelites the clear-cut lines of the stern god who threatens the disobedient, but who also rewards the faithful. More impressive still is the uniqueness of personality in those cases in which a multiplicity of gods causes the development of diverse and partly opposed characteristics in the various gods. How individual are the gods of the Greeks with respect to one another! Under the influence of poetry every god has here become a clearly defined personality, whose individuality was fixed by formative art. Thus, the error of the demon theory or, as it might also be called, the three-stage theory, lies in the fact that it effaces the essential distinctions between god and demon, retaining as the chief characteristic of the multitude of resulting deity-conceptions only the most external quality, that of *permanence*. For the 'god of a moment' is characterized merely by his extreme transitoriness, the 'particular god' is the 'god of a moment' become somewhat more enduring but not yet possessed of sufficient stability to develop personal traits; the true or personal god, finally, owes his distinctive attribute solely to the permanence of his characteristics. Because of this confusion of the concepts 'god' and 'demon,' there is lacking precisely that which is of most importance for a psychological investigation—namely, an answer to the question as to the *intrinsic* marks that differentiate a god, in the proper and only true sense of the word, from demons, ancestors, and souls—in short, from all other creations of mythological thought.

Herewith we come to a question which will bring us closer to an answer respecting the origin of gods. By what characteristic marks is a mythological conception to be distinguished as that of an actual god? The question might also be stated in a more concrete form. What characteristics differentiate a god from a *demon,* who is not yet a god because he lacks personality, and from a *hero,* who is regarded by the age in which gods originate as somewhat approximating a god but as nevertheless still a man? Or, briefly expressed, how does the god differ from the demon and from the ideal man? The criteria thus demanded are to be found in the traits that are universally ascribed to gods wherever any complete deity mythology and a corresponding religion have been developed. The god is always distinguished by three characteristics. The first of these is that his *place of abode* is other than that of man. He may occasionally visit man on the earth, but this occurs only rarely. So far as he himself is concerned, the god lives in another world. In this sense, the idea of a 'beyond' is closely bound up with that of gods. As a rule, the 'beyond' is the heavenly world. But gods may dwell also in the regions of the air and clouds between the heaven and the earth, on high mountains, on distant islands, or, finally, under special circumstances, in the depths of the earth. Secondly, the gods lead a *perfect* life, free, on the whole, from the evils and infirmities of earthly existence. A perfect life, however, is always regarded as primarily a life without death and without sickness. There then develops, though doubtless gradually, the idea of something even more perfect than is involved in this merely negative conception of immortal and painless existence. But at this point ideas begin to differ, so that, in reality, the most universal characteristics of the gods are that they know neither death nor sickness. There are occasional exceptions, however, just as there are with respect to the supra-mundane place of abode. The Greek as well as the Germanic deity sagas represent the gods as possessing a particular food and a particular drink, an idea connected with that of the anthropomorphic nature of these gods. The Germanic gods, especially, are described as capable of maintaining their perfect life only by far exceeding the human measure of food and drink. This, however, is but a subordinate feature. More important is the fact that if, by any unfortunate circumstance, food and drink are lacking, the gods waste away and meet the universal lot of human existence—death. But, even apart from this connection, the Germanic sagas, or at any rate the poetry inspired by them, tell of a decline of gods and of the rise of a new divine hierarchy. It is not to be assumed, of course, that this represents an original element in Germanic mythology. All records of Germanic deity sagas, as we know, date from Christian times. Even though the ancient skalds, as well as those historians who regarded the saga as a bit of actual history, may have made every effort to preserve for posterity the memory of this departed world, they could, nevertheless, hardly have avoided mingling certain Christian ideas with tradition. In view of the actual decline of the former gods, the thought of a *Götterdämmerung*, in particular, must almost inevitably have forced itself upon them. At any rate, inasmuch as this particular conception represents the gods as subject to death, it contains an element that is bound up with the anthropomorphic nature of the divine beings, though this, of course, is irreconcilable with the immortality originally conceded to them. We are thus brought to the most important characteristic of gods, which is connected with this very fact of their similarity to man. The god is a *personality* ; he has a specific personal character, which gives direction to his will and leads him to send blessings or misfortunes to mortals. These purely human characteristics, however, he possesses in an exalted and complete measure. His will-acts, as well as the emotion from which they spring and the insight by which they are guided, are superhuman in power. But this power is not equivalent to omnipotence. This it cannot be by very reason of the multiplicity of gods, each of whom has a particular sphere of activity. Frequently, moreover, omnipotence is rendered impossible by the idea—likewise carried over from the terrestrial to the supermundane world—of a *destiny* an impersonal power behind the wills of gods no less than those of men. This is a conception which deity beliefs inherit from the earlier demon beliefs. True, polytheistic myth itself takes a step in the direction of transcending this limitation when it here also transfers the conditions of the human order to the divine world, and creates for the latter a monarch, a supreme deity ruling over gods and men. But this very projection of human relations into the divine realm prevents the chief deity from being an unlimited ruler. On the one hand, he shares authority with a deliberative assembly consisting of the remaining gods ; on the other hand, even behind him there lurk those demoniacal powers which, to a certain extent, continued to assert themselves even after they had been superseded by the gods. For here also it holds true that whatever lives in folk-belief must retain a foundation in myth. The advent of gods nowhere led to the complete banishment of demons. What occurred was that, due to the power of the gods, certain of the demons likewise developed into mighty forces of destiny, though continuing to remain impersonal.

Thus, the god possesses three characteristics : a special dwelling-place, immortality, and a superhuman, though at the same time a human, personality. Leaving out of regard the tribute exacted even of the gods by the last-mentioned of these characteristics, human nature, we have before us the marks which distinguish the god both from the demon and from the hero. The demon, however powerful he may be, lacks the attribute of personality; the hero, as thoroughly human, shares the universal lot of man as regards dwelling-place, length of life, and liability to sickness and death. This places the god midway between the demon and the hero, though, of course. by combining the attributes of both he is really exalted above them. The demon, in the sense in which the Greeks employed this term, is a fundamental element in the development of all mythologies. There can be no doubt, moreover, that demons appeared far earlier than gods, if we exclude from among the latter those indefinite and transitory personifications of natural phenomena that have wrongly been classed with them—such personifications as those of rocks, hills, clouds, stars, etc., which were widely current even among peoples of nature. According to a belief which has not entirely disappeared even among cultural peoples, the soul leaves the corpse in the form of a demon; the wandering ghost is a demon; demons dwell in the depths, in the neighbourhood of streams, in solitary ravines, in forests and fields, upon and beneath the earth. They are usually threatening, though sometimes beneficent, powers. In every instance, however, they are absolutely impersonal embodiments of the emotions of fear and hope, and it is these emotions, under the assimilative influences of impressions of external nature, that have given rise to them. Thus, demons are usually mundane beings, or, at any rate, have their abode near the surface of the earth; with few exceptions, the most distant realm which they occupy is that of the clouds, particularly the dark rain and thunder clouds. True, the heavenly bodies may manifest demoniacal powers, just as may also the gods. As a rule, however, celestial phenomena are far from belonging to the class of demons proper; they are too constant and too regular in their changes and movements to be thus included. The activity of demons relates exclusively to the welfare of man. Hence it is but natural that demons should be primarily man's co-inhabitants on earth. Usually invisible, they assume sensuously perceptible forms only in the darkness of night, or, more especially, under the influence of heightened emotions. Sometimes they are audible even when invisible. Only in those narratives which tell of demoniacal beings that are not immediately present do demons acquire fairly definite forms. Thus, even soul beliefs—which the fear of the uncanny activity of the departed soul transforms directly into a sort of demon belief—represent the soul in the form of a bird, a snake, or of other specific 'soul animals.' The demons of sickness lurking within the diseased body are usually portrayed as fantastic animals, whose monstrous forms reflect the terrible distress and the torturing pains of sickness. These animals hinder respiration and bore into and lacerate the intestines. Thus, they objectify both the pain of the sickness and the fear aroused in the community by the behaviour of the sick person. No less, however, can the impression of the desert, the dark forest, the lonely ravine, or the terror of an approaching storm cause demons, which are in first instance invisible, to assume definite shapes. Where there is a more highly developed sense of nature, such as begins to manifest itself in the heroic age, this objectification of impressions occurs not only under the influence of strong excitement but also in connection with the peaceful landscape. Here it gives rise to more friendly beings, in the case of whom those characteristics, at least, which made the original demon an object of terror, are moderated so as to find expression in magic of a playful sort. This is the origin of satyrs, sylphs and fauns, of gnomes, giants and dwarfs, elves, fairies, etc., all of whom are debarred from personality by their very multiplicity, while their generic character accurately reflects the mood which led to their creation. The individualization of certain of these beings is, in general, due to poetry. But even poetry does not entirely succeed in freeing the demon from the generic character which once for all represents its nature. Thus, it is the contrast between genericalness and individual personality that differentiates the demon from the god.

Every gnome resembles every other, and all nymphs are alike; hence these beings are generally referred to in the plural. Their multiplicity is such that they are imaged in only indefinite forms, except in cases where particularly strong emotions excite a more lively imagination. Indeed, they may be present to consciousness solely as a peculiar feeling associated with particular places or occasions, such as is the case with the Lares, Manes, and Penates of the Romans, and with the similar guardian spirits of the house and the field common among many peoples. Some of these guardian spirits are not very unlike the ancestors of cult. But this only indicates that the ancestor worshipped in cult also approximates to the demon, acquiring a more personal character only in occasional instances in which memory has preserved with considerable faithfulness the traits of a particularly illustrious ancestor. Here, then, we have the condition underlying the origin of gods. Gods are universally the result of a *union of demoniacal and heroic elements*. The god is at once demon and hero; since, however, the demoniacal element in him magnifies his heroic attributes into the superhuman, and since the personal character which he borrows from the hero supersedes the indefinite and impersonal nature of the demon, he is exalted above them both: the god himself is neither hero nor demon, because he combines in himself the attributes of both, in an ideally magnified form.

The resemblance of demons to gods is due primarily to the magic power which they exert. The demons of sickness torture and destroy men; the cloud demons bring rain and blessing to the fields, or plot ruin when rain does not relieve the drought of the burning sun. By means of magic incantations and ceremonies, these demons can be won over, or, when angry, reconciled. Their own activity, therefore, is magical, and, as regards the effects that it produces, superhuman. In their fleeting and impersonal character, however, they are subhuman. Since the dominant emotions that call them into being are fear and terror, they are generally regarded as enemies not only of man but even of the gods. The struggle between gods and nature-demons is a recurrent theme in the cosmogonies of all cultural peoples. This hostility between demons and gods is connected with the contrast in the feelings evoked by darkness and radiant brightness. Hence the mighty nature-demons are, as a rule, consigned to gloomy abysses, from which they rise to the sky only occasionally, as, for example, in the case of thunder-clouds. The abode of the gods, however, is in the bright celestial realms, and they themselves are radiant beings upon whose activity the harmonious order of nature and the happiness of mankind are dependent. In the strife which the demons carry on with gods, they occasionally develop into counter-gods, as occurred in the case of the Persian Ahriman and the Jewish-Christian Satan. Yet it is significant of the almost insuperable lack of personality characteristic of the demon, that even these counter-gods of darkness and evil are wanting in *one trait* which is indispensable for a completely developed personality —namely, changes in motives and the capacity to determine at will the nature of these changes. Herein, again, is reflected the fact that the demon has but a *single* source—namely, fear.

Very different from the relation of the god to the demon is his relation to the hero. The hero, to a greater extent even than the god, is the complete opposite of the demon. For the hero is an idealized man. He is subject to all human destinies, to sickness and death, to afflictions of the soul, and to violent passions. Yet in all these instances the experiences are of a more exalted nature than in the case of ordinary human life. The life as well as the death of the hero are of wide import ; the effects of his deeds extend to distant lands and ages. But it is just because the hero is the ideal man himself that he possesses all the more markedly the attribute which the demon lacks—namely, *personality*. This, of course, does not prevent his character from exhibiting generic differences and antitheses. But herein also the hero is only the idealized counterpart of man, for, despite all its uniqueness and individuality, man's character usually conforms to certain types. Thus, legend introduces the strong, all-conquering hero, and, in contrast with him, the hero who is resourceful and overcomes his enemies through subtle cunning. It tells of the aged man, superior in wisdom and experience, and also of him who, in the unbroken strength of youth and with stormy passion, overthrows all opponents. It further portrays the hero who plots evil, but who is nevertheless characterized by a sharply defined personality.

When we survey these various heroic figures in both their generic and their individual aspects and compare them with the god-personalities, we are struck by the fact that the god was not created directly in the image of a man, but rather in that of the hero, man idealized It is the hero who gives to the gods those very characteristics which the demon lacks from the outset. Of these, the most important are personality, self-consciousness, and a will controlled by diverse and frequently conflicting motives. This multiplicity of motives has a close connection with the multiplicity of gods. Polytheism is not an accidental feature which may or may not accompany the belief in gods ; it is a necessary transitional stage in the development of the god-idea. Folk-belief, which never frees itself entirely from mythology, always retains a plurality of divine beings. Hence true monotheism represents a philosophical development of the god-idea. Though this development was not without influence on the theological speculation which was dominated by traditional doctrines, it was never able to uproot the polytheistic tendency involved in the god-idea from the very beginning. There are two sources from which this tendency springs. Of these, one is external and, therefore, though of great importance for the beginnings of religious development, is transitory. It consists in the influence exerted by the multiplicity of natural phenomena, through the nature myth, upon the number of gods. More important and of more permanent significance is the second or *internal* motive, namely, the fact that the psychical needs that come to expression in the demand for gods are numerous. There cannot be a single god-ideal any more than a single type of hero. On the contrary, as heroes exhibit the diversity of human effort on an exalted plane, so, in turn, does the realm of gods represent, on a still higher level, the world of heroes. This advance beyond the hero-ideal becomes possible to the mythological imagination only because the very endeavour to exalt the hero above the human itself brought the hero-idea, at the very time of its origin, into connection with the demon-idea. For the demon is a superhuman being, magic-working and unpredictable, affecting in mysterious ways the course of nature and of human destiny. But it lacks the familiar human traits which make the hero an object not only of fear but also of admiration and love. Thus, the fusion of hero and demon results in the final and the greatest of mythological creations, the conception which represents the birth of religion in the proper and ultimately only true sense of the word. I refer to *the rise of gods*.

The god-idea, accordingly, is the product of *two* component factors. One of these, the demoniacal, has had a long history, extending back to the beginnings of mythological thought ; the other, the heroic, begins to assert itself the very moment that the figure of the hero appears. This implies that god-ideas are neither of sudden origin nor unchangeable, but that they undergo a gradual development. The direction of development is determined by the relation which its two component factors sustain to each other. The earliest god-ideas are predominantly demoniacal in nature—personal characteristics are few, while magical features are all the more pronounced. Then the heroic element comes to the fore, until it finally acquires such dominance that even the magical power of the god appears to be a result of his heroic might, rather than a survival of the demoniacal nature which was his from the very beginning. In connection with this change, it is significant to note that, as the god loses his original demoniacal character, he comes to be attended by subservient beings who remain, in every respect, demons. On the one hand, these beings execute the divine commands ; on the other hand, however—as an echo, one might say, of the age of demons which precedes that of gods—they are superior even to the gods in that they possess magical powers. These beings must be regarded as survivals of the age of demons. Between them and the gods proper there are intermediate beings, just as there are between heroes and gods, those of the latter sort being exemplified particularly by such heroes as have been exalted into deities. Inasmuch as all the intermediate forms that arise in the course of this transition continue in existence even up to the culmination of the development, the gods constantly become more numerous. Side by side with the gods, demons maintain their sway. At times, they contend with the gods ; in other instances, they are subservient to them ; again, as in the earliest periods of mythological thought, they are without any knowledge whatsoever of the existence of gods. The hero also is invariably associated with the god. With the decline of the heroic age, therefore, the realm of gods also disappears. Though the religious developments that ensue have their origin in deity beliefs, they nevertheless discard the original nucleus of these beliefs—namely, the gods themselves—or, at any rate, they retain gods only in a greatly altered form.

That gods belong essentially to the heroic age appears also in the fact that the divine realm mirrors in detail the relations of political society developed subsequently to the beginning of the heroic age. The world of gods likewise forms a divine *State*. It is at most at an early period that the tribal gods of various peoples betray the influence of the ancient tribal organization that preceded the State. In the supremacy of a single god, however, the idea of rulership, which is basal to the State, is transferred also to the divine realm. This is true whether the ruling deity exercises command over a subservient host of demons and subordinate gods, or whether he has at his side a number of independent gods, who represent, in part, an advisory council, such as is found associated with the earthly ruler, and, in part, since the different gods possess diverse powers, a sort of celestial officialdom. Finally, the multiplicity of independent States is mirrored in the multiplicity of the independent realms ruled over by the gods. The differentiation, in this latter case, corresponds with the main directions of human interest. The development is influenced, moreover, by those natural phenomena that have long factored in the capacity of assimilative elements. Over against the bright celestial gods are the subterranean gods who dwell in the gloomy depths. For the inhabitants of the sea-coast and of islands, furthermore, there is a ruler of the sea. The importance of the god of the sea, however, is subordinate to that of the rulers of the celestial and the nether worlds, so that those over whom he holds sway never develop into clearly defined personalities, but always retain more of a demoniacal character. All the more important, therefore, are the contrasts between the celestial and the nether worlds, as the two realms which include the real destiny of man. At death, man must enter the nether world; to rise from the gloom of this realm of the dead to the heaven and immortality of the celestial gods becomes his longing. Thus, deity beliefs enter into reciprocal relations with soul conceptions. The further stages of this development carry us far beyond the heroic age, and reflect the influence of a diversity of motives. The discussion of this point will occupy our attention in later pages.

12. THE HERO SAGA.

If the gods be described as personalities, each one of whom possesses a more or less definite individuality, it is at once evident that the conception of an animated natural phenomenon—the idea, for example, that the setting sun is a being which a dark cloud-demon is devouring—cannot in and of itself as yet be called a god-idea. Just as the character of a man may be known only from the manner in which he reacts towards the objects of his experience, so also is the nature of a god revealed only in his life and activity, and in the motives that determine his conduct. The character of the god is expressed, not in any single mythological picture, but in the *myth* or mythological tale, in which the god figures as a personal agent. It is significant to note, however, that the form of myth in which god-ideas come to development is not the deity saga, in the proper sense of the term, but the *hero saga*, which becomes a combined hero and deity saga as soon as both gods and heroes are represented as participating in the action. The deity saga proper, which deals exclusively with the deeds of gods and demons, is, as we shall see below, only of secondary and of later origin. It is not to such deity sagas, therefore, that we must turn if we would learn the original nature of gods. This circumstance in itself offers external evidence of the fact that gods did not precede heroes, but, conversely, that heroes preceded gods. Or, at least, to be more accurate, the idea of the divine personality was developed in constant reciprocity with that of the hero personality, in such wise, however, that with reference to details the hero paved the way for the god, and not conversely.

But how did the idea of hero arise? Was it a free and completely new creation of this age, based merely on actual observations of individuals who were paragons of human ability? Or did it have precursors in the totemic era? As a matter of fact, this second question must be answered unqualifiedly in the affirmative. The hero was not unknown in the preceding age. At that time, however, he was not a hero in the specific sense which the word first acquired in the heroic age; on the contrary, he was a *mörchen*-hero, if we may use the word ' hero ' in connection with the concepts of this earlier period. On the threshold of the heroic age, the märchen-hero changes into the hero proper. The former represents the central theme of the earlier form of myth narrative, the märchen-myth, as does the hero that of the more developed form, the saga. The marks that distinguish the märchen-hero, as he still survives in children's tales, from the hero of saga, are important ones and are fraught with significance for the development of myth as a whole. The märchen-hero is usually a *child*. In the form in which he gradually approximates to the hero proper, he is more especially, as a rule, a boy who goes forth into the world and meets with adventures. In these adventures, he is aided by various powers of magic, which he either himself possesses or which are imparted to him by friendly magical beings. Opposed to him are hostile, demoniacal beings, who seek his destruction. It is in their overthrow that the action usually consists. Thus, fortune comes to this hero, in great part, from without, and magic plays the decisive rôle in his destiny; his own cunning and skill may be co-operating factors, but they rarely determine the outcome. Not so the hero of the saga. This hero is not a boy, but a *man*. The favourite theme of the saga is particularly the young man in the bloom of life. In his acts, moreover, this hero is dependent, for the most part, upon himself. True, he, as well as the märchen-hero, is familiar with magic and miracle, but it is primarily by his own power that he overcomes the hostile forces that oppose him. A suggestive illustration of this is Hercules, that figure of Greek saga who is pre-eminently the typical hero among the most diverse peoples and in widely different ages. Hercules is an entirely self-dependent hero. He indeed performs marvellous deeds, but these are never more than extreme instances of what an ordinary man might do were his strength multiplied a hundred or a thousand fold. Hercules is not a magician, but a being of transcendent power and strength. As such, he is able even to carry the weight of the sky on his shoulders; as such, he can overcome monsters, such as the Nemean lion and the Lernæan hydra, or bring Cerberus, the most terrible of these monsters, from the nether world. These are deeds which surpass every measure of human power, but which nevertheless still lie in the general plane of human actions. Thus, just as the magic-working boy was superseded by the man of might, so also does the true magical hero disappear from mythology. The saga, then, differs from the märchen-myth in the character of its hero. The Hercules saga itself, however, is an illustration of the fact that the former may have no connection whatsoever with historical events, any more than has the latter. Moreover, the earliest sagas, particularly, not infrequently still remind one of the märchen in that they are obviously a composite of several narratives. Of this fact also, the saga of Hercules offers a conspicuous example. The deeds of the hero appear to have but an accidental connection with one another. True, later sagas represent these deeds as adventures which the hero undertook at the command of King Eurystheus of Mycene. But even here we obviously have only a loose sort of framework which was at some later period imposed upon the original tales in order to bind the cycle together as a whole. It is not improbable that these various sagas of a hero who vanquished monsters, rendered lands habitable, and performed other deeds, originated independently of one another. Not only may their places of origin have been different, but their narratives may have had their settings in different localities. Possibly, therefore, it was not until later that the sagas were combined to portray the character of a single individual, who thus became exalted into the national hero. But, though the hero saga resembles the märchen in the fact that it grows by the agglutination of diverse legendary materials, it differs from it in the possession of a characteristic which is typical of this stage of development. That which binds together the separate elements of the hero saga is a unitary thought, generally associated with great cultural changes or with historical events.

There is a further differentia of the saga as compared with the märchen. Wherever magic enters into the saga to affect the course of events, the chief vehicle of magical powers is not the hero himself—at most, he has been equipped by others with magical powers and implements. Such demoniacal powers as the saga may introduce into its narrative are usually vested in accessory persons. This fact is closely connected with the self-dependent character of the hero-personality, who may, it is true, employ magic in so far as he has received such power from external sources, but who himself possesses none but human attributes. The saga of the Argonauts, for example, is so replete with magic as not to be surpassed in this respect even by the magical märchen. Moreover, the various elements incorporated in the saga are all pure märchen motives—the golden fleece, the talking ship, the closing cliffs, as well as the sorceress Medea and the whole wonderland of Colchis. Those who man the Argo, however, are not magicians, but heroes in the strictly human sense of the word. The same fact stands out even more strikingly in the case of the saga of Odysseus, at any rate in the form in which the Homeric epic presents it. We may here discern an entire cycle of tales, whose separate elements are also to be found elsewhere, some of them in wide distribution. But in the midst of this märchen-world stands the absolutely human hero, contrasting with whom the fabulous events of the narrative run their course as a fantastic show. The hero overcomes all obstacles that block the course of his journey by his own never-failing shrewdness and resourcefulness. Herein again the märchen-myth gives evidence of being preparatory to the hero saga. At the time when the hero ideal arose, the old märchen ideas were as yet everywhere current. Together with the belief in demons and magic, they, also, found their way into the heroic age. For a long time they continued to be favourite secondary themes, introduced in portraying the destiny of heroes. Nevertheless märchen ideas became subordinate to the delineation of heroic figures, whose surpassing strength was described, very largely, in terms of victory over demoniacal powers. Thus, in the course of the development, the heroic elements gradually increased ; the märchen ideas, on the other hand, disappeared, except when some poet intentionally selected them for the enrichment of his tale, as was obviously done by the author of the Odyssey.

The disappearance of the elements derived from the

märchen-myth, however, must in part be attributed to another factor. This factor, which is closely bound up with the entire culture of the heroic age, consists in the increasing influence of *historical recollections*. Particularly illuminative, as regards this point, are the Greek and Germanic sagas. The sagas of Hercules and the Argonauts, which, from this point of view, belong to a relatively early stage, are purely mythical creations. So far as one can see, no actual events are referred to by them. The Trojan saga, on the other hand, clearly exhibits the traces of historical recollections; its historical setting, moreover, seems to cause the events that transpire within it to approximate more nearly to the character of real life. Even here, indeed, ancient magical motives still cast their fantastic shadows over the narrative. Occasionally, however, the miracle appears in a rationalized form. The magician of the märchen gives place to the seer who predicts the future. What the miracle effected is now accomplished by the overpowering might and the baffling cunning of the strong and wily hero. In this change, the external accessories may sometimes remain the same, so that it is only the inner motives that become different. Thus, it is not impossible that the wooden horse which was said to have been invented by Odysseus and to have brought into Troy the secreted warriors of the besieging hosts, was at one time, in märchen or in saga, an actual magical horse, or a help-bringing deity who had assumed this form. In this case, the poet may possibly be presenting a rationalistic reinterpretation of an older magical motive, with the aim of exalting the craftiness of his hero. In the account of Achilles' youth, on the other hand, and in the story of Helen which the poet takes as his starting-point, the märchen-idea of the saga obviously affects the action itself, though it is significant to note that these purely mythical features do not belong to the plot so much as to its antecedent history. In so far as the heroes directly affect the course of action, they are portrayed as purely human. The same is true of the German *Niebelungen* saga. Just as Achilles, a mythical hero not at all unlike the märchen-hero, was taken over into the historical saga, so also was Siegfried. But here again the märchen motives, such as the fight with the dragon, Siegfried's invulnerability through bathing in its blood, the helmet of invisibility, and others, belong to the past history of the hero, and are mentioned only incidentally in the narrative itself. By referring these specifically märchen miracles to the past, the saga seems to say, as it were, that its heroes were at one time märchen-heroes.

In this course of development from the purely mythical to the historical, the saga may approach no more closely to historical reality than does the purely mythical tale. But while this may be the case, it is nevertheless true that the saga more and more approximates to that which is *historically possible*. Moreover, it is not those sagas which centre about an historical hero that are particularly apt to be free from elements of the original märchen. Very often the reverse is true. An original märchen-hero may become the central figure of an historical saga, and, conversely, the account of an historical personality may become so thoroughly interwoven with märchen-like tales of all sorts that history entirely disappears. A striking antithesis of this sort occurs in Germanic mythology. Compare the *Dietrich* saga with the later development of the *Niebelungen* saga in the form rendered familiar by the *Niebelungenlied*. Siegfried of the *Niebelungen* saga originates purely as a märchen-hero; Dietrich of Bern is an historical personage. But, while the *Niebelungenlied* incorporates a considerable number of historical elements—though, of course, in an unhistorical combination—the Dietrich of the saga retains little more than the name of the actual king of the Goths. There are two different conditions that give rise to sagas. In the first place, historical events that live in folk-memory assimilate materials of ancient märchen and sagas, and thus lead to a connected hero saga. Secondly, an impressive historical personality stimulates the transference of older myths as well as the creation of others, though these, when woven into a whole, resemble a märchen-cycle rather than a hero saga proper.

An important intermediate phenomenon of the sort just mentioned, is not infrequently to be found in a specific form of myth whose general nature is that of the hero saga, even though it is usually distinguished from the latter because of the character of its heroes. I refer to the *religious legend.* Some of these legends, such as the Buddha, the Mithra, and the Osiris legends, border upon the deity saga. Nevertheless, the religious legend, as exemplified also in the mythological versions of the life of Jesus, represents an offshoot of the hero saga, springing up at those times when the religious impulses are dominant. That it is a hero saga is evidenced particularly by the fact that it recounts the life and deeds of a personality who is throughout exalted above human stature, but who, nevertheless, attains to divinity only through his striving, his suffering, and his final victory. In so far, the religious hero very closely resembles the older class of heroes. Nevertheless, instead of the hero of the heroic period, pre-eminent for his external qualities, we have the religious hero, who is exalted by his inner worth into a redeeming god. But it is only because these divine redeemers fought and conquered as men—a thing that would be impossible to gods proper who are exalted from the beginning in supermundane glory—that they constitute heroes of saga, in spite of the fact that they fought with other weapons and in other ways than the heroes of the heroic age. And, therefore, none of these redeemer personalities, whether they have an historical background, as have Jesus and Buddha, or originate entirely in the realm of the mythological imagination, as in the case of Osiris and Mithra, belong to the realm of the saga once they are finally elevated into deities. Even Buddha's return in the endless sequence of ages is not to be regarded as an exception to this rule, for the hope of salvation here merely keeps projecting into the future the traditional Buddha legend. The redeeming activity of the one who is exalted into a god is to be repeated in essentially the same manner as the saga reports it to have occurred in the past.

Contrasting with the redemption legend is the *saint*

legend. The former portrays the fortunes and final victory of a god in the making; the latter tells of the awakening of a human being to a pure religious life, of his temptations and sufferings, and his final triumph. Thus, it has a resemblance to the redeemer legend, and yet it differs from it in that its hero remains human even when he ascends into heaven to receive the victor's crown; the lot that thus befalls him is identical with that of all the devout, except that he is more favoured. This leads to further differences. The hero of the redemption legend is conscious of his mission from the very beginning; in the case of the saint, conversion to a new faith not infrequently forms the starting-point of the legend. Common to the two forms however, is the fact that suffering precedes the final triumph. The traits that we have mentioned constitute the essential difference between these forms of the legend and the hero saga proper. The latter, also, is not without the element of suffering; the Greek saga has developed the specific type of a suffering hero in the figure of Hercules, as has the German saga in that of Balder. In the case of religious legends, however, the strife-motives of the saga are transferred to the inner life; similarly, the suffering of the saint, and especially that of the redeemer, is not merely physical but also mental. Indeed, the original form of the Buddha legend, which is freest from mythological accretions, is an illustration of the fact that this suffering may be caused exclusively by the evils of the world to be redeemed. The suffering due to a most intense sympathy is so intimate a part of the very nature of the redeeming god-man, that it is precisely this which constitutes the most essential difference between the religious legend and the ordinary hero saga, whose interest is centred upon the actions and motives of external life. And yet the external martyrdom of the redeemer intensifies this difference in a twofold way. In the first place, it directly enhances the impression of the inner suffering; secondly, it gives heightened expression both to the evil which evokes the sympathy of the redeemer, and to the nobility of this sympathy itself. In all of these characteristics, however, the redemption legend belongs to the following era rather than to hero saga and the heroic age.

The saint legend exhibits a number of essential differences. It is frequently only through a miracle of conversion, due to external powers, that the saint *becomes* holy ; moreover, it is not, as a rule, through miracles of his own performance that he manifests himself as a saint in the course of his later life and sufferings. The miracles that transpire come as divine dispensations from without, whether they effect his conversion or surround him, particularly at the close of his life's journey, with the halo of sanctity. Thus, to whatever extent the saint may come, in later cult, to supersede the protective undergods and demons of early times, he nevertheless remains human. It is for this very reason, however, that magic and miracle gain a large place in his life. The latter is all the more possible by virtue of the fact that the mythological imagination is not bound by any fixed tradition, and need, therefore, set itself no limits whatsoever either in the number of saints or in the nature of their deeds. Moreover, the legend is almost totally lacking in those factual elements which the hero saga acquires, in its later development, as a result of the historical events that are woven into it. This is not the case with the legend. Here it is at most the name of an historical personality that is retained, while everything else clearly bears the marks of imagination and of myth creation. Hence the saint legend is not to be counted among the factors that underlie the development from the purely mythical tale to the saga, whose content, though not real, is at any rate possible. On the contrary, the tendency of the saint legend is retrogressive, namely, toward a return to the märchen stage of myth. This is all the more true, not merely because elements that are generally characteristic of märchen are disseminated from legend to legend, but also because the saint legend appropriates widely current märchen conceptions. Märchen of very diverse origins found their way into the Christian, as well as the Buddhistic, legends ; moreover, occasional Buddhistic legends, with the clear marks of an Oriental origin upon them, were changed into Christian legends. Thus, the saint legend combines two characteristics. As compared with the hero saga, its motives are internalized; moreover, it represents a decided relapse into the pure märchen form of myth. Though apparently contradictory, these characteristics are really closely related, inasmuch as the internalization of motives itself removes any barriers imposed by historical recollection upon the free play of the mythological imagination.

13. Cosmogonic and Theogonic Myths.

In view of the relationship of heroes and gods, not only with respect to origin but also as regards the fact that they both embody personal ideals, it would appear but natural, having treated of the hero saga, that we inquire at this time concerning the corresponding deity saga. A search for the latter, however, will at once reveal a surprising fact. There is no deity saga at all, in the sense in which we have a hero saga that has become a favourite field of epic and dramatic poetry. The reason for this lack is not difficult to see. There can be no real deity saga because, in so far as gods possess characteristics which differentiate them from men, and therefore also from heroes, they have no history. Immortal, unchangeable, unassailable by death or sickness, how could experiences such as befall the hero also be the lot of gods? If we examine the narratives that approach somewhat to the deity saga, we will find that they consist, not of a connected account of the experiences of the gods, but of isolated incidents that again centre about human life, and particularly about the beneficent or pernicious intervention of the gods in the destinies of heroes. We may recall the participation of the Greek gods in the Trojan war, or the interest of Jahve, in Israelitic saga, in the fortunes of Abraham, Jacob, etc. These are isolated occurrences, and not history; or, rather, we are given the history of heroes, in which the gods are at times moved to intervene. In so far, therefore, as there are approximations to deity saga, these, in their entirety, are woven into hero saga;

apart from the latter, the former but report particular actions, which may, doubtless, throw light on the personal character of the god, but which of themselves do not constitute a connected history. Greek mythology offers a clear illustration of this in the so-called Homeric hymns. These hymns must not be ascribed to Homer or merely to singers of Homeric times. They are of later composition, and are designed for use in cult. Their value consists precisely in the fact that they portray the god by reference to the various directions of his activity, thus throwing light partly on the nature of the god and partly, and especially, on his beneficent rulership of the human world. It is this last fact that gives these poems the character of religious hymns.

Nevertheless, there is *one* class of myths in which the gods themselves actually appear to undergo experiences. I refer to those sagas and poems which are concerned with the birth of the gods, and with the origin of their rulership over the world and over the world-order which they have created, namely, to the *cosmogonic* and *theogonic* myths. These myths relate solely to a world of demons and gods, and they deal, as a rule, with an age prior to the existence of man, or with one in which the creation of man is but a single episode. Again, however, one might almost say that the exception proves the rule. For upon close examination it will be found that the gods who figure in these cosmogonies are not those with whose traits the hero saga, and the hymnology connected with it, have made us familiar. The gods whom the cosmogonic myths portray differ from those who protect and direct human life. They are not real gods, even though they bear this name, but are powerful demons. Except in name, the Zeus of Hesiodic theogony has scarcely anything in common with the Zeus of the Homeric hierarchy of gods. This fact does not reflect any peculiarity of the poet, as it were, but is due to the nature of the subject-matter itself. Even though theogonic myths were not elaborated into poetic form until a relatively late period, they are nevertheless of a primitive nature. Analogues to them had existed among primitive peoples long before the rise of the hero saga, hence at an age when the preconditions of god-ideas proper were still entirely lacking. The cosmogonic gods of the Greeks and Germans, as well as those of the ancient Babylonians, are of the nature of purely demoniacal beings. They lack the chief attribute of a god, namely, personality. Moreover, the myths themselves—if we disregard their form, which was the product of later literary composition—are not at all superior to the cosmogonies of the Polynesians and of many of the native tribes of North America. Obviously, therefore, it betokens a confusion of god-ideas proper with these cosmogonic beings, when it is maintained, as sometimes occurs, that the mythology of these primitive peoples, especially that of the Polynesians, is of a particularly advanced character. This should not be claimed for it, but neither may this be said of the Hesiodic theogony or the Babylonian creation myths. It is true that these myths are superior to the earlier forms of demon belief, for they at least develop a connected view of the origin of things. Primitive myth accepts the world as given. The origin of the world-order as a whole still lies beyond its field of inquiry. Though it occasionally relates how animals came into being, its imagination is essentially concerned with the origin of man, whom it regards as having sprung from stones or plants, or as having crept up out of caves. Even when this stage is transcended and an actual cosmogony arises, the latter nevertheless remains limited to the circle of demon conceptions, which are essentially the same in the myths of civilized peoples as in those of so-called peoples of nature. According to a cosmogonic myth of the Polynesians, for example, heaven and earth were originally a pair of mighty gods united in embrace. The sons who were born to these gods strove to free themselves and their parents from this embrace. Placing himself on the floor of mother earth, therefore, and extending his feet toward the heavens, one of these sons pushed father heaven upward, so that ever since that time heaven and earth have been separated. This mistreatment aroused another of the divine sons, the god of the winds. Thus a strife arose, whose outcome was a peaceful condition of things. This is a cosmogonic myth whose essential elements belong to the same circle of ideas as the cosmogony of the Greeks. In the latter also, Uranus and Gæa are said to have held each other in an embrace, as the result of which there came the race of the Titans. One might regard this as a case of transference were the idea not obviously a grotesque development of a märchen-motive found even at a more primitive period. According to the latter, heaven and earth were originally in contact, and were first separated by a human being of prehistoric times—an idea undoubtedly suggested by the roofing-over of the hut. The Babylonian myth gives a different version of the same conception. It ascribes the separation of heaven and earth to the powerful god Marduk, who cleaves in two the original mother Thiamat. From one part, came the sea; from the other, the celestial ocean. As in many other nature myths, heaven is here conceived as a great sea which forms the continuation, at the borders of the earth, of the terrestrial sea. This then suggests the further idea that the crescent moon is a boat moving over the celestial ocean.

In all of these myths the gods are given the characteristics of mighty demons. They appear as the direct descendants of the ancient cloud, water, and weather demons, merely magnified into giant stature in correspondence with their enormous theatre of action. Thus, as regards content, these cosmogonic myths are märchen of a very primitive type, far inferior to the developed märchen-myths, whose heroes have already acquired traits of a more personal sort. In form, however, cosmogonic myths strive towards the gigantic, and thus lie far above the level of the märchen-myth. Though the complete lack of ethical traits renders the gods of cosmogonic myths inferior in sublimity to gods proper, they nevertheless rival the latter in powerful achievement. Indeed, however much cosmogony may fail to give its gods the characteristics requisite for true gods, it does inevitably serve to enhance the divine attribute of power. A further similarity of cosmogonic and theogonic myths to the most primitive märchen-myths appears in the fact that they seem directly to borrow certain elements from widely disseminated märchen-motives. I mention only the story of Kronos. Kronos, according to the myth, devours his children. But his wife, Rhea, withholds the last of these—namely, Zeus—giving him instead a stone wrapped in linen; hereupon Kronos gives forth, together with the stone, all the children that he had previously devoured. This is a märchen of devourment, similar or derivative forms of which are common. For example, Sikulume, a South African märchen-hero, delays pursuing giants by throwing behind him a large stone which he has besmeared with fat; the giants devour the stone and thus lose trace of the fugitive.

But there is also other evidence that cosmogonic myths are of the nature of märchen, magnified into the immense and superhuman. In almost all such myths, particularly in the more advanced forms, as found among cultural peoples, an important place is occupied by *two* conceptions. The first of these conceptions is that the creation of the world was preceded by *chaos*. This chaos is conceived either as a terrifying abyss, as in Germanic and particularly in Greek mythology, or as a world-sea encompassing the earth, as in the Babylonian history of creation. In both cases we find ideas of terrible demons. Sometimes these demons are said to remain on the earth, as beings of a very ancient time anteceding the creation—examples are Night and Darkness, described in Greek mythology as the children of Chaos. Other myths represent the demons as having been overcome by the world-creating god. Thus there is a Babylonian saga that tells of an original being which enveloped the earth in the form of a snake, but whose body was used by the god in forming the heavens. As a second essential element of cosmogonies we find accounts of *battles of the gods*, in which hostile demons are vanquished and a kingdom of order and peace is established. These demons are thought of as powerful monsters. They induce a live consciousness of the terrors of chaos, not only by their size and strength but often also by their grotesque, half-animal, half-human forms, by their many heads or hundreds of arms. Obviously these Titans, giants, Cyclopes, and other terrible beings of cosmogony are the direct descendants of the weather demons who anteceded the gods. Does not the idea of a world-catastrophe that prepares the way for the rulership of the gods at once bring to mind the image of a terrible thunderstorm? As the storm is followed by the calm of nature, so chaos is succeeded by the peaceful rulership of the gods. Inasmuch, however, as the gods are the conquerors of the storm demons, they themselves inevitably revert into demoniacal beings. It is only after the victory has been won that they are again regarded as inhabiting a divine world conceived in analogy with the human State, and that they are vested with control over the order and security of the world.

All this goes to show that cosmogonic myths, in the poetic forms in which cosmogonies have come down to us, are relatively late mythological products. True, they represent the gods themselves as demoniacal beings. Nevertheless, this does not imply that god-ideas did not exist at the time of their composition ; it indicates merely that the enormous diversity of factors involved in the creation of the world inevitably caused the gods to lose the attributes of personal beings. The cosmogonies of cultural peoples, however, differ from the otherwise similar stories of those semi-cultural peoples whose mythology consists exclusively of such cosmogonic märchen. In the latter case, real god-ideas are lacking. The gods have remained essentially demons. In the higher forms of this semi-culture, where political development has had an influence on the world of gods, as was once the case among the peoples of Mexico and Peru, divine beings may approximate to real gods. In cosmogonic myths themselves, however, this never occurs. Thus, these myths invariably constitute a stage intermediate between the mythology of demons and that of gods ; they may originate, however—and this is what probably happens in the majority of cases—through a relapse of gods into demons An illustration of the latter is the Hesiodic cosmogony. The weather-myth which the poet has elaborated obviously incorporated ancient märchen-myths that do not differ essentially from the original märchen as to content, but only as respects their grotesque and gigantic outlines. Compared with the gods of the hero saga, therefore, the cosmogonic myths of cultural peoples are of relatively late origin; to discuss the latter first, as is still done in our accounts of the mythology of the Greeks, Germans, etc., may easily lead to misconceptions. Of course, the creation of the world came first, but it is not at all true that the myth of the world's creation anteceded all others. On the contrary, the latter is a late and sometimes, perhaps, the last product of the mythological imagination. This is particularly apt to be the case where, as so clearly appears in the Biblical account of the creation, there is involved a specific *religious* impulse that is seeking to glorify the world-creating god. This religious impulse imposes upon the older mythical material a new character. Hence we find that, of the two elements universally characteristic of the cosmogonic myth, it is only the idea of chaos that is retained, while the account of struggles with the monsters of earliest times disappears. Nevertheless, though the creating god has lost his demoniacal character, he has not yet attained a fully developed personality—this is precluded by the enormity of the world, which transcends all human measure. He himself is in every respect an unlimited personal will, and is, therefore, really just as much a *superpersonal* being as the battling gods of other cosmogonies are subpersonal. That such a cosmogony, unique in this respect, may be original, is, of course, impossible. Indeed, the dominant conviction of Oriental antiquarians to-day is that the Biblical account of the creation rests on older and more primitive ideas derived from the Babylonian cosmogony, whose main outlines we have described above. This may doubtless be true, and yet no compelling proof of the contention can be adduced, for it is precisely those features in which both accounts are identical—namely, chaos, the original darkness, and the separating and ordering activity of the god—that are common property to almost all cosmogonies. The

Biblical account of the creation, however, may not be classed with myths. It is a religious production of priests who were dominated by the thought that the national god rules over the people of Israel and over the world. Hence alone could it substitute a creation out of *nothing* for the ordering of a chaos, though the latter feature also persists in the Biblical account. The substitution, of course, dates from a later time than the myth, and represents a glorification of divine omnipotence which is entirely impossible to the latter.

A sort of offshoot of cosmogonic myths, though in striking antithesis to them, is the *flood saga*. This still retains, in their entirety, the characteristics of the original märchen-myth. It belongs to a variety of widely prevalent myths which, like the creation myths, appear to some extent to have originated independently in various parts of the earth, but also to have spread widely from one region to another. Evidence indicative of the independent origin of many of these sagas is to be found in the fact that, in many tropical regions, accounts of a flood, or so-called deluge sagas (*Sintflutsagen*), are represented by sagas of conflagration (*Sintbrandsagen*), according to which the world was destroyed, not by a general deluge, but by fire. In neither word has the prefix *Sint* any connection with *Sünde* (sin), with which popular etymology commonly connects it. *Sint* (old high German *sin*) is a word that has disappeared from modern German and means 'universal.' A *Sintflut*, thus, is a *universal*, in distinction from a merely local, flood. In so far, the sagas of universal flood and conflagration already approximate to the myths relating to the destruction of the world. Now, the Biblical story of the flood has so many elements in common with that of the Babylonians that we are compelled to assume a borrowing, and hence a transference, of material. The rescue of a single man and his household, the taking of animals into the ship, its landing upon the summit of a mountain, the dispatching of birds in quest of land—of these elements, some might possibly have originated independently in different parts of the earth. The rescue of individuals, for example, is included in almost all flood and conflagration legends, the direct source of the idea being the connection between the antediluvian and postdiluvian worlds. Of the combination of all of these elements into a whole, however, we may say without hesitation that it could not have arisen twice independently. The universal motive of the flood saga and that which led to its origin in numerous localities, without any influence on the part of foreign ideas, is obviously the rain as it pours down from the heavens. For this reason flood sagas are particularly common wherever rain causes devastating and catastrophic floods, whereas they are lacking in such regions as the Egyptian delta, where there are periodic inundations by the sea, as well as in the Arabian peninsula and in the rainless portions of Africa. As a rule, therefore, they are both rain sagas and flood sagas. They naturally suggest, further, the idea of a boatman who rescues himself in a boat and lands upon a mountain. According to an American flood myth which has preserved more faithfully than that of western Asia the character of the märchen, the mountain upon which the boatman lands rises with the flood and settles again as the flood subsides.

The flood sagas of cultural peoples, however, combine these very ancient märchen elements with a projection of the cosmogonic myth into a later event of human history. The flood deluging the earth is a return to chaos; indeed, often, as in the sagas of western Asia, chaos itself is represented as a mighty abyss of water. This is then connected with the idea of a punishment in which the god destroys what he has created, preserving from the universal destruction only the righteous man who has proved worthy of such salvation. Thus, the universal flood (*Sintflut*) actually develops into a sin flood (*Sündflut*). This change, of course, represents an elaboration on the part of priests, who projected the religious-ethical feature of a divine judgment into what was doubtless originally a purely mythological saga, just as they transformed the creation myth into a hymn to the omnipotence of the deity. But this prepares the way for a further step. The counterpart of these cosmological conceptions is projected not merely into a past which marks the beginning of the present race of men, but also into the future. Over against the transitory world-catastrophe of the universal flood, there looms the final catastrophe of the actual destruction of the world, and over against a preliminary judgment of the past, the final judgment, at which this life ends and that of the yonder world begins.

Thus, we come to the *myths of world destruction,* as they are transmitted in the apocalyptic writings of later Israelitic literature and in the Apocalypse of John, who betrays the influence of the earlier writers. At this point we leave the realm of myth proper. The latter is always concerned with events of the past or, in extreme cases, with those of the immediate present. No doubt, the desires of men may reach out indefinitely into the future. Myth narrative, however, in the narrower sense of the term, takes no account of that which lies beyond the present. In general, moreover, its scene of action is the existing world, however much this may be embellished by the imagination. Myth reaches its remotest limit in cosmogonies. Even here, however, no absolute limit is attained, for the world-creation is represented as having been preceded by chaos. The idea of a creation out of nothing, which dislodges the idea of an original chaos, arises from religious needs and is not mythological in character. Similarly, the apocalyptic myth of world-destruction has passed beyond the stage of the myth proper. It is a mythological conception, which, though combining elements of the cosmogonic myth with fragments of märchen and sagas, is, in the main, the expression of a religious need for a world beyond. These myths, therefore, are not original myth creations, as are the cosmogonic myths, at least in part. They are the product of religious reflection, and, as such, they are dominated primarily by the desire to strengthen the righteous in his hopes and to terrify his adversary. Thus, the history of the cosmogonic myth here repeats itself in a peculiarly inverted form. With the exception of occasional survivals, the religious hymn, which is the ripest development of the cosmogonic myth, excludes the struggles of demons and wild monsters of the deep ; the myth of the destruction of the world, on the other hand, constantly seeks, by its fantastic imagery, to magnify fears and punishments, as well as blessed hopes. As a result, all these accounts clearly bear the traces of a laborious invention seeking to surpass itself and thus to atone for the lack of original mythological imagination. We may call to mind the monster which the Book of Daniel describes as coming forth from the sea, provided with enormous iron teeth, and bearing on its head ten horns, among which an eleventh horn appears, which possesses eyes, and a mouth that speaks blasphemous words. Such things may be invented by the intellect, but they are impossible as natural creations of the mythological imagination. The motives underlying such exaggerations beyond the mythologically possible are to be found in factors which, though extending far back into the beginnings of mythology, nevertheless attain their development primarily in this age of gods and heroes. These factors are the *ideas of the beyond*.

14. The Belief in Souls and in a World Beyond.

Closely connected with the cosmogonic myth are the ideas of a world beyond into which man may enter at the close of the present life. Before such ideas could arise, there must have been some general world-conception into which they could be fitted. The ideas of a beyond, therefore, are but constituent elements of cosmogonic conceptions ; indeed, they are confined to relatively advanced forms of the latter. This is indicated by the fact that the earlier mythological creations contain no clearly defined notions of a beyond. Where there is no definite world-view, such conceptions, of course, are impossible. Thus, the two ideas mutually reinforce each other. The cosmogonic myth gives a large setting to the ideas of a beyond ; the latter, in turn, contribute to the details of the world picture which the cosmogonic myth has created. At any rate, when poetry and philosophy, in their endeavour to construct a coherent cosmogony, began to appropriate celestial myths, ideas of a life after death and of a world beyond were already in existence. Some of these ideas, indeed, date back to an early period.

It is an extremely significant fact that, wherever we can trace their development at all, these ideas of a beyond follow the same definite and orderly course. The direction of this development is determined not only by the cosmogonic myth but also by the ideas regarding the soul. The formation of ideas of a beyond is impossible without a world-view transcending the limits of earthly existence ; the latter, however, results from the need of ascribing to the soul a continuance after death. This need, of course, is not an original one, but is essentially conditioned by the age of gods. Among primitive peoples, the beginnings of a belief in a life after death are to be found chiefly in connection with the fear of the demon of the dead, who may bring sickness and death to the living. But just as the fear is of short duration, so also is the survival after death limited to a brief period. On a somewhat more advanced stage, as perhaps among the Soudan peoples, most of the Melanesian tribes, and the forest-dwelling Indians of South America, it is especially the prominent men, the tribal chiefs, who, just as they survive longest in memory, are also supposed to enjoy a longer after-life. This conception, however, remains indefinite and of a demoniacal character, just as does that of the soul. In all of these conceptions, therefore, the disembodied soul is represented as remaining within this world. It continues its existence in the environment ; as yet there is no yonder-world in the strict sense of the word. It is important, moreover, to distinguish the early ideas of a beyond from the above-mentioned celestial märchen which narrate how certain human beings ascended into heaven. The latter are purely märchen of adventure, in which sun, moon, stars, and clouds, as well as the terrestrial monsters, dwarfs, gnomes, etc., are conceived of as belonging to the visible world. Indeed, these celestial travellers are not infrequently represented as returning unharmed to their terrestrial home. Thus, these tales generally lack the idea which, from the outset, is essential to the conception of a yonder-world—the idea, namely, of *the sojourn of the soul at definite places,* whether these be thought of as on, under, or above the earth. Here again it is characteristic that at first this region is located approximately midway between this world and the one beyond. The belief takes the form of a *spirit-village,* a conception prevalent especially among the tribes of American Indians. Inaccessible to living beings and in some secret part of the earth, there is supposed to be a village. In this village the spirits of the dead are thought to assemble, and to continue their existence in precisely the same manner as before death, hunting and fighting just as they did in their earthly life. The spirit-village itself is described as exactly like an ordinary village. Characteristic of the totemic setting which all of these ideas still possess, is the fact that among many of the Indians of the prairies there is thought to be not only a spirit-village but also a buffalo-village, where the dead buffaloes congregate, and into which, according to the märchen, an adventurous youth may occasionally stray. Sometimes, moreover, these tales give more specific accounts of the way in which such villages are rendered inaccessible. A river spanned by an almost impassable bridge, or a dense, impenetrable forest, separates the spirit-village from the habitations of the living. Ravines and mountain caves may either themselves serve as the dwelling-places of the spirits or form the approaches to them. In addition to these conceptions, there are also others, which have, in part, found a place even in later mythology. The dead are represented as dwelling, not in some accessible part of the earth, but on remote islands. Such ideas are common in Polynesia, and also in other island and coast regions. Even in Homer we come upon the picture of a distant island. It is here that Menelaus found rescue on his return from Troy. The island is described as a place of happiness, where only the privileged among mortals are granted a blessed future.

A second and, on the whole, an obviously later form of

ideas of a beyond, are the *myths of the nether world.* These for the first time tell of a beyond which is by its very nature inaccessible to human beings, or which is visited by only a few divinely privileged heroes, such as Hercules, Odysseus, and Æneas. As a third and last form of ideas of a beyond, we may mention those of a *heaven,* where dwell the dead, in the presence of the gods. As a rule, however, this heavenly beyond does not lead to the disappearance of the nether world. Rather are the two worlds set over against each other, as the result of the enhancement of an antithesis which arose even in connection with the realms of the nether world. The heaven becomes the abode of the blessed, of the devout and righteous, the favoured of the gods ; the underworld continues, at the outset, to be the lot of the majority of human beings. The growing desire to participate in the joys of blessedness, then causes the privilege which was at first enjoyed only by a minority to become more universal, and the underworld is transformed into the abode of the guilty and the condemned. Finally, heaven becomes possible even for the latter, through the agency, more particularly, of magical purification and religious ecstasy.

Of the various ideas of the beyond that successively arise in this development, those regarding the underworld are the most common and the most permanent. This is probably due in no small measure to the custom of *burying the corpse.* Here the entrance into the underworld is, to a certain extent, directly acted out before the eyes of the observers, even though the mythological imagination may later create quite a different picture of the event. The custom of burial, however, cannot have been the exclusive source of these ideas, nor perhaps even the most important one. In the Homeric world, the corpse was not buried, but burned. And yet it is to Homer that we owe one of the clearest of the older descriptions of the underworld, and it can scarcely be doubted that the main outlines of this picture were derived from popular conceptions. As a matter of fact, there is another factor, purely psychological in character, which is here obviously of greater force than are tribal customs. This is the fear of death, and the terror of that which awaits man after death. This fear creates the idea of a ghostly and terrible region of the dead, cold as the corpse itself and dark as the world must appear to its closed eyes. But that which is thought of as dark and cold is the interior of the earth, for such are the characteristics of mountain caves that harbour uncanny animals. The underworld, also, is stocked with creations of fear, particularly with subterranean animals, such as toads, salamanders, and snakes of monstrous and fantastic forms. Many of the terrible beings which later myths represent as living on the earth probably originated as monsters of the underworld. Examples of this are the Furies, the Keres, and the Harpies of the Greeks. It was only as the result of a later influence, not operative at the time of the original conceptions of Hades, that myth permitted these beings to wander about the upper world. This change was due to the pangs of conscience, which transforms the ghosts of the underworld into frightful, avenging beings, and then, as a result of the misery visited even upon the living because of the crimes which they have committed, transfers them to the mundane world. Here they pursue particularly the one who has committed sacrilege against the gods, and also him whose sin is regarded as especially grievous, such as the parricide or matricide. Thus, with the internalization of the fear impulse, the demoniacal forms which the latter creates are brought forth from the subterranean darkness and are made to mingle with the living. Similarly, the joyous and hope-inspiring ideas of a beyond are projected still farther upward, and are elevated beyond the regions of this earth into heavenly spaces that seem even more inaccessible than the underworld. Prior to the age, however, which regards the heaven as the abode of the blessed, many peoples—possibly all who advanced to this notion of two worlds—entertained a different conception. This conception represents, perhaps, the surviving influence of the earlier ideas of spirit-islands.

For the underworld was itself regarded as including, besides places of horror, brighter regions, into which, either through the direct favour of the gods or in accordance with a judgment pronounced upon the dead, the souls of the pure and righteous are received. As a result of the division which thus occurred, and of the antithesis in which these images of the beyond came to stand, pain and torment were added to the impressions of horror and hopelessness which the original conceptions of the underworld aroused. The contrasts that developed, however, did not prevent the underworld from being regarded as including both the region of pain and that of bliss. This seems to have been the prevalent notion among Semitic as well as Indo-Germanic peoples. The Walhalla of the Germans was also originally thought to be located in the underworld, and it is possible that it was not transferred to the heavens until the advent of Christianity. For, indeed, we are not familiar with Germanic mythology except as it took form within the period in which Christianity had already become widespread among the German tribes.

An important change in the ideas of the beyond now took place. The separation of the abodes of spirits gradually led to a distinction between the deities who were regarded as the rulers of the two regions. Originally, so long as only the fear of death found expression in the unvarying gloom of the underworld, these deities were but vaguely defined. The conceptions formed of them seem to have reflected the ideas of rulership derived from real life, just as was true in the case of the supermundane gods. Indeed, the origin of the more definite conception that the underworld is a separate region ruled by its own gods, must probably be traced to the influence of the ideas of celestial gods. But there is a still more primitive feature of myths of the beyond, one that goes back to their very beginnings, and that long survives in saga and märchen. This is the preference shown by myths of the nether world for *female* beings, whether as subordinate personifications of fear or as deities. Not only is the ideal of beauty and grace thought of as a female deity, an Aphrodite perhaps, but the psychological law of the intensification of contrasts causes also the fearful and terrifying sorts of deities to assume the feminine form. Such a gruesome and terrible goddess is exemplified by the Norse Hel, or, widely remote from her in time and space, by the Babylonian Ereksigal. In the Greek underworld also, it is Persephone who rules, and not Pluto, her consort. The latter seems to have been introduced merely in order that the underworld might have a counterpart to the celestial pair of rulers, Zeus and Hera. If the fear-inspiring attributes are not so pronounced in the Greek Persephone, this is due to the fact that in this case agricultural myths have combined with the underworld myths. To this combination we must later recur, inasmuch as it is of great significance for cult. The dominant place given to the female deity in the underworld myth, again brings the nether world into a noteworthy contrast with the supermundane realm of gods. In the latter, male gods, as the direct embodiments of a superhuman hero-ideal, are always predominant.

It is not alone the inner forces of fear and horror that cause the realm of the dead to be thought of as located in the interior of the earth. There is operative also an external influence imparted by Nature herself, namely, the perception of the setting sun. Wherever particular attention is called to some one entrance to the underworld, or where a distant region of the earth is regarded as the abode of the dead, this is located in the west, in the direction of the setting sun. We have here a striking example of that form of mythological association and assimilation in which the phenomena of external nature, and particularly those of the heavens, exert an influence upon myth development. It would, of course, be incorrect to assert that the setting sun alone suggested the idea of an underworld. We must rather say that this phenomenon was obviously a subordinate and secondary factor. Its influence was not clearly and consciously apprehended even as affecting the location of the underworld, though this location was determined solely by it. Because of its connection with approaching night, the setting sun came to be associated with all those feelings that caused the underworld to be regarded as a realm of shadows and of terrifying darkness. It was the combination of all these factors, and not any single one of them—least of all, a relatively secondary one, such as the sunset—that created and so long maintained the potency of this most permanent of all the ideas of a beyond.

Mention should also be made of the influence exerted, even at an early time, by soul-ideas. At the beginning of the heroic age, it was almost universally believed that after death *all* human beings lead a dull, monotonous life under the earth, or, as Homer portrayed it, heightening the uniformity, that all lapse into an unconscious existence. Obviously these ideas were determined, in part, by the phenomena of sleep and dreams. Just as death seemed a protracted sleep, so did the dream come to foreshadow the life after death. The characteristics of dream images, therefore, came to be attributed to the souls of the underworld. The latter, it was thought, are visible, but, like shadows, they elude the hand that grasps them and move about fleetly from place to place. This shadow-existence is a fate that is common to all. It is only exceptionally flagrant transgressions against the gods that call forth punishments which not merely overtake the guilty in this world but may also continue in the next. Such figures, therefore, as are described in connection with Odysseus' journey to Hades—Sisyphus, who must unceasingly roll uphill a stone that is constantly rolling back, and Tantalus, who languishes with hopeless desire for the fruits suspended above his head—are not as yet to be regarded as expressing ideas of retribution, even though they may be anticipatory of them. Perhaps, also, it is not without significance that these accounts are probably later accretions, of which the Homeric poems contain a considerable number, particularly the Odyssey, which is so rich in märchen elements.

Gradually, however, that which at first occurs only in occasional instances becomes more universal; the distinction in destinies comes to be regarded as applying generally. The earlier and exceptional cases of entrance into a world of the blessed or of particular punishments in Hades were connected with the favour or anger of the gods. Similarly, that which finally makes the distinction a universal one is religious cult. The object of cult is to propitiate the gods; their favour is to be won through petitions and magical acts. The gods are to grant not merely a happy lot in this world but also the assurance of permanent happiness in the next. Before this striving the shadows of the underworld give way. Though the underworld continues, on the whole, to remain a place of sorrow, it nevertheless comes to include a number of brighter regions in which the righteous may enjoy such happiness as they experienced in this world, without suffering its distresses and evil. It was this that early led to the formation of cult associations. Even during the transition of totemic tribal organization into States and deity cults, such religious associations sprang up out of the older totemic groups. During this period, the conditions of descent and of tribal segregation still imposed limitations upon the religious associations. These limitations, however, were transcended on the stage of deity cults, as appears primarily in the case of the Greek mysteries and of other secret cults of the Græco-Roman period, such as the mysteries of Mithra, Attis, Osiris, and Serapis. No doubt, the extreme forms of the cults prevalent in an age thoroughly conscious of a deep need for salvation were bound up with the specific cultural conditions of that age. And yet these cults but bring out in particularly sharp relief certain traits which, though they are not clearly apparent until later, are quite universally characteristic of the deity-worship of the heroic era. These cults arise only when the early heroic ideal, embodying certain external characteristics, has disappeared, having given way more and more to inner ideals, connected with religion and morality. This, however, occurs at the very time when minds are beginning to be more deeply troubled by the terrors of the underworld, and when, in contrast with this, the imagination creates glowing pictures of the future, for whose realization it turns to the gods. Thus arises the idea of a special region of the underworld, allotted to those cult-associates who have been particularly meritorious in the performance of religious duties. These will enter into Elysium, a vale of joy and splendour which, though a part of the underworld, is nevertheless remote from the regions of sorrow. Here the blessed will abide after death. This Elysium is no longer a distant island intended as a refuge for occasional individuals, but belongs to the established order of the underworld itself. In the sixth book of the Æneid, Virgil has sketched, with poetic embellishments, a graphic picture of this abode of the blessed as it was conceived, in his day, under the confluence of ancient mythical traditions and new religious impulses—a portrayal which forms perhaps the most valuable part of the whole poem. For, in it, the poet presents a living picture of what was believed and was striven for by many of his contemporaries.

In closest connection with this separation of realms in the underworld, is the introduction of judgeship. It devolves upon the judge of the underworld to determine whether the soul is to be admitted to the vale of joy or is to be banished into Orcus. It is significant that, in his picture of the underworld, Virgil entrusts this judgeship to the same Rhadamanthus with whom we are familiar from the Odyssey as the ruler of the distant island of the blessed. Obviously the poet himself recognized that these later conceptions developed from the earlier idea that salvation comes as a result of divine favour. After the separation of the region of the blessed from that of the outcasts, a further division is made; the two regions of the underworld are partitioned into subregions according to degrees of terror and torment, on the one hand, and of joy and blessedness, on the other. Gradations of terror are first instituted, those of blessedness following only later and in an incomplete form. The subjective factor, which precludes differences in degree when joy is at the maximum, is in constant rivalry with the objective consideration that the merits of the righteous may differ, and, therefore, also their worthiness to enjoy the presence of the deity. In contrast with this, is the much stronger influence exerted by the factor of punishment. The shadowy existence of souls in Homer's Hades is not regarded as a penalty, but merely as the inevitable result of departure from the circle of the living. Only when the hope of Elysium has become just as universal as the fear of Hades, does the latter become a place of punishment, and the former a region of rewards. Just as language itself is very much richer in words denoting forms of suffering than in those for joy, so also does the mythological imagination exhibit much greater fertility in the portrayal of the pains of the underworld than in the glorification of the Elysian fields. All the horrors that human cruelty can invent are carried over from the judicial administration of this world into that of the beyond. Gradations in the magnitude of punishments are reflected in the location of the regions appointed for them. The deepest region of the underworld is the most terrible. Above this, is the place where those sojourn who may enter Elysium at some future time, after successfully completing a period of probation.

The contrast which first appears in the form of a separation of the realms of torment and blessedness, of punishment and reward, is then carried to a further stage, again by the aid of ideas of a spacial gradation. No longer are all mortals compelled to enter the underworld; this not only loses its terrors for the blessed, but the righteous and beloved of the gods are not required to descend into it at all. Their souls ascend to heaven—a lot reserved in olden times exclusively for heroes who were exalted into gods. With this, the separation becomes complete: the souls of the righteous rise to the bright realms of heaven, those of the godless are cast into the depths. Among both the Semitic and the Indo-Germanic peoples, the antithesis of heaven and hell was established at a relatively late period. Its first clear development is probably to be found among the ancient Iranians, in connection with the early cosmogonic myths. Here the battle which the creation-myths of other cultural peoples represent as being fought between gods and demons is portrayed as the struggle of *two* divine beings. One of these is thought to rule over the regions of light above the earth and the other over the subterranean darkness. True, this contrast is also brought out in the battles described by other peoples as between gods and demons, and this surely has been a factor leading to the incorporation of the Iranian myth into the ideas of the beyond elsewhere entertained. The distinctive feature of Iranian cosmogony and that which gave its dualism an unusual influence upon religion and cult is the fact that the original cosmic war was restricted to a single hostile pair of gods, Ormuzd (Ahuramazda) and Ahriman (Angramainju). Here also, however, Ahriman is the leader of a host of demons—a clear indication that the myth is based on the universal conception of a battle with demons. This similarity was doubtless all the more favourable to the influence of the Iranian dualism upon other religions, inasmuch as the separation of ideas of the beyond had obviously already quite generally taken place independently of such influence, having resulted from universal motives of cult. The fact, however, that the battle was not waged, as in other mythologies, between gods and demons, but between two divine personalities, led to a further essential change. The battle no longer takes place on the earth, as did that of Zeus and the Titans, but between a god of light, enthroned on high, and a dark god of the underworld. This spacial antithesis was probably connected by the ancient Iranians with that of the two ideas of the soul, the corporeal soul, fettered to earth, and the spiritual soul, the psyche, soaring on high. Herein may possibly lie the explanation of a curious custom which markedly distinguished the Iranians from other Indo-Germanic peoples. The former neither buried nor burned their dead, but exposed them on high scaffolds, as food for the birds. It almost seems as though the 'platform-disposal,' commonly practised in totemic times and mentioned above (p. 216), had here been taken over into later culture; the only change would appear to be that, in place of the low mound of earth upon which the corpse was left to decompose, there is substituted a high scaffolding, doubtless designed to facilitate the ascent of the soul to heaven. Furthermore, many passages in the older Avesta point out that the exposure of the corpse destroys the corporeal soul, rendering the spiritual soul all the freer to ascend to heaven. This is the same antithesis between corporeal soul and psyche that long continues to assert itself in later conceptions. Indeed, it also occurs, interwoven with specifically Christian conceptions, in many passages of the Epistles of the Apostle Paul, where the corporeal soul survives in the idea of the sinfulness of the flesh, and where, in the mortification of the flesh, we still have a faint echo of the Iranian customs connected with the dead.

Thus, the ideas of a twofold beyond and of a twofold soul mutually reinforce each other. Henceforth the heavenly realm is the abode of the pure and blessed spirits ; the underworld, that of the wicked, who retain their sensuous natures even in the beyond, and who must, therefore, suffer physical pain and torment in a heightened degree. The thought of a spacial gradation corresponding with degrees of merit, though first developed in connection with the pains and punishments of the underworld, then comes to be applied also to the heavenly world. In this case, however, the power of the imagination seems scarcely adequate to the task of sufficiently magnifying the degrees of blessedness. Hence the imagination is forced ; it becomes subservient to reflection, which engenders an accumulation of apocalyptic imagery that completely defies envisagement. In Jewish literature, one of the earliest examples of such apocalyptic accounts of the beyond is to be found in the Book of Enoch. The idea of a journey to the underworld, developed in ancient history, here apparently suggested a journey to heaven ; as a result, the celestial realm was divided into various regions, graded according to height, as were those of the underworld according to depth, and leading to places of greater blessedness, as did those of the latter to increasing torment. We here have one of those dream-journeys to which dream association readily gives rise in the expectant and excited consciousness of the sleeper. Indeed, it is not improbable that the narrative is based on actual dream images. Had not the appearance of the dead in dreams already led to the belief in a shadow-soul, which now journeys to this distant world? The division of the celestial realms, in these mythical works, fluctuates between the numbers three and seven—the two numbers held sacred *par excellence*. In the Second Epistle to the Corinthians, the Apostle Paul tells of a dream-vision in which, years before, he was caught up to the 'third heaven' of paradise.

Under the influence of expiatory rites, which were zealously practised even by the ancient mystery cults, these two worlds, the subterranean hell and the celestial paradise, were supplemented by a *third* region. This development was also apparently of Iranian origin. The region was held to be a place of purification, where the soul of the sinner might be prepared, through transitory punishments and primarily through lustrations, for entrance into the heavenly realm. Purgatorial lustration, after the pattern of terrestrial cult ceremonies, was believed to be effected by means of fire, this being regarded as the most potent lustrical agency, and as combining the function of punishment with that of purification. Dante's "Divine Comedy" presents a faithful portrayal of these conceptions as they were finally developed by the religious imagination of mediæval Christianity out of a mass of ideas which go back, in their beginnings, to a very ancient past, but which continually grew through immanent psychological necessity. Dante's account of the world beyond incorporates a further element. It tells of a *guide*, by whom those exceptional individuals who are privileged to visit these realms are led, and by whom the various souls are assigned to their future dwelling-places. The first of the visitors to Hades, Hercules, was accompanied by deities, by Athena and Hermes. Later it was one of the departed who served as guide. Thus, Virgil was conducted by his father, and Dante, in turn, was led by Virgil, though into the realms of blessedness, closed to the heathen poet, he was guided by the transfigured spirit of Beatrice. The rôle of general conductor of souls to the realms of the underworld, however, came to be given to Hermes, the psychopomp. Such is the capacity in which this deity appears in the Odyssey, in an exceedingly charming combination of later with very ancient soul-conceptions. After Odysseus has slain the suitors, Hermes, with staff in hand, leads the way to the underworld, followed by the souls of the suitors in the form of twittering birds.

These external changes in the ideas of the beyond, leading to the separation of the two realms, heaven and hell, and finally to the conception of purgatory, an intermediate realm, are dependent also on the gradual development of the *idea of retribution*. This is not a primitive idea. It arises only in the course of the heroic age, as supplementary to the very ancient experiences associated with the fear of death and to the notions concerning the breath and shadow souls. Moreover, it is especially important to notice that at the outset the idea was not ethical in character, but *purely religious*—a striking proof that morality and religion were originally distinct. The transference of the idea from religion to morals represents the final stage of the development, and occurred long after other-world mythology had reached its zenith. The first traces of the retributive idea are to be found in connection with those unusual dispensations of favour by which a hero who has won the favour of the gods is either taken up into their midst or is granted admittance to some other region of blessedness; the conception may, however, also take the form of punishments attached to certain particular offences directed against the gods. These latter exceptions already form a prelude to the more general application of the retributive idea in later times. But, even at this stage, the idea did not at once include *all* men within its scope, but found expression only in the desire to gain some exceptional escape from future suffering or some peculiar claim to eternal joy in the future. True, the natural impulse toward association, and the hope that united conjurations would force their way to the ears of the gods more surely than individual prayers could do, early led to cult alliances, whose object it was to minister to these other-worldly hopes. None of these alliances, however, was concerned with obtaining salvation for all ; on the contrary, all of them sought to limit this salvation to a few, in the belief that by such limitation their aim would be more certain of realization. These cults, therefore, were shrouded in secrecy. This had a twofold purpose. On the one hand, it increased the assurance of the members in the success of their magical incantations—a natural result of the fact that these rites were unavailable to the masses ; on the other hand, it augmented the magical power of the incantations, inasmuch as, according to an associative reaction widely prevalent in the field of magical ideas, the mysterious potency of magic led to a belief in the magical effect of secrecy. The influence of these ideas had manifested itself in much earlier times, giving rise, on the transitional stage between totemism and the deity cults, to the very numerous secret societies of cultural and semi-cultural peoples. At this period, these societies were probably always the outgrowth of the associations of medicine-men, but later they sometimes included larger circles of tribal members. As is evident particularly in the case of the North American Indians, such societies frequently constituted restricted religious groups within the clans—groups which appear to have taken the place of the earlier totemic associations. In harmony with this, and, perhaps, under the influence of the age-groups in the men's clubs, there was originally a gradation of the members, based on the degree of their sanctification and on the extent of their participation in the mystic ceremonies. In peculiar contradiction to the secrecy of such associations, membership in one of its classes was betrayed, during the festivals of the cult groups, by the most striking external signs possible, such as by the painting of the body or by other forms of decoration. Moreover, on the earlier stages of culture, the interest of all these secret societies was still centred mainly on things connected with this world, such as prosperity of crops, protection from sickness, and success in the chase. Nevertheless, there was also manifest a concern regarding a future life, especially wherever a pronounced ancestor worship or an incipient deity cult had been developed.

It is the idea of the beyond, however, that gradually crowds out all secondary motives and that gives to the mystery cults proper their characteristic stamp, bringing them into sharp contrast with the dominant ideas of the early heroic age. In the earlier period, the idea of the beyond had been enveloped in hopeless gloom ; now, it fills the mystic with premonitions of eternal happiness. In striving for this experience, the mystic wishes for a bliss that is not granted to the majority of mortals. Once more all the magic arts of the past are called into play in order that the initiate may secure entrance into the portals of the yonder world ; it is thither that he is transported in the ecstasy induced by these magical means. No longer is admiration bestowed upon the heroes of the mythical past, upon a Hercules and a Theseus, as it was in ancient times. The change came about slowly, and yet at the great turning-point of human history, marked by the Hellenistic age, it spread throughout the entire cultural world. Radiating far beyond the Eleusinian and Orphic mysteries, which these hopes of a yonder-world raised to new life, the same idea was appropriated by the cults of Osiris, Serapis, Attis, and Mithra. The *idea of redemption,* born of the longing to exchange this world, with its sufferings and wants, for a world of happiness in the beyond, took possession of the age. It is the negation of the heroic age, of the heroes which it prized, and of the gods which it revered. Along with this world, these cults of the beyond repudiate also the previously existent values of this world. The ideals of power and of property fade. Succeeding the hero ideal, as its abrogation and at the same time its consummation, is the ideal of humanity.

At first it is only *religious* ideals that manifest this shift in values. The enjoyment of the present gives way to hopes for the future, the portrayal of which welds religious feelings into a power that proves supreme over all other impulses. It is for this very reason that the future, which the mystic already enjoys in anticipation, comes to be exclusively the reward of the *devout*. It is not vouchsafed to the moral man who stands outside the pale of these religious associations, for his activity centres about this world. At a much earlier period, however, these ideas became combined with ethical motives of retribution. If, accordingly, the two motives again become entirely distinct at this decisive turning-point of religious development, this only signifies that, in themselves, they are of different origin, and not that from early times forward there were no forces making for their union. These forces, however, were not so much internal as external in character. They did not spring from the religious experiences themselves, nor, least of all, from the ideas of the beyond. Their source is to be found primarily in a transference of the relations of the earthly State to the divine State, as a result of which the ruler of the latter was exalted to the position of lawgiver in the kingdom of men no less than in that of the gods. Proofs of this transference are to be found in the most ancient customs and legal enactments of all regions. Either the ethical and religious commandments are, both alike, supposed to be the very utterances of the deity, as in the case of the Mosaic decalogue, or, as is illustrated by the Babylonian code of Hammurabi, an earthly ruler expressly promulgates his law in the name of the deity, even though this law is essentially restricted to legal and ethical norms. Thus it came about that every ethical transgression acquired also a religious significance. The ethical norm was not, at the outset, religious in sanction, as is usually believed ; it acquired this character only through the medium of the world-ruling divine personality. Nevertheless, the union of the ethical and the religious gradually caused the idea of retribution, which originally had no ethical significance whatsoever, to force its way into the conceptions of the beyond. It was essentially in this way that ethical transgressions came to be also religious offences, whereas, on the other hand, the rewards of the other-world continued to be restricted to the devout, or were granted to the moral man only on condition that he be devout as well as moral.

In conclusion, we must consider an offshoot of other-world ideas—the belief in the *transmigration of souls.* This belief is ultimately grounded in the more general ideas of soul-belief, even though its developed form appears only as a product of philosophical speculation, and has, therefore, found only a limited acceptance. In its motives, the belief most closely resembles the conception of purgatory, in so far as the latter involves the notion that the occupation of animal bodies is a means, partly of transitory punishment, and partly of purification. The idea of lustration, however, is not involved in that of metempsychosis. In its place, there is a new and unique element. It consists in the thought, expressed in Plato's "Republic," that it is proper that man should retain after death the character manifested during life, and that he should therefore assume the form of the animal which exhibits this character. There is thus manifested the idea of a relationship between man and the animal. In the distant past this idea gave rise to the animal totem; in this last form of the animal myth, it leads to the conception of the transmigration of souls. Thus, a complete inversion of values has here taken place. The significance of the totem as an ancestral animal and as an object of cult caused it to be regarded as superior to man. The animal myth, on the other hand, represents transformation into an animal as degrading, even as a severe punishment. It is precisely this difference which makes it probable that the idea of transmigration was not a free creation of Hindoo philosophers—for it was they who apparently first developed it, and from whom it passed over to the Pythagorean school and thence to Plato—but that it, also, was connected with the general development of totemic conceptions. Of course, it is not possible to trace a direct transition of the totem animal into the animal which receives the soul of a human being who is expiating sins that he has committed. It is not probable, moreover, that such a transition occurred.

Doubtless, however, the idea of transmigration is connected with the fact that, beginning with the totemic age and extending far down into the period of deity beliefs, the value placed on animals underwent a change. For the Australian, the animal is an object of cult, and the totem animal is frequently also regarded as the incarnation of an ancestor or of some magical being of antiquity; the American Indian calls the animals his elder brothers; Hercules, the hero of the heroic age, is honoured because, among other things, he was instrumental in exterminating wild animals. This change, moreover, is reflected in animal myths even more than in these general evaluations. Indeed, transformation into animals is a dominant characteristic of these myths. Tracing the conception of this magical process, however, we find, step by step, a progressive degradation of the animal. In Australian legends, animal and man are either absolute equals or the animal is the superior, being endowed with special magical powers. In American märchen-myths also, we still frequently find the same conception, although transformation into an animal is here sometimes regarded as a disgrace. Finally, in many African myths, and, particularly, in those of the cultural peoples of the ancient world, such a transformation is regarded either as a serious injury resulting from evil magic or as a punishment for some crime. We may well suppose, therefore, that the Brahmans, who first incorporated this idea into the religious conceptions of retribution, were influenced by the ideas current in popular belief, which, on their part, represented the last development of earlier totem conceptions. These ideas may also have been reinforced by the belief (not even yet entirely extinct) in soul animals, into which the psyche disappears at the moment of death. Whether the Brahmans had as yet come to the notion that transformation into an animal is a simpler and more natural way of conceiving the future of the soul than ideas of a supermundane and a subterranean beyond, need not concern us. In any event, it is noteworthy that, after science had closed the path to heaven as well as that to Hades,

Lessing and, in a broader sense, taking into account nature as a whole, Goethe himself, regarded metempsychosis as the most probable hypothesis concerning the way in which the desire for an endless survival of the soul will be satisfied.

15. The Origin of Deity Cults.

Psychologically, myth and cult are closely interrelated. The *myth* is a species of *idea*. It consists of ideas of an imaginary and an essentially supersensuous world that constitutes a background for the phenomena of sensuous reality. This supersensuous world is created by the imagination exclusively from sensuous materials. It finds portrayal throughout the various stages of myth development, first in the märchen-myth, then in the heroic saga, and finally in the deity saga. In the latter, there are interwoven ideas of the origin and destruction of things, and of the life of the soul after death. *Cult*, on the other hand, comprises only *actions*. These relate to the demons or the gods whose lives and deeds are depicted by mythology, at first only in fragmentary sketches, but later, especially in the deity saga, after the pattern of human life. Now, inasmuch as action is always the result of feeling and emotion, it is these subjective elements of consciousness that are dominant in cult, whereas cognition plays its rôle in connection with myth. This contrast is important because of its close bearing on the development of myth as well as on that of religion, and on the essential differentiæ of the two. Not every myth has a religious content. In fact, the majority of the myths prevalent, or once prevalent, in the world, have absolutely no connection with religion, if we give to the latter any sharply defined meaning at all. At the setting of the sun, a flaming hero is swallowed by a dusky demon—this conception of nature mythology may possibly be incorporated in religious conceptions, but, in itself, it possesses no religious significance whatsoever, any more than does the idea that the clouds are demons who send rain to the fields, or that a cord wound about a tree may magically transfer a sickness to it. These are all mythological ideas, yet to call them religious would obviously leave one with a most vague conception of religion. Similarly, moreover, not every cult relating to things beyond immediate reality is a religious cult. Winding a cord about a tree, for example, might constitute part of a magic cult which aims at certain beneficent or pernicious results through the aid of demons of some sort. There is no ground, however, for identifying these cult activities with deity cult. From the very beginning, of course, every cult is magical. But there are important differences with respect to the objects upon which the magic is exercised. The same is true with respect to the significance of the cult action within the circle of possible magic actions and of the derivatives which gradually displace the latter. In view of this, it is undeniable that, in *deity cult*, the cult activity, in part, assumes new forms, and, in part, and primarily, gains a new content. Prior to the belief in gods, there were numerous demon cults, as well, particularly, as single, fragmentary cult practices presupposing demoniacal powers. Moreover, these demon cults and the various activities to which they gave rise, passed down into the very heart of deity cult. The question therefore arises, What marks shall determine whether a deity cult is *religious* in character? These marks, of course, may be ascertained only by reference to that which the general consensus of opinion unites in calling religious from the standpoint of the forms of religious belief prevalent to-day. From this point of view, a religious significance may be conceded to a deity conception if, in the first place, it possesses by its very nature—that is, objectively—an *ideal* worth, and, since the ideal transcends reality, a *supersensuous* character; in the second place, it must satisfy the subjective need of man for an ideal purpose of life. To one outside of the particular cult community, the value of this ideal may be but slight; to the community, however, at the time when it is engaged in the cult practices, the ideal is of highest worth. As the embodiments of the ideals just mentioned, the gods are always pictured by the mythological imagination in human form, since it is only his own characteristics that man can conceive as magnified into the highest values in so absolute a sense. Where the deity does not reach this stage, or where, at the very least, he does not possess this ideal value during the progress of the cult activities, the cult is not religious in nature, but prereligious or subreligious. Thus, while myth and cult date back to the beginnings of human development, they acquire a religious character only at a specific time, which comes earlier in the case of cult than in that of the myth. The gods are created by the religious emotion which finds expression in cult, and myth gives them the character of ideal personalities, after the pattern of the heroic figures of actual life. The entire life of man, with all its changes of destiny, is placed in their hands. Their cult, therefore, is no longer associated merely with special circumstances or various recurrent events, as were primitive magic and the conjuration of demons, but is concerned with the whole of life, which is now subordinated to a divine legal order fashioned after the political government. Thus, the god is soon succeeded by the *divine State*, and by the cult festivals dedicated to the latter. As an idealized counterpart of the human institution peculiarly characteristic of the heroic era, religious cult appears, from this point of view also, as the most distinctive creation of the age of heroes and gods.

If a conception proves to be too narrow to cover all the phenomena which fall within its sphere, it is legitimate, of course, to broaden it, to a certain extent, to suit our needs. Nevertheless, once we admit that not every mythological conception or magical practice is religious in character, we can no longer doubt that there was never a more significant change in the development of these phenomena than occurred in the case of the myths and cults directly connected with the heroic age. Primarily, therefore, it was the cults of the Babylonians, Egyptians, Israelites, and also those of the Greeks, Romans, Aryans, and Germans, that were religious in the full sense of the word. In the

Old World, the Semitic and Indo-Germanic peoples must be regarded, to say the least, as the most important representatives of religious ideals ; in the New World, prior to the coming of the Europeans, this distinction belongs to the cultural peoples of the Andes, the Mexicans and the Peruvians. Though the religion of these latter races, no less than the other phases of their culture, was of a cruder sort than that of the former peoples, it frequently throws a remarkable light upon the initial stages of many forms of cult. Of course, there is never a sharp separation of periods ; intermediate stages are always to be found. The latter result, particularly, from two conditions. On the one hand, a deity cult may be inaugurated by the introduction of elements of a celestial mythology into the still dominant magical cults. In this case, it is important to note, deity myth is usually far in advance of deity cult. This is exemplified in Polynesia, where we find a rich theogony alongside of cults that have not advanced essentially beyond the stage of totemic magic beliefs. On the other hand, however, a people whose civilization is still, on the whole, totemic, may be influenced by the deity cults of neighbouring cultural peoples, and, as a result, fusions of various sorts may occur. Of this, also, the New World affords instructive examples, namely, the Pueblo peoples of New Mexico and Arizona, who were influenced by Mexican culture.

In the soul-life of the individual, *action*, together with the feelings and emotions fundamental to it, have the primacy over ideation. The same psychological fact universally accounts for the superior importance of deity cult over deity myth. It is action that constantly influences ideas, changing and strengthening them, and thus arousing new emotions which stimulate to further activities. Thus, the elevation of the gods into ideal beings must be ascribed, in great part, to religious cult, for it came about as a result of the influence which the emotions associated with cult exercised upon the ideas of the gods. Even less than the mythological thought from which it develops does religious reflection consist simply of ideas. The mythical tales and legends into which ideas are woven excite primarily the feelings and emotions. These it is that cause the exaltation of the religious consciousness, giving rise to action, which, in turn, enhances the emotions. If anywhere, therefore, it is in the psychology of religion that intellectualism is doomed to failure. The intellectualist is unable to explain even the fact of cult, to say nothing of those effects upon religion by virtue of which cult becomes religion's creative force. While, therefore, there are cults—namely, those of magic and demons—which, for specific reasons, we may call prereligious, there is no religion without some form of cult, even though, in the course of religious development, the external phases of cult may diminish in significance. In so far, cult is to be regarded as *moulding*, rather than as permanently expressing religious emotions; and it is not merely an effect, but also a source of religious ideas. It is in cult that deity ideas first attain their full significance. By giving expression to his desires in prayer and sacrifice, man enjoys a foretaste of their satisfaction, and this, in reaction, enhances not only the desires but also the mythological conceptions fundamental to them. It is precisely this relationship of myth to cult that extends far back into the totemic age and that causes the dominant magic cults of this period to be displaced by deity cults as soon as gods have arisen through a synthesis of heroes and demons. This accounts for the fact that, in the beginnings of religion, the worship of gods always contained elements that derived from the age of demons. But even the demon cults frequently exhibit one feature, particularly, that remains characteristic also of religion: in the cult the individual feels himself one with the object of worship. This is clearly shown in the case of primitive vegetation festivals. Those who execute the orgiastic cult dances regard themselves as one with the spirits of vegetation, whom they wish to assist, by their actions, in increasing the productive forces of nature. Such vegetation festivals have already been described in our account of totemic cults. Inasmuch, however, as they represent not only the highest of the totemic cults but even partake, in part, of the character of deity cults, it was necessary to refer to them again at this point. Vegetation festivals still prevail in richly developed forms among some of the tribes of North and Central America. It is clear that they represent primarily a transitional stage, for, in addition to totemic ideas, demon and ancestor beliefs are everywhere mingled with elements of a celestial mythology. Spirits of ancestors are thought to be seated behind the clouds, urging the rain demons to activity. Above them, however, are celestial deities, whose abode is in the heavens, and to whom is attributed the supreme control over destiny.

Even these relatively primitive vegetation cults manifest still another trait, which later comes more and more to characterize all cult, namely, the *union of many cult motives*. The great vegetation festivals of Central America attract not only those in health but also the sick. The latter are in search of healing. Hence there come to be special cults alongside of those that serve more universal needs. Moreover, the initiation of youths into manhood is also celebrated during these great festivals. Finally, the individual seeks to expiate some sin which he has committed in the past. Thus, numerous supplementary and subsidiary cults cluster about the great cult festivals. This was true even of the cults that reach far back into the age of magic and demon beliefs, when gods still played a secondary rôle, and conditions remained the same up to the time of the highest forms of deity cult. Furthermore, the incentive, or impelling motive, which originally brought cult members together for these comprehensive festivals seems everywhere to have been the same. The aim in view was to secure the prosperity of the crops, for, on the threshold of this higher civilization, these formed man's chief food-supply. The prominence of this motive in the earliest deity cults, moreover, indicates that the latter were genuine products of the general culture of this period. The roving hunter and nomad were giving place to the settled tiller of the soil, who utilized the animal for the services of man, and thus engaged more systematically in the breeding of domestic animals, though also perfecting, in addition to the arts of peace, the agencies of war. The motives that gradually elevated vegetation cults to a higher plane consisted in every case of those that at the outset found expression in the subsidiary cults. The concern for the *spiritual welfare* of mankind finally supplanted materialistic purposes. This is clearly shown by the history of the Greek mystery cults. These, however, were obviously influenced, particularly at a later time, by the similar cults of the Egyptians, as well as by the Babylonians and other peoples of western Asia. Among all these peoples, the chief cults were vegetation cults, and, as such, they occurred at stated seasons. In the Orient, particularly, the festivals were held at the solstices. Surviving remnants of seed-time and harvest festivals—which were solstice festivals and were prevalent throughout the entire Oriental world—allow us to conclude, even with respect to many regions in which a complete historical tradition is lacking, that agricultural festivals probably represent the earliest deity cults. Hence it is that these remnants still contain so many elements characteristic of demon beliefs.

It is the contrast of spring, of newly awakened Nature and its sprouting and growing crops, with winter and its dying vegetation, that first finds expression in the deity myths which inspire the vegetation festivals. The more permanent significance of these cults, however, is due to the fact that the gods of vegetation gain an increasing sphere of influence. The reason for this is obviously to be found in the fact that subsidiary motives come to be incorporated into the main cults of the earliest cultural peoples. *One* factor is of particular importance. Though inconspicuous in the earliest of these cults, it becomes increasingly prominent as the cults become more highly developed. I refer to *hopes of a beyond*. Of course, many phases of the cult remain hidden to us. Due to the combinations already mentioned and to the incorporation, in this case, of magical and mystical elements, these cults acquired a secret nature in proportion as they concerned themselves with the riddle of the beyond. The more carefully the individual cult member guarded the secrets of the group, the richer the blessings that he might hope to receive. Nevertheless, the general psychological motives underlying this development enable us to supplement the historical tradition. In this way it is possible to gain a fairly positive knowledge of the process by which, with an apparently almost universal uniformity, vegetation cults came to combine with soul cults. The ideas of changing seasons, of summer and winter, of the budding and the withering of grain, are naturally associated with those of life and death. Winter and bleak nature resemble death; and, just as lifeless nature is again resuscitated in the spring, so also will the soul awaken to a bright and joyous existence in the future. The connection is so obvious that poetry and even myth itself everywhere refer to it. Hence also it could not have been overlooked by the mythologists. Generally, however, this has been regarded as an ingenious allegory by means of which man sought to gain a vivid realization of the resurrection of the soul. In fact, such allegorical reinterpretations occur in later cult legend itself. Particularly characteristic of this is the legend of the Eleusinian mysteries. Persephone, the daughter of Demeter, goddess of the crops, is stolen by Pluto, ruler of the underworld, and the goddess-mother wanders about on the earth seeking her child. Resentfully she withdraws from the heavens and avoids the assemblages of the gods. During this period of mourning, however, she devotes all of her care to mankind. She protects not only the vegetation but also the germinating human life, the child. Thus she becomes a benefactress upon earth. The gods, however, mourn her absence, and Zeus makes a compact with the lord of the underworld. Persephone is to remain in the underworld with her husband, Pluto, during only one-half of the year; during the other half she is to return to her mother. Appeased, Demeter herself returns to the heavens. The allegorical significance of this legend cannot fail to be recognized, nor the fact that it was probably only as a result of a poetical elaboration of the mythological material that this allegorical character was acquired. The same is true of all other similar cult legends, from the descent into hell of the Babylonian Ishtar down to the legends of Dionysos and Osiris, and other vegetation legends of the Hellenistic period. In the form in which these have come down to us, they are all products of priestly invention, replete with a conscious symbolism such as cannot be ascribed to the original mythical material upon which they were based. Nevertheless, it is customary not only to regard all of this original content as allegorical, but also to surpass even the traditional legend itself, if possible, in allegorical interpretation. In the legend of Demeter, for example, Demeter is supposed to be the mother earth, and Persephone the seed that is thrown into the earth to grow up and blossom. Analogously, he who participates in the cult hopes that, while his soul, similarly, is at first buried in the earth with his body, it will later ascend to heaven as did Demeter. Back of the myth, therefore, there is supposed to be a symbolical allegory, and to this is attributed the original union of the soul cult with the vegetation festival. When, then, the former lost its influence, the symbolism it thought to have remained as the chief content of the mystery. No original cult, however, shows the least sign of connection with such subtle allegories. On the other hand, there are many indications that the vegetation cults developed into these higher forms of soul cults in an entirely different way. Soul cults of a lower order had, of course, long been prevalent. But these were absolutely distinct from any vegetation myths that may have existed. They pictured souls as demons, against whom it was necessary to be on one's guard, or, at a later stage, as beings whom one might conciliate and win over as helpful spirits. Now, the cults of Demeter practised in Eleusis had as their aim, not only an increased productiveness of the soil, but also success in the interests and activities of this world. Since they related to happiness in general, it was but natural that, as soon as the ideas of a beyond reached a point of development at which the yonder-world became the focus of desires and hopes, the cults also should necessarily concern themselves with happiness in a life after death. Thus, interest in the beyond came to be one of the further cult motives that linked themselves to the dominant vegetation cults. The latter, however, held the primacy, as is still clearly apparent by reference to the vegetation festivals of the semi-cultural peoples of America. It is only natural that this should have been the case. When agriculture was in its beginnings, the most pressing need of life was that of daily bread. For the tiller of the soil, moreover, the changes of seasons marked by seedtime and harvest, represent sharply defined periods, suitable above all others for the festivals to which tribal associates assemble from near and far. The later allegories connected with these cults had nothing to do with their transition into soul cults, but, as their whole character indicates, were creations of the priestly imagination. As a result of the reaction of cult activities upon the emotions, however, concern for the future happiness of the soul finally came more and more to overshadow the desires connected with this world. Thus, the cults of Demeter eventually passed over, in all essentials, into cults of the beyond. The same is true of the Dionysos cults of the Greeks, of the Egyptian worship of Isis and Osiris, of the Persian Mithra cult, and of many other mystery cults of Oriental origin. All of these express the same passion for a future bliss that shall begin at the close of earthly life and endure endlessly.

The character of these cults is shaped, in a decisive measure, by other influences, whose source is to be found in the hopes of a beyond. Even in the vegetation festivals of the semi-cultural peoples of America, with their elements of totemism and ancestor worship, an important place is occupied by *ecstatic* features—by the orgiastic dance, and by the ecstasy that results from sexual excitement and from narcotic poisons, such as tobacco. Conjurations, prayer, sacrifice, and other cult ceremonies aid in stirring the emotions. Doubtless it was due to these ecstatic elements that the cult of Dionysos gained supremacy over the older cults of Demeter in the Greek mysteries, and that Dionysos himself was eventually given a place in the Demeter cult. For is he not the god of wine, the most potent of all the means for creating a condition of bliss that elevates above all earthly cares? In the mystery cults, however, the central feature of the cult activity was the vision experienced in the ecstasy. The mysterious equipment of the place, the preliminary ascetic practices, the liturgic conjurations and sacrifices, the wine, which originally took the place of the blood sacrifice, and, among the Hindoos, the soma, which was itself deified—all of these served to transport consciousness to another world, so that the cult became increasingly concerned with the world beyond, and finally devoted itself exclusively to this interest. As a result of this change, the hopes centring about the beyond forced their way overpoweringly into cult, whereas the cult, in turn, reacted in an important measure to enhance these hopes.

Over against the tendency toward unification inherent in vegetation cults and in the other-world cults which sprang from them, the increasing diversity of needs and interests now introduces influences toward a progressive differentiation of cults. Separate deity cults come to be fostered by the various social groups and classes, just as had occurred in the case of the totem cults of the preceding age, which differed according as they were practised by the tribe, the sex, or the individual. The desire for protection against dangers and for security in undertakings gives rise to guardian gods no less than it did to guardian demons. Since, however, this more general desire branches out into a considerable number of special desires, advancing culture results in a progressive differentiation of cults. The foundation of cities and the separation into classes and occupations lead to special cults for each of these divisions of society. The personal characteristics of the gods and the purposes of the cult come to be affected, each by the other. Each specific cult chooses from among the members of the pantheon that god who best suits its purpose, and it then modifies his character according to its needs. The characteristics of the gods thus undergo a change of significance analogous to that of the forms of speech and custom. This change, however, is due mainly to cult, and to the fact that the human beings who practise the cult have need of protection and aid. The influence of saga and poetry is only secondary, being, at best, mediated through cult.

In addition to the increasing diversity of human interests, and interplaying with it in various ways, are two further factors that tend toward the differentiation of cult. In the first place, divine personality as such awakens man to the necessity of establishing a cult. As a personal being who transcends human stature, the god calls for adoration by his very nature, even apart from the special motives which are involved in the specific deity cults and which, in the further course of development, give to the latter their dominant tone. Pure deity cults, thus, are the highest forms of cult, and give best expression to ideal needs. Outstanding examples of this are the Jahve cult of the Israelites, and the cults of Christ and Buddha. The latter, in particular, show the great assimilative power of cults that centre about an objective ideal, in contrast with those that are subjective in nature, springing entirely from human desires and hopes, and especially with that most subjective of all cults, the cult of the beyond. Moreover, this idealizing impulse may also create new cults, by deifying heroes who were originally conceived as human. Besides the ancient hero cults, the most prominent examples of such cults are again those of Christ and of Buddha. For there can be no doubt that Christ and Buddha alike existed as human beings and that originally they were also regarded as such. The fact that their heroic character consists entirely in the spiritual qualities of their personalities does not preclude them from consideration in this connection. These qualities proved all the more effective in bringing about the exaltation of the human into the divine. Thus, they enable us to understand how it was possible for the cult of the original deities to be crowded into the background by that of those who later came to be gods. This is emphatically brought out in the Buddha legends, many of which represent the ancient Hindoo gods of the Veda as the servants of the divine Buddha.

In addition to the fact that divine personalities call forth homage by their very nature, the multiplication of cults results also from the fusion of the gods of various peoples. This is the most external factor, and yet it is by no means the least potent one. It not infrequently happens that cults gain their supreme importance only in the territory into which they have been transplanted. Dionysos, for example, was a god introduced from elsewhere into Greece. Through his connection with the mystery cults, however, he later came to surpass all other Greek gods in religious significance. The original cults of the native Italian deities, with their numerous elements carried over from the age of demoniacal and ancestral spirits, were but few in number. Through the assimilation of Greek deities, however, and later, at the time of the empire, of Oriental gods, differing widely in character, Rome acquired a multiplicity of cults to which history doubtless affords no parallel. Yet we must not overlook the fact that in certain other cases—such, for example, as the Babylonian-Assyrian and the Egyptian cults—the fusions may perhaps have become more complete at an early period, and thus have precluded the juxtaposition of the many separate cults that existed in the Rome of the Empire.

16. The Forms of Cult Practices.

This multiplicity of cults, increasing with the advance of civilization both as regards the ends that are desired and the gods who are worshipped, is by no means paralleled by the number of *cult agencies*. The only possible exception might be in the case of the means which the cults of the beyond employed for arousing ecstasy. Even here the difference lies not so much in the means themselves as in the extent to which they were used. Moreover, the secrecy surrounding these cults is itself an external indication of the fact that they differed from the cults concerned with the things of this world, for the latter generally sought publicity. And yet there was no form of cult in which ecstatic features were altogether lacking; such features are inherent, to a certain extent, in cult practices as such and, in so far, are absolutely universal. Differences in the specific purposes of the cults and in the deities to whom the acts were dedicated did indeed cause certain variations. These, however, we may here neglect, inasmuch as they do not affect the essential nature of cult itself. From early times on, there were certain activities that were universally characteristic of deity cults, and their fundamental purposes remained the same, namely, to gain the favour of the deity and thereby to obtain the fulfilment of personal wishes. As regards this motive, the *three* cult agencies—*prayer, sacrifice*, and *sanctification*—are absolutely at one. In this order of sequence, moreover, these agencies represent a progressive intensification of the religious activity of cult.

In the records of ancient civilized peoples we meet with a great number of *prayers*, representing all the forms developed by this simplest and most common of the means of cult. The most primitive form of prayer is *conjuration*. Conjuration passed over from demon cult into the beginnings of deity cult, and is intermediate between a means of magic and a petition. This also indicates the direction of the further development of the prayer. Conjuration is succeeded by the *prayer of petition*, whose essential differentia consists in the fact that, however earnestly the suppliant may strive for the fulfilment of his desires, he nevertheless ultimately commits them to the will of the deity. The development of the prayer of petition out of conjuration becomes possible only because gods possess a characteristic which demons lack—namely, personality. Once this personality attains to its ideal sublimity, the exercise of magical power over the deity ceases to be possible, or is so only under the presupposition that the will of the deity is in itself favourably inclined toward the suppliant. The idea underlying conjuration nevertheless continues for a time to remain a supplementary factor in the prayer of petition; even where no clearly conscious trace of it appears, it survives in the depth of emotion that reinforces the petition. That conjuration blends with petition is particularly evident in the case of *one* characteristic, whose origin must be traced to magical conjuration. I refer to the fact that the *words of the petition* are *repeated* in the same or in a slightly changed form, and that, at a later stage of development, there is a constant recurrence of the same content, even though this is variously expressed. This is a derivative characteristic of the prayer of petition. Originally, it was thought that repetition brought about an intensification of the magical effect, particularly in the case of word-magic. We are already familiar with conjurations of this sort as elements of totemic cults. With but few changes, they recur in the older songs of the Avesta and Veda, as well as in some of the Biblical Psalms. In these cases, however, the repetitions are somewhat more extensive, for there is a more detailed statement of that which is desired. And yet the Biblical Psalms, particularly, are an illustration of the fact that, with submission to the will of the deity, the petition becomes less urgent in tone. Even when the petition is repeated the expression more and more assumes a somewhat altered form. It is probably this enhancement through repetition—itself, in turn, due to the dynamic character of the emotions of desire—that accounts for the so-called 'parallelism of members,' characteristic especially of Hebrew poetry. The view, once entertained, that this is a sort of substitute for the rhythm arising from emphasis and sentence arrangement is doubtless incorrect, for recent investigations demonstrate the ingenious rhythm of Hebrew poetry. We would not, of course, deny that the repetition of the thought in a changed form intensifies the rhythmic expression. The real basis of the repetition, however, lies not in this fact but in the motive underlying petition. This is clear, above all, from the fact that repetition is most pronounced particularly in those psalms and prophetic songs which are of the nature of a prayer of petition and of the praises closely connected with it. Later, repetition was also employed in other forms of religious expression. In the case of the hymn of praise, particularly, the tendency to repetition is augmented, by virtue of the enthusiastic exaltation of the divine personality whom the hymn extols.

Besides the prayer of petition we find the *prayer of thanksgiving*. Petition and thanksgiving are properly correlative, the one expressing a wish to the deity and the other acknowledging its fulfilment. Not infrequently, therefore, they are combined, particularly in the more advanced forms of the prayer cult, into a single prayer of thanksgiving and petition. He who prays returns thanks for the blessings which he has received and adds a request for further divine aid. This combination occurs very frequently in the Psalms, but it is to be found also in other hymnodies. The extent to which the request for further favours is subordinated to the thanksgiving for past aid, is a measure of the humility involved, and represents a fair criterion of the maturity of the religious feeling underlying the prayer. Nevertheless, it may also be noticed that he who prays always aims first to gain the divine favour through his thanksgiving, in the hope that the gods may thereby be rendered more disposed to grant his request. Typical examples of this are to be found, not only in the Biblical Psalms, but also in the ancient Babylonian texts which recent discoveries have brought to light. That the prayer of thanksgiving is a higher form of prayer than is petition, is shown by the very fact that it occurs in deity cult alone. More clearly even than petition does thanksgiving presuppose a personal being, capable of appreciating the feeling of gratitude. It is at most in the fact that the prayer of thanksgiving still seeks to obligate the deity to future favours, that demon-conjuration has left its traces upon it. And yet deity cult is characterized precisely by the fact that the compulsion of magical conjuration has entirely disappeared in favour of the free volition of the deity. That prayer is regarded as imposing an obligation upon the god no less than upon man, is extremely well brought out in the conception that the relation of the two is that of a contract, or of a covenant sealed in the cult. This idea, reinforced by the national significance of the deity, is fundamental in the Jahve cult of the Israelites.

Praise, or, as it is called in its poetic forms, the *hymn*, is an even more pronounced feature of deity cult than is the prayer of thanksgiving. The hymn is not usually classified as a form of prayer because, when externally regarded, it may entirely lack the motive of petition, and it is from the latter that the prayer has derived its name. In view, however, of the continuity of the development of the cult forms which find expression in speech, we cannot escape including also the song of praise. Indeed, it generally adduces the blessings conferred by the god as an evidence of his glory ; not infrequently, moreover, it concludes with a hope for the future favour of the deity. Artistically perfect examples of such prayers are the compositions known as the Homeric Hymns, which, of course, belong to a much later age than the Homeric epics. They are pæans in praise of Demeter, Apollo, Dionysos, and Hermes, in which the laudation of the beneficent activity of these deities takes the form of a recital of some incident in their lives, followed by a prospective glance at the favour which they may be expected to bestow in the future.

In these cases, the song of praise clearly represents a development of the prayer of thanksgiving. The final and most mature form of prayer, however, the *penitential prayer*, or, as it is usually called, the *penitential psalm*, may in a certain sense be called a subform of the petitional prayer. In it, either external need or the consciousness of personal guilt leads the individual to call upon the gods for mercy and for forgiveness of the committed sin. Typical examples are again available in the Hebraic and Babylonian psalms. These psalms contain, in the first instance, prayers of cult, which were offered on the occasion of national disasters and needs, such as crop failure or drought, or, as in the case particularly of the Israelites, were repeated at stated times in penitence for the sins of the community. Such being the motives, the most universal form of prayer, that of petition, may here also be discerned in the background. Not only is the penitential psalm in and for itself a particular form of petition, containing as it does a plea for the forgiveness of committed sins, but it is frequently combined with a direct prayer for the favour of the deity and for renewed manifestations of grace through a fortunate turn of destiny. In spite of this egoistic strain, however, which, just as in the case of the song of praise, is seldom absent, the penitential prayer is, religiously speaking, the highest form of prayer, and may be found only at an advanced stage of deity cult. Above all other forms of prayer, its emphasis falls on the inner life; where it comes to expression in its purity, it seeks not external goods, but only peace of conscience. Moreover, more than anywhere else, we find in it a resignation to the will of the deity. This resignation, in turn, draws its strength from the belief that human destiny is in the absolute control of the gods, everything experienced by the individual or by the cult community being interpreted as a divine punishment or reward. Thus, the penitential prayer is closely bound up, on the one hand, with the idea of a divine providence and, on the other, with ideas of retribution. Neither the idea of providence nor that of retribution is to be found in early deity cult; both are products of the subsequent religious development. Moreover, the issue is not changed by raising the question whether the retribution is regarded as occurring here or in the beyond. As a matter of fact, the retributive idea is far from being implicated with other-world hopes. The conviction that punishment will overtake the guilty man even in this world, because of the direct connection between present fortune and misfortune and the worship of the gods, is itself the immediate source of the idea of a divine power ever controlling the destinies of mankind.

In addition to prayer, however, and usually bound up with it, there is a second important form of cult practice, namely, *sacrifice*. The usual conception of sacrifice is altogether too narrow—just as is the case with prayer. Hence the origin and significance of sacrifice have been misunderstood. In view of one of its prominent features in the more highly developed cults, sacrifice is usually regarded as a gift to the deity, and the various meanings that a gift may have are then simply held to apply to sacrifice itself. Accordingly, the purpose of sacrifice is limited either to disposing the god favourably toward the sacrificing individual or community, or to obtaining forgiveness for committed sins. In the Priests' Code of the Israelites, this second form of sacrifice—the trespass or sin-offering—also served the former purpose, thus acquiring the significance of an act of reconciliation which at the same time blotted out any transgressions of the past. The sin-offering, on the other hand, was concerned with purification from a single, definite sin for which the forgiveness of the deity had to be obtained. The peace-offering, therefore, was a cult that was celebrated in common and on a specific day, whereas the sin-offering was brought only on special occasions, when an individual or a restricted group felt the burdens of conscience because of a committed sin. Corresponding to the different purposes indicated by the words 'reconciliation' and 'forgiveness' was the manner in which the sacrifice was brought. The peace-offering was taken to definitely established centres of cult, primarily to the temple at Jerusalem. Those bringing the sacrifice shared its enjoyment with the deity in the sacrificial meal, which was an expression of the covenant concluded with the deity for the future. The sin-offering was made whenever occasion demanded, and the sacrifice was designed for the deity alone. After the removal of the portion reserved for the priesthood, the remainder was burned—those making the sacrifice could enjoy none of it. If we regard both kinds of sacrifice as forms of gift, the peace-offering would correspond more closely to an actual gift with a certain tinge of bribery, though this conception is rendered less crude by the fact that the sacrifice represents also a covenant which receives expression in the sacrificial meal. The sin-offering, on the other hand, is more of the nature of a penalty, similar to that which a judge imposes in satisfaction of a crime.

It must be granted that there is a stage in the development of sacrificial cult in which the gift motive is dominant. Nevertheless, even here there are concomitant phenomena which clearly indicate that the sacrifice cannot originally have had the significance of a gift. On the contrary, there has been, in part, a change in meaning and, in part, an arbitrary reinterpretation of phenomena. The Jewish peace-offering was not a true gift. This is evidenced by the fact alone that one of its chief features was the sacrificial feast, which involved the idea of the deity's participation in the meal. In connection with this idea of communion with the deity, the offering of parts of the consumed sacrifice was manifestly only a secondary motive. Nor was the renunciation required of the sacrificer in connection with the Jewish sin-offering a feature which had anything in common with a gift. It was similar rather to punishment. Moreover, all resemblance whatsoever to a gift disappears when we call to mind the earliest forms of sacrifice, as well as the objects that were offered. One of the oldest sacrifices, found even within totemic culture, was that offered to the dead. In its broadest sense, this comprehends everything that was given over to the deceased, or that was burned with him, in case cremation was practised. Such objects originally included some of the belongings of the deceased, particularly his weapons and personal decorations. After despotic forms of government arose, the death of a chief or of a person of influence demanded also the sacrifice of his animals, slaves, and wives. We are already familiar with the change of motives that here occurred. At first, the aim was to keep the deceased from approaching the living; later, it was to equip him with whatever might be of service in his future life. The sacrifice then became an offering to the demon of the deceased, designed to win his aid for the living. Finally, it was devoted to the gods, whose favour was sought both for the deceased and for the survivors.

A survey of the development as a whole shows that the gift motive was at first entirely lacking, and that even later it was of relatively little importance. The idea of magic was predominant. The aim was to bring the power of magic to bear upon the deceased and his demon, and finally upon the gods. The demon was to be kept at a distance, just as in the case of burial and of the binding of the corpse, and the gods were to be won over to a friendly attitude. This appears even more clearly when we consider the objects that were sacrificed. In this respect, there was an important change, first mediated, probably, by the cult of the dead, and thence carried over to sacrifice in general. The sacrificer offered such parts of his own body as were held to be the specific vehicles of the soul. Homer tells us that Achilles deposited the two locks of hair, which he had once promised to his native river god, upon the dead body of Patroclus. The use as a sacrifice to the dead of a gift dedicated to a god, clearly indicates that the two forms of sacrifice possessed an identical significance. The deceased takes with him into the underworld part of the person of the sacrificer. Similarly, it was believed that the psychical powers of the deity are, on the one hand, strengthened through the soul which he receives in sacrifice, and are, on the other hand, inclined toward the one who brings the offering. In animal sacrifice, the blood was poured out beside the sacrificial stone for the enjoyment of the god. Of the inner parts of the bloody sacrifice, it was again those that were in ancient times regarded as the chief vehicles of the soul, the kidneys with the surrounding fat, that were particularly set aside for the god. Closely connected with this is the sacrifice which, through self-mutilation, the priests and temple servants offered in the case of ecstatic cults (pp. 294 f.). In all of these instances the ideas of magic and of gift intermingle. The soul-vehicles which are offered are also gifts to the deity, intended for his enjoyment. In partaking of them, however, a magical influence is released by means of which the will of the deity is controlled, or, in the view of a more advanced age, is favourably inclined toward the sacrificer.

The same idea prevails when public sacrifice demands a human being, instead of an animal, as a vicarious offering for the sacrificing community. Indeed, human sacrifice also has its prototype in the sacrifice to the dead, though the sacrificial idea is in this case kept in the background, inasmuch as the dominant purpose is to equip the deceased with that which he requires for his further life. Human sacrifice proper, therefore, is at most connected with faint survivals of this older practice. In contrast with the latter custom, the individual sacrificed to the deity serves as a *substitute* for the community. In this form, however, human sacrifice does not antedate animal sacrifice, as has been believed, but follows upon it. Still later, of course, it was again displaced by the latter, as is graphically portrayed in the Biblical legend of Abraham and Isaac. The priority of animal sacrifice is attested, first of all, by its incomparably wider distribution. Human sacrifice, and traditions indicative of it, appear to be altogether restricted to the great agricultural festivals and solstice-cults in which the one who is sacrificed serves, on the one hand, as a substitute for the sacrificing community which offers itself to the deity in his person, and, on the other hand, as the representative of the god himself. Convincing proof of this is furnished by the traditions regarding the seasonal cults of the ancient Mexicans, as these have been reported by K. Th. Preusz. Prior to the sacred festival at which an individual was offered in sacrifice, he was himself reverenced as a god. The twofold significance of the human sacrifice becomes perfectly intelligible in the light of the above-mentioned fusion of the ideas of gift and of magic. Dedication to the deity and union with him merge so completely that they become a single conception. Even the blood poured out upon the sacrificial altar was not merely an offering, but, as a vehicle of the soul, was supposed to transfer to the deity who received it the desires of the offerer. What was true of the blood was quite naturally pre-eminently true when the object of sacrifice was the person himself.

In this case, all the organs were offered, and, therefore, the entire soul. This is the most extreme form of the sacrificial idea, and occurs only in the sacrificial cult of fairly large political and religious communities. As is characteristic of legend, the 'Abraham and Isaac' story individualizes the ancient tradition, construing the latter as an account of a test of obedience to the god—an interpretation very obviously to be regarded as an invention of later priestly wisdom. On the other hand, the Roman Saturnalia, the Persian festival of Sacæa, and other agricultural cults of the ancient world, exhibit traces of the sacrifice of a human being who represents the deity himself. Along with these we might probably mention also the Babylonian festival of Tammuz and the Jewish feast of Purim. Finally, the Christian conception of the sacrificial death of Jesus combines the same ideas, though their religious significance is transformed and reinforced by the thought of redemption, which has displaced the older protective and fortune-bringing magic. The sacrificial community has here become the whole of mankind, and the one who by his death brings about a reconciliation with the deity is himself the god. For this reason dogma insists—with a logic that is perhaps unconscious and mystical in nature, yet all the more compelling—on the unity of the divine personality with that of the redeemer who died the sacrificial death. This fusion of sacrificial conceptions thus gave rise to the most impressive and effective story that the human mind ever conceived.

Herewith we reach the culminating point in the development of the idea of a gift offered to the deity, and here also the sacrificial object attains its highest *worth*. That the sacrificer, however, is little concerned with the value of the objects which he brings, is obvious from the fact that these are frequently without any objective value whatsoever. Such, for example, are the small pictures offered in Chinese ancestor cult, and also the miniature representations of desired objects which are placed on votive altars—instances in which, of the two ideas combined in sacrifice, that of the gift again entirely vanishes, leaving as the sole motive the more primitive idea of magic, which never completely disappears. Wherever sacrifice is dominated by the idea of a gift offered to the deity, the sacrificer, in turn, seeks to gain certain ends in return for the value of his gifts. The scale of values may be either quantitative or qualitative, or both combined. Even in the case of the bloody sacrifice both criteria are, as a rule, involved. At the great festivals of Athens and other Greek cities, one hundred steers were sacrificed to the gods, the greater part of the sacrifice, of course, serving as food for the people. In Israel, the rich man sacrificed his bullock, the poor man, his young goat. It was the conception of value that caused especially the fruits of the field, as well as the products of the cattle industry, milk and butter, to become objects of sacrifice. Later, sacrificial offerings were also made in terms of jewels and money. These were brought to the temple for the decoration of the house of the god and for the support of the cult or the relief of the poor. This development was influenced by another change, connected with the transition from the earlier bloody sacrifice to the bloodless sacrifice. Prior to the influence of the sacrificial customs, the bloody sacrifice involved the loss of the sacrificial animals. These were either entirely burned and thus given to the gods, or their flesh was consumed by the cult members at the sacrificial feast, the god receiving only those parts that were prized as the vehicles of the soul. Now, bloodless sacrifice belongs to a higher stage both of culture and of cult. In general, it presupposes an advanced agricultural and cattle industry, as well as the existence of more extensive cult-needs whose satisfaction the sacrifice is designed to secure. Thus, the two conditions mutually reinforce each other. The products of agriculture cannot be directly offered to the deity as can the burnt offering, which ascends to heaven in the smoke. On the other hand, the cult cannot dispense with certain means, and these are obtained by utilizing in its interests the economic foresight which has been acquired by the agriculturist and the cattle-raiser in the course of their work. In place of the direct products of husbandry, the succeeding age more and more substitutes costly jewels and money. Thus, the development which began with the burnt offering concludes with the money offering. This later offering is no longer made directly to the deity or, at most, this occurs in the accompanying prayer ; the offerer bestows his gifts upon the temple, the priests, or the poor. By so doing he hopes to win the divine favour indirectly, through the merit which such gifts possess or through the cult activities which are purchased by means of them.

The earliest forms of sacrifice are thus more and more displaced by cult agencies which, to a certain extent, themselves approximate to purification ceremonies. This transformation, however, cannot suppress the original sacrificial purpose, which was solely that of exercising a direct magical influence upon the deity. We now meet with phenomena in which this purpose asserts itself all the more potently because of the above development—phenomena from which the idea of a gift possessing objective value is entirely absent. We refer particularly to votive and consecration gifts. These very names, indeed, are evidence of the confusion which a one-sided emphasis of the gift-idea has introduced into the interpretation of sacrifice. For votive and consecration gifts generally consist of artificial objects which are ordinarily devoid of any artistic or other value. They are deposited on the altars of the gods, or, in the Catholic cult, on those of the saints, either to make known a wish, as does the 'gift of consecration,' or, less frequently, to render thanks for the fulfilment of a desire, as in the case of the 'votive offering.' Although these offerings, even in their beginnings, are inseparable from a fairly developed deity cult—since they presuppose altars upon which they are placed, and, therefore, temples consecrated to the gods—it is practically the amulet alone that may be said to rival them in extent of distribution. They occur in ancient Egypt, as well as in Greece and Rome. They were known also to Germanic antiquity, from whence they probably found their way into the Catholic cults of Mary and the saints. The consecration gift corresponds to the prayer of petition, the votive offering to the prayer of thanksgiving ; these prayers, accordingly, are spoken when the object is placed upon the altar. The gift of consecration is the earlier and more common, just as the prayer of petition precedes that of thanksgiving. The peculiarity of this cult, however, consists in the fact that the object offered as a sacrifice is an artificially fashioned image, usually reduced in size, of the object in connection with which aid is sought. This obviously gives it a certain relationship with the fetish, on the one hand, and with the amulet, on the other. As a matter of fact, the so-called 'consecration gifts' are not in the least real gifts. The sick man presents a figure of the diseased part of his body, fashioned of clay, bronze, or wax, and the peasant who has suffered a loss of cattle brings a representation of the animal. In themselves, these objects are valueless ; nor can they be of service to the deity to whom they are brought, as was doubtless believed by the sacrificers to be true in the case of the animal that was slaughtered, as well as of the blood, and doubtless also of the fruits which were offered. The significance of such a gift of consecration lies solely in its subjective value, just as does that of the primitive amulet, which is likewise an article without any objective worth. To believe, however, that this value consists in the fact that the consecration gift symbolizes the submissive reverence of the offerer would be to read back a later stage of religious thought into an age to which such symbols are entirely foreign. Moreover, the purposes of this sacrifice make such an interpretation impossible. The vast majority of consecration sacrifices have another similarity to amulets, in addition to that just mentioned ; those who bring them seek healing from disease. Hence, in ancient times, such offerings were brought chiefly to the temple of Æsculapius. Just as the amulet, in its most common forms, is designed as a protection against dreaded sicknesses, so also does the consecration gift aim at relief from actual suffering. The amulet, however, may be traced far back into the period of demon-cult, and its characteristic types, therefore, are patterned on the more prevalent expressions of demon-belief, such as cord magic. The consecration gift, on the other hand, is associated with deity cult, and takes the form of sacrifice. Moreover, it reverts to the most primitive kind of sacrifice, to the purely magical offering. The leg of wax offered by the lame is simply a means of magic. Since it possesses no objective value, it is worthless as a gift, and, as a means of magic, it is again of the most primitive sort. The sacrificial object is regarded as having a soul, quite in the sense of early animism. Through its immanent psychical power it is to exercise magical coercion over the soul of the god or the saint. Its potency is precisely the same as that which the soul of the sacrificial animal or human being is supposed to possess. The only difference is that the external characteristics of animistically conceived objects ordinarily force into the background the idea that the sacrifice magically becomes identical with the deity who receives it, whereas this conception comes out with especial clearness when the offering consists of an animal or of a human being. This is strikingly shown by the above-mentioned sacrificial festivals, in which, prior to being offered as a sacrifice, the individual was himself reverenced as the god to whom he was to be offered. True, the fact that the human individual, as well as the animal, possesses a value for those who bring the sacrifice, also introduces the idea of a gift; added to this, moreover, in the case of human sacrifice, is the further thought that the sacrifice is a substitution for the sacrificial community.

Thus, the idea of a magical effect upon the deity is combined with that of a gift designed to gain his favour. This appears also in connection with the sacrifice of the *first-fruits of the harvest* or, with what is only a transference from the fruits of the field to the animal used in its cultivation, that of the first-born of the cattle. From the standpoint of the gift theory, such an offering is regarded as a particularly valuable gift. But this greater value is again exclusively of a subjective nature. Objectively speaking, the mere fact that it is the first of the fruits or the first-born of the cattle that is offered does not give the sacrifice any additional value. Very probably the decisive factor is the preference which man gives the gods in the enjoyment of the fruits of the field. It certainly cannot be denied that this motive is operative, particularly in later development. That it was the original notion, however, is improbable. Obviously, this offering is closely related to the custom, common even to-day, of leaving the last sheaf in the harvest-field. This custom, which W. Mannhardt was able to trace from ancient times down to rural festivals that are still prevalent, is also of the nature of a sacrifice. On such occasions, an egg, a piece of bread, or the picture of a human being or of an animal, is sometimes tied to the first or to the last sheaf of the harvest and left upon the field. Such acts are obviously due to the need of attributing to the garnered grain life and a soul, as well as the ability to influence by its soul the vegetation demons of the field, and, in later times, the gods who protect the cultivated soil. The custom could scarcely have originated except for the presence, from the very outset, of the idea of a psychical power resident in the sprouting seed. Later, the idea of a gift here also forced the magical motive into the background. Indeed, it may well be that this caused the sacrificial usages which originally, as it appears, marked the end of the harvest, to be put forward to its beginning.

It is only ideas of magic, furthermore, that can account for the practice of *divination*. Connected with sacrifice are various phenomena that are accidental in nature and unforeseeable on the part of the sacrificer. These phenomena are such as to be sometimes regarded as indications of the acceptance or the rejection of the sacrifice on the part of the deity, while at other times they are interpreted from a different point of view, as general prophetic signs. In the case of the burnt offering, for example, the direct ascent of the smoke to the heavens was regarded as a sign that the deity graciously accepted the offering. Similarly, the examination of entrails, common among Oriental as well as Occidental peoples, originally, doubtless, had the purpose of discovering whether the animal possessed a nature pleasing to the gods. Later, however, it became one of a large class of general prophetic signs (*prodigia*), such as the flight of birds, lightning, clouds, and other incalculable phenomena of nature by which the future was predicted, particularly in respect to the success or failure of enterprises about to be undertaken. Because of the general relationship of magic and divination, the sacrificial cult borders upon the *oracle*. In the oracle, man wishes to read the future ; in the sacrifice, he wishes to influence it by his action. This of itself implies that sacrifice occupies the higher plane. The belief in prophetic signs passed over from demon cult to deity worship with relatively little change, except that it became connected with particular gods or priesthoods and was therefore more strictly regulated. The hopes of a beyond, which were involved in the ecstatic practices of the orgiastic cults, opened up a new field to prophecy, and supplied divination with additional methods—the dream and the vision. Though connected in various ways with sacrificial cult, these phenomena are far from containing the wealth of religious motives involved in the former. Nor do they develop any common cult. This is due particularly to the fact that ecstatic visions are dependent upon a certain psychological predisposition, a fact which also enables us to understand the influence exercised by the individual seer and prophet upon religion and cult.

A third, and the highest, form of cult practice consists in *sanctification ceremonies*. Just as sacrifice is bound up with the various forms of prayer—conjuration, petition, thanksgiving, and penitence—so, in turn, is the sanctification ceremony closely connected with both sacrifice and prayer. On the one hand, it is reinforced by accompanying prayers ; on the other, it results directly from sacrifice, particularly whenever the latter takes the form of a cult practice that brings mankind into association with the deity. In this event, the ceremony of sanctification represents an activity supplementary to sacrifice. The impulse to sanctification gains the dominance over the sacrificial idea as soon as the desires relating to the personal worth of the sacrificer himself gain ascendancy over the external motives which at first prevailed. This subjective interest, of course, appears only after the religious life has become relatively mature ; at the outset, moreover, it is still everywhere combined with sacrificial practices that centre about external possessions. Once it has finally freed itself, and has become purely a sacrifice designed to enhance personal worth, it becomes a *means of sanctification*. When sacrifice has reached this highest stage, however, the idea of a gift presented to the deity by the sacrificer completely disappears—in so far, there is a resemblance to the very earliest sacrifices, which were of a purely magical nature and were in no sense intended as gifts. If, therefore, the sacrifice of self-sanctification retains any connection at all with the conception of a gift, the sacrificer must not only be said to offer himself to the deity but the deity must likewise be regarded as giving himself to the sacrificer.

Nevertheless, the origins of sanctification ceremonies and of sacrifice are essentially diverse. At the outset, moreover, these cult practices adopt different paths, meeting only at the height of their development. True, the sanctification ceremony is rooted in magic belief, just as is sacrifice. In primitive sacrifice, however, the magic is directed externally ; in the case of sanctification, on the other hand, the object of the magic is the human being himself who performs the cult action or who permits it to be performed upon him. Even in the earliest stages of these practices, therefore, the sanctification ceremony occupies the higher level ; hence, also, this ceremony is subsequent in origin to sacrifice. And yet practices presaging sanctification may be found in much more primitive cults, in the *purification ceremonies*, whose beginnings may be traced far back into the totemic age. We have already mentioned the fact that water and fire were used as means of magical purification even in the period of demon-belief (pp. 201 ff). So long as they retain this significance, they may both be classed as agencies of counter-magic. Their function is to counteract the evil spells that result from contact with a corpse or with some other object that is regarded as taboo. Purification by fire has the same significance. Because of the more elaborate preparations which it requires, however, such purification tends, from the very beginning, to take the form of a public cult celebration. As a result, it passes over directly from the field of counter-magic into that of magic proper—a reversal common in the field of magical usage. At this point, purification becomes sanctification. For, the original purpose of the means which the latter employs is always that of affording protection against *future* attacks on the part of the demoniacal powers that threaten man from without, or, in a later and a religiously purified interpretation, against personal transgressions resulting from man's inner nature. Herewith the development reaches the stage of the sanctification ceremony proper. The belief that sanctification is necessary for the individual can arise only in connection with deity beliefs, for it is bound up with ideas of retribution. The latter, in turn, depend upon the feeling of the personal guilt of the individual no less than upon the belief in the existence of personal gods who avenge the sins that are committed. Precisely the same change that takes place in the development of purification by fire transpires also in the case of water, the second and more common means of lustration. Here this transition is most clearly evident in connection with *baptism*. True, even Christian baptism still partly retains the idea of lustration. For, though the newborn child who is baptized is not himself conscious of any wrongdoing, he is nevertheless tainted, according to the doctrine of inherited guilt, by the original sin from which he must be cleansed. Baptism thus incorporates the meaning both of purification and of sanctification. The latter conception, however, asserts its dominance. And yet the Anabaptists, though insisting that man is unworthy of the sacred act unless he submits to it of his own free will, have also wished to preserve, along with the idea of sanctification, the idea of purification, which is both more original and, for sense perception, more real. Moreover, baptism also occurs with this twofold meaning outside the pale of Christianity, not only among the Hebrews, to whom the Christian religion is indebted for the cult, but even elsewhere, particularly among Semitic and African peoples. Sometimes it occurs alongside of another very common custom, that of *circumcision* ; sometimes, as in Christendom, it is found where the latter is lacking ; in still other regions, circumcision is practised, whereas there is no real baptism aside from the ordinary rites of lustration. This diversity itself testifies to the essential difference between the two cult practices—for that circumcision also must be classed as such there cannot be any doubt. Circumcision, however, is not a means either of purification or of sanctification, but is of the nature of a *sacrifice*. Along with the offering of hair in the cult of the dead and with the pouring out of blood in connection with deity worship, it belongs to that form of sacrifice in which the sacrificial object gains its unique value by virtue of its being the vehicle of the soul. Thus, the object of sacrifice, in the case of circumcision, may perhaps be interpreted as a substitute for such internal organs as the kidneys or testicles, which are particularly prized as vehicles of the soul but which can either not be offered at all, on the part of the living, or whose sacrifice involves serious difficulties.

Originally, sanctification and lustration not only employed the same means but also followed identical methods. The need frequently came to be felt, however, of an external distinction between these two cult practices. Ablution thus came to be regarded as the proper method of actual purification, whereas *sprinkling* was adopted in connection with sanctification. This also indicates the antithetical positions which the two hold with respect to magic and counter-magic. Lustration aims to remove moral, or, in the last analysis, demoniacal impurity · sanctification furnishes him who seeks its blessings with water possessed of magical powers. For this reason purification water fell into disuse with the disappearance of belief in demoniacal impurity. On the other hand, it was believed that sanctification water must remain as available as possible to him who stands in need of its virtues. Just as baptism is a cult agency whose purpose is intermediate between purification and sanctification, so also does the priest who conducts it lay emphasis, now on the one, and now on the other of these phases. When sprinkling comes to be employed as a means of sanctification, the magical significance of the act leads to a further change. Ordinary water, such as is generally used in lustration, no longer suffices—the water itself needs sanctification if it is to serve the purpose for which it is designed. Even in the ancient mystery cults, therefore, one of the chief elements in the ceremonies of sanctification consisted in sprinkling the members with water from sacred springs. The Jordan festival of the Greek Catholic Church still employs water from the river after which it is named, or ordinary water that has magically been converted into Jordan water. The relation of the burning of incense to lustration by fire is the same as that of sprinkling to lustration by water. And yet, in the case of incense, the idea of sanctification has almost entirely suppressed the earlier aim of purification. The purpose of sanctification finds its specific expression in the belief that the smoke cannot have a sanctifying effect without the addition of certain other elements. Balsamic substances were therefore used. First and foremost among these, even in ancient times, was incense resin, whose exciting and narcotic odour enhances the magical effect. The herbs and resins that were thrown into the flames, however, were also generally regarded as sacrificial gifts to the gods, whose delight in the ascending odours would, it was thought, render them favourably disposed toward the offerer.

Thus, sanctification ceremony and sacrifice become merged. The highest form of sanctification, moreover, originates in sacrifice itself. It appears as soon as the idea of intercourse with the deity becomes elevated to that of communion with him. This occurs especially in the *sacrificial feast*. When the sacrificial food is sanctified by virtue of the fact that the deity partakes of it, this sanctification is imparted to those human individuals who receive a share of the sacrifice. In proportion as the worth of the sacrifice increases, so does also the degree of sanctification. The latter reaches its culmination in *human sacrifice,* where the person sacrificed is the representative both of the sacrificial community and of the deity himself. Sanctification here becomes deification for every participant in the sacrifice. Following the disappearance of human sacrifice, this idea was maintained in connection with the sacred animal that was substituted for man, and finally, after bloody sacrifice was entirely abandoned, in connection with the bread which constituted the sacrificial food. In the most diverse cults of the Old and of the New World, this bread was moulded into the form, sometimes of a human being and sometimes of an animal. In this case again, the sacrificial cult of Christianity unites the various elements. When taken as a whole, the different interpretations that have been given to sacrifice in the Christian world include conceptions representing all the various stages of development. The bread and wine of the sacrament perpetuate the memory of the most exalted human sacrifice known to religious tradition, since, in this case, the idea of the unity of the sacrificial person with the deity continues to survive in the cult of the redeeming deity. In this sacrificial meal, moreover, elements of related sacrificial cults survive—the idea of the paschal lamb, borrowed from the Jewish Passover, and the substitution of wine, as in the Dionysian mysteries, for the blood of the sacrificed god. To the Christian, moreover, this sacrificial sanctification has had *three* distinct meanings, though these, of course, have frequently been intermingled. There have been magical, mystical, and symbolical interpretations—a series of stages through which all sanctification ceremonies pass. To the uncritical mind, he who receives the bread of the sacrament partakes of the actual body of Christ. Following upon this stage of miracle and magic, is the idea that the cult act effects a mystical union with the Redeemer, a union that is not corporeal but spiritual. At the third stage, the cult action finally becomes the symbol of a religious exaltation of spirit.

This exaltation is regarded as possible in itself without the external manifestation ; nevertheless, it is reinforced by the latter, in accordance with the general relationship that obtains between inner needs and external actions. Moreover, in each of these three cases, participation in the common sacrificial meal is evidence of membership in the religious society—a feature common to all firmly organized religious associations. Such membership must be attested by participation in the cult celebrations. Of the ceremonies in which expression is given to one's religious affiliations, the sacrificial meal has been regarded, from early times on, as the most important. The end of the development thus returns to its beginning. The meal, enjoyed in common at fixed times, differentiates cultural man from the man of nature. Among all meals in which a relatively large community unites, however, the sacrificial feast is probably the earliest, just as the cult festival is the earliest festival celebration.

17. The Art of the Heroic Age.

A survey of the various phases of human interest will show that they are all present from the very beginning in the mental organization of man. Moreover, they are throughout so interconnected that an advance in one field of interest will lead to progress in general. Nevertheless, we are unable to escape the further observation that, in the life of the individual, certain capacities develop earlier than others. Precisely the same is true of the life of humanity. The phenomena in which the character of ages and peoples receives its chief expression differ in each of the periods through which the development of mankind passes. The secondary phenomena, in each case, either occur only in their beginnings or, where we are dealing with later stages of culture, are being perfected along lines already established. In this relative sense, we may doubtless say of the three eras following that of primitive man, that totemism is the age of the *satisfaction of wants*, the heroic age, that of *art*, and the succeeding period of the development to humanity, that of *science.* Of course, there were many art productions, some of them admirable, even in the totemic age—we need mention only the artistic cult dances, or the high perfection to which the semi-cultural peoples of the period attained in the decoration of the body and of weapons. It must be admitted also that the heroic age already laid imperishable foundations for science. Nevertheless, the main achievements of the totemic age relate exclusively to the satisfaction of the external needs of life. The modes of procuring and preparing food, and the forms of clothing, adornment, implements, and weapons—all originated in the totemic age, and, however great may have been the advances made by succeeding eras along these several lines, the beginnings had nevertheless been made. A manner of dress suitable to the climate had been developed. The preparation of food by means of fire, the manufacture of the fundamental and permanent implements and weapons—the hammer, the axe, the saw, the chisel, the knife—and, finally, the differentiation between weapons of close and of long range, had all been introduced. Moreover—and this is perhaps most significant of all—art itself was governed absolutely by the motive of satisfying needs. Articles of adornment, tattooing, the dance, song, and music, were first of all means of magic, and as such they served the most urgent needs, such as man by himself was unable to satisfy. These needs were protection against sickness and success in the chase and in war. Only gradually, through a most remarkable heterogeny of ends, were many of these agencies of magic transformed into *pure means of adornment.* Such transformations, of course, occurred also in the heroic age. But by this time the necessities of life had in part changed and, of the new interests, those connected with cult and with political organization gained an increasing importance. Æsthetic value came to be more and more appreciated as an independent feature of objects. As a result, articles were produced of a nature such as to minister both to the needs of life and to æsthetic enjoyment. But, again, this occurs pre-eminently within the field of spiritual needs, particularly in connection with deity cult, on the one hand, and in the glorification of human heroes, on the other. The construction of the temple, the plastic reproduction of the human form and its idealization into the divine image, and, finally, the forms of literature—the epic, the hymn, and the beginnings of the religious drama, with their accompanying music—all of these spring from the spiritual needs of this age, among which needs cult is the foremost. With these various activities, art begins an independent development, gaining a value of its own, and conquering fields that had previously been untouched by æsthetic influences. This conquest of new fields by the higher forms of art is indicative also of an increasing appreciation of the æsthetic, and, along with this, of a spiritualization of life as a whole, such as results, in a particular measure, from art, and only partly, and at a much later period, from science. The first subjects of this art are heroes and gods—that is, those figures which the imagination creates at the threshold of the heroic age, under the influence of the new conditions of life. Gradually art then concerns itself with the human personality and with the objects of man's environment. In correspondence with a change which transpired in the totemic age, in which means of magic were transformed into articles of adornment, the objects of nature and culture are now more and more stripped of their mythological significance and elevated into pure objects of æsthetic appreciation. Thus, the heroic age includes the two most important epochs in the entire history of art. These are the origin of a true religious art, and the attainment of an æsthetic independence which allows art to extend its influence to all departments of human life. Religious art made its appearance with the beginning of the heroic age; æsthetic independence represents a later achievement. This explains why the totemic age seems to us a vanished world, no less with regard to its art than in other respects. It can arouse our æsthetic interest only if we attribute the final product of this period—namely, decoration freed from its original magical significance—to the motives that really underlie artistic activity. The art with which we are still familiar and whose motives we can all still appreciate, begins only with the heroic age. The tattooing of the man of nature and the amulet about his neck are to us adornments of low æsthetic value. A Greek temple, however, may even to-day arouse the mood of worship, and the battles of the Homeric heroes and the tragedy of a Prometheus overtaken by the wrath of the gods may still impress us as real. However remote the age may be which these products of art represent, the general spirit which animated it has not vanished. The greatest turning-point in the spiritual history of man consists in the stupendous achievement which inaugurates the heroic age. I refer to the creation of the ideal man, the hero, and of the god in whom heroic characteristics are magnified into the superhuman and demoniacal. Here lies the beginning of a real history of art; everything earlier is prehistoric, however important it may be for a psychological understanding of art—an importance greater than is generally supposed, since it is only these earliest phenomena that can disclose the conditions underlying the first manifestations of the artistic imagination. Since we may assume that the facts of the history of art are generally familiar, it may here suffice to consider these originating factors and their relation to the general character of the heroic age.

The first and most striking characteristic of the new era is the development of *architecture*. This is a new art, not to be found in the preceding age, or at most only in very meagre beginnings. The gabled and the conical hut, as well as the tent and the wind-break from which they developed, are not artistic creations, but are products of the most urgent needs of life. The impulse to erect a building for any higher purpose than this, manifested itself first of all when, here and there, the need of the living was attributed also to the dead. For the shelter of the dead, soul and ancestor cults demanded the erection of more permanent structures. Hence there appeared the burial chamber, built of solid stone. Its walls, designed to afford protection from without, were likewise constructed of stone, and constantly became more massive. This stimulated a sense of the sublime and eternal, which reacted on the construction of the monuments and gave them a character far transcending the need that called them into being. The development of the gigantic Egyptian pyramids out of the simple walled tomb, the mastaba, tells us this significant story in pictures that impress the imagination more vividly than words. But the cult of the dead, which this history records, was itself intimately connected with deity cult. The preservation of the mummy involved every possible protection of the corpse from the destructive agencies of time. This fact reveals a concern relating to incalculable ages, and thus gives evidence of an idea of a beyond into which the deceased is supposed to enter. Besides the house of the dead, therefore, there is the house belonging to the deity, and this is even more directly and universally characteristic of the age. This edifice, into which man may enter and come into the presence of the deity, stimulates the incomparably deeper impulse to build a structure worthy of the deity for whom it is erected. Thus, then, we have the *temple,* designed at the outset for the protection of the sacrificial altar, which had originally been erected in the open, upon consecrated ground. Since it is located at the seat of government, at the place where the citizens assemble for the conduct of political affairs and for purposes of trade, the temple is indicative also of the city and of the State. Secular interests likewise begin to assert themselves. Hence there appears a second mark of the city, the *castle,* which is the seat of the ruler and of the governing power, and is generally also the final defence, when hostile attacks threaten the city and State. Closely connected with the castle, in all regions in which the ruler lays claim to being a terrestrial deity—as he did, for example, in the ancient realms of the Orient—is the *royal palace.* In harmony with the twofold position of the ruler, his dwelling is architecturally intermediate between the castle and the temple. Thus, it is the temple, the castle, and the palace, whose development not only awakens the æsthetic sense for architectural forms, but also gives impetus to the other arts, especially to sculpture and to ornamentation. The latter had previously found material for its expression in the utensils of daily use. Enriched through its connection with architectural forms, it now recurs to the miniature work of utensils and implements, where it more and more serves a purely æsthetic need. Of the works of architecture belonging to the early part of this period, it is the temple which proves the greatest æsthetic stimulus. This is due not only to its more exalted purpose, but also to the impetus derived from the fact of the multiplicity of gods. The castle represents the unity of the State. Hence the State contains but one such structure, erected, whenever possible, upon a hill overlooking the city. The temple, from early times on, is the exclusive possession of a single deity. The idea of harbouring several deities in a single structure could arise only later, as a result of special cult conditions and of the increasing size of the sacred edifices. Even then, however, the need for unity in the cult generally caused each temple to be dedicated to a specific deity, the chief god of the temple. Hand in hand with this went a striving for richness and diversity in architecture. The temple, therefore, expresses in a pre-eminent degree not only the character of the religious cult, but also the mental individuality of the people to whom the gods and their cult owe their origin.

Closely connected with temple construction is ***sculpture***, for, in it, the importance which the human personality receives in this age finds its most direct expression. Sculpture, moreover, clearly exhibits the gradual advance from the generic to the individual, from a value originally placed on man as such to absorption in the particular characteristics of the individual. The early, 'generic' figure is generally a representation of the divine personality who has inspired the artist to create an image for the sacred shrine. Art does not aim at the outset to copy man himself; it transfers his characteristics to the deity, and only thus, and after laborious efforts, does it attain its mastery over the human form. True, the gods are conceived as human from the very beginning. So long, however, as the sacrificial stone and the altar stand in the open field, this humanization leads but to inartistic images, similar to fetishes. While these images indicate the presence of the gods at the sacred places, they are not intended as likenesses of the deities themselves. In their external appearance, therefore, the fetishes of early deity cult still impress one as survivals of the totemic age, even though the gods are no longer represented after the fashion of demons, namely, as subhuman, possessing animal or grotesque human forms. The conditions obtaining in life generally were repeated in the realm of art. For the transference of purely human characteristics to the image took place in the case of the hero—or, what amounts to the same thing in the great Oriental civilizations of antiquity, in that of the ruler—earlier than in the case of the deity. The ruler is glorified by means of drawings which represent processions of the hunt and of war, and which are executed on the walls of his palaces. Similarly, the religious impulse expresses itself in the erection of an anthropomorphic image of the deity. This image is placed either in the temple, which is regarded as the dwelling-place of the deity, or in some commanding part of the city which reverences the god as its protector. Here, however, we come upon a noteworthy proof of the fusion of the hero with the demon as described above. From Babylonian and Egyptian monuments we learn that the ruler and his retinue were already represented in human form at a period when deity cult still retained hybrid forms of men and animals, sometimes of the nature of animal demons with human faces, or again as human figures with animal heads. Thus, art strikingly confirms the view that the gods arose from a fusion of the hero personality with the demon. When these external characteristics, due to the past history of gods and their connection with demon beliefs, came to be superseded, the divine image at first reproduced only the typical features of man. In addition to overtowering size, external marks, such as dress, weapons, and sacred animals, were the only evidences of deity.

The first step in the transition from the generic figure to the gradual individualization of personality occurs in connection with the facial expression. It is surprising to note the uniformity with which, in all the civilizations of the Old World, the images of the gods, as well as those of the heroes and rulers, acquire an expression of kindliness and gentleness. This trait, however, is again of a generic nature. The stiff, expressionless form has indeed disappeared, but the expression that supervenes is uniform. Though we have referred to this transition as universal, this is true at most as regards the fact that, on the one hand, the expression of complete indifference gives way to one manifesting emotion, and that, on the other, this emotion, though pronounced, again exhibits uniformity. In the quality of this feeling, differences in the character of peoples may come to light, just as they do in myth and religion, with which sculpture in its first stages is closely connected. In the two great cultural regions of the New World, Mexico and Peru, there is a similar transition. The cults of these peoples, however, emphasize the fear-inspiring character of the gods. Hence, in their art, the terrifying grimace of the earliest divine images becomes moderated into an expression of gloomy, melancholy seriousness—a change such as the art of the Old World approximates only in occasional productions that fall rather within the province of the demoniacal, such as the image of the Egyptian sphinx or the gorgon's head of the Greeks. Thus, the transition from features that are entirely expressionless to such as are generic, and then to those that characterize the individual personality, occurs in connection with a change in the quality of the emotions. To illustrate the relative uniformity of this development we might likewise refer to the early Renaissance. Here again it was necessary to seek a path to the concrete wealth of personality that had been lost. Art reached this goal by way of the pathetic expression of humble submission. As soon as plastic art departs from the typical form, we find not only that a change occurs in the expressions of the face, but also that the entire body becomes more lifelike. Along with this, the themes of plastic art pass from the gods, rulers, and heroes to the lower levels of every-day life. Even here art at first continues to be fascinated by the great and conspicuous, though it later gains more and more interest in the *significant*. This striving for reality in its wealth of individual phenomena is characteristic not only of sculpture, however, but also of painting. Disregarding the bodily form in favour of the portrait, painting first acquires new means of characterization in colour and shading; then, passing from man to his natural environment, it wins from nature the secrets of perspective, and thus gains a far greater mastery over the depths of space than was possible to sculpture. *Landscape painting*, moreover, unlocks for art that rich world of emotions and moods which man may create from the impressions of nature, and which attain to purity of expression in proportion as man himself disappears from the artistic reproduction of his environment. Thus, the final product of pictorial art, together with such paintings as those of still life and the interior, all of which are psychologically related inasmuch as they express moods, represent the most subjective stage of art, for they dispense with the subject himself whose emotions they portray. All the more, therefore, are these emotions read into nature, whose processes and activities now constitute the content of personal experience. Once it attains to this development, however, landscape art is already far beyond the borders of the heroic age. Indeed, the Renaissance itself advanced no farther than to the threshold of this most subjective form of pictorial art. This art represents the hero—however broad a conception of him we may form—as in all respects a human individual. Thus, art again returns to the being whose ideal enhancement originally gave rise to the hero.

The changes which the forms of æsthetic expression undergo within the field of formative art, are paralleled, on the whole, by those of the *musical* arts. By this term, as above remarked, we wish to designate all those arts which depend from the outset upon the *external* factors of tone and rhythm ultimately employed most freely in music (cf. p. 262). In the preceding age, only *one* of these arts, the *dance*, really reached any considerable development. Of the two elements of the musical arts, rhythm was as yet predominant. The dance received but little melodic support from the voice ; noise instruments had the ascendancy over musical instruments. The further development of these arts leads to continued progress, particularly with respect to the melodic forms of expression. These begin with the language of speech, and gradually pass on to the pure clang formations produced solely by manufactured instruments. Corresponding with this external change is an inner change of motives, influenced, of course, by the varying materials which enter into the creations of the musical arts. From the very beginning, the character of this material is involved in constant change, as is also language, which is the basis of all these arts, and whose rhythmical-melodic forms cannot be arrested at any moment of its living development. The attempt to render permanent some of the movements of this flowing process, by means of literary records or definite symbols, is but an inadequate substitute for the enduring power with which the mute creations of sculpture and of architecture withstand the destructive influences of time. Just because of this plasticity of their working material, however, the musical arts are enabled all the more faithfully to portray the thoughts and feelings that move the artist and his age. Particularly where these thoughts and feelings are directly reproduced in language, the work, even though coming down from a long-departed past, has an incomparably greater power to transport us to its world than is ever possible to plastic art. How much more vividly do we not experience the life of the Homeric heroes while reading the Iliad than when viewing the Mycenian art of that period !

Of all the products of the verbal arts, it is the epic that most faithfully mirrors the character of the heroic age as a whole. The human hero here stands in the forefront of action. His battles and fortunes and a laudatory description of his qualities constitute the main themes of the poem. In the background, appears the world of gods. It receives no attention apart from its relation to the action. The gods, it is true, take a hand in the destinies of the heroes—they quarrel about them, or, when the need is greatest, descend to the earth and, though unrecognized, assist them in battles. As for the rest, however, their life lies outside the sphere of the epic narrative ; it appears to be an even and undisturbed course of existence into which change enters only in so far as there is a participation in the affairs of the terrestrial world. Such is the epic at the zenith of its development and as it receives expression in the Homeric poems. Though such poetry be traced back to its beginnings, the gods will not be found to play any greater rôle, as we should be led to expect were the theory of many mythologists true that the hero saga developed out of the deity saga and, correspondingly, the heroic epic out of the deity epic. In confirmation of our assertion, we might point to the Russian and Servian romances, and also to the songs of the Kara-Kirghiz and to the Finnish Kalewala, though the Kalewala has not come down to us in quite its original form. The Norse Edda, which has been at the basis of certain misconceptions regarding this question, should not here be drawn into consideration, though, were it examined, it would substantiate, if anything, the opposite of what is supposed. It dates from a later period, which no longer believed, as we may assume that the Homeric rhapsodists did, in the gods and heroes of which it sang. The Norse skalds dealt, in their songs, with a departed world, whose memory they endeavoured to renew ; they drew their material from märchen-myths and from folk-sagas. If, now, we turn to that poetry of the Slavic and Turkish tribes which is really preparatory to epic poetry, we find certain radical differences. Here also, of course, there are imaginary beings who either take a hand in the battles and destinies of the heroes or, through the magic over which the human hero as yet still frequently disposes, come to identify themselves with heroes. These beings, however, are not gods, but demons. They possess no personal traits whatsoever. Such traits are lacking also to the hero in proportion as he makes use of magical powers rather than of an enhanced measure of human ability. Thus, it is the *world of demons*, not that of gods, which forms the background of the early epic. As regards the hero himself, it is apparent from his characteristics that he is on the border-line between the hero of märchen and the epic hero. This development of the epic again mirrors the development of the hero saga described above. But, since epic poetry gives permanence to the unstable characters of the folk-saga, and thus, in turn, reacts upon the saga itself, its development is all the more capable of presenting a clear picture of that fusion of demon with human hero which gave rise to the god. It is by virtue of his human characteristics that the hero of the early epic is distinguished from the demons whose world as yet always forms his scene of action. These human characteristics are then more and more transferred to the demons. Throughout all these changes of environment, the hero remains the central figure of epic poetry, and continues to develop purely human characteristics. Hence it is that, at a later period, the gods again completely disappear from the action, and the destinies of human heroes come to be the exclusive concern of the epic. At this stage, it is no longer external factors that determine the destiny of the hero, as they did when demons and, later, gods were supreme ; inner motives, whose source lies within the hero himself, are of paramount importance. When this occurs, however, epic poetry has already passed beyond the boundaries of the heroic age.

At one time it was held that the Homeric epic, so far from marking the climax of a development in which the world of heroes was brought into relation with that of the gods, really inaugurated epic poetry. During this period, the rhythmic-melodic form of Homer was regarded as the beginning of all narrative. Indeed, at times it has been thought to represent the beginning of language. Following the view of Jacob Grimm, it was maintained that poetry was the earliest form of speech, and that prose came through a process of deterioration analogous to that by which prehistoric deity and hero sagas passed into the märchen. This theory, of course, is just as untenable for the history of language and poetry as it is for that of the saga. The original narrative is the märchen-myth that passes artlessly from mouth to mouth. The transition to a form which is at first loosely constructed and then more strictly metrical, is clearly bound up with the transition from the hero of the märchen to the hero of the saga. Coincident with this, gods also gradually gain a place in epic poetry. This development is accompanied by *two* important external changes. The first of these involves the transformation of the every-day prose, in which the märchen-myth had been expressed, into rhythmic-melodic forms. These are reinforced by a simple musical accompaniment that gives to the diction itself the character of a recitative melody. The second change consists in the fact that separate narratives are joined into a series, the basis of connection being, in part, the heroes who participate in the action and, in part, the content of the action itself. Thus, a romance-cycle arises, which, when supplemented by connecting narratives, finally develops into a great epic. As might be supposed, it is primarily the first and the last stage of this development that are accessible to direct observation—the romances of the early epic, preserved in folk-poetry, and the perfected poems, such as the Homeric epics and the *Niebelungenlied*. As regards the formation of these epics out of their separate elements, we can do no more than to frame hypotheses on the basis of somewhat uncertain inferences relating to differences in style and composition. There can be no doubt, however, that the more important step as regards the form of the epic, namely, the development of rhythmic-melodic expression, was directly bound up with its very first stage, namely, with the appearance of the earliest form of the heroic narrative—a form resembling the romance.

But how may we account for this origin? Does the narrative of itself rise to song because of the more exalted character of its content? Or, is the rhythmic-melodic form imposed upon it from other previously existing types of poetry? Such poetry exists. The simple songs of primitive man we have already come to know; besides these, there are the cult-song, whose conjurations and petitions were addressed to demons prior to the advent of gods and heroes, and, finally, the work-song. This at once indicates that we must postulate a transference from the lyric type of song, taken in its broadest sense, to the narrative. Nevertheless, the first of the above-mentioned factors must not be disregarded. The heroic hero, of course, arouses far greater admiration and enthusiasm than did the märchen-hero. Here, as in the case of the song, the intensification of mental excitement causes its verbal expression to assume rhythmic forms, precisely as the dominance of festive and joyous emotion in the dance transforms the external movements of the body into rhythmical pantomime. Doubtless, therefore, it was primarily from the cult-song, and under the influence of a related poetic ecstasy, that a sustained rhythmical form was carried over to the portrayal of the hero personality and his deeds. And so, as is clearly shown by the romance-like beginnings of epic composition, the metrical form of the epic first follows current song-forms, and then gradually adapts these to the specific needs of the narrative. Now, the earliest characteristic of the song, and that which at a primitive stage constitutes almost its only difference from ordinary speech, is the refrain. In the epic, the rhythm becomes smoother. The refrain disappears entirely, or occurs at most in the case of regularly recurring connective phrases or of stereotyped expressions relating to the attributes of the gods and heroes. These aid the rhapsodist in maintaining an uninterrupted, rhythmic flow of speech, and also continue to be used as means for intensifying the rhythmic impression.

Epic poetry thus develops out of the earlier forms of lyric composition, through a process by which the exalted mood of the song is transferred to the portrayal of the hero personality. Finally, however, the epic itself reacts upon the lyric.

Here again the cult-song occupies the foreground. When it reaches the stage of the hymn, its most effective content is found in narratives that centre about divine deeds which far transcend human capacities, or about the beneficent activity of the deity toward man. The tendency to incorporate such narratives is particularly marked in the song of praise and thanksgiving, which comes to occupy the dominant place in religious cult for the very reason that the mood which it expresses is at the basis of the common cult. At this point, cult acquires a further feature, the preconditions of which, however, date back to the age of demon cults. Even in the case of demons, aid was sought not merely by means of conjurations but also by means of *actions* that imitated, in dances and solemn mask processions, the activities of demons. In the great vegetation festivals of New Mexico and Arizona, which are intermediate between demon and deity cults, there were imitative magical rites connected with the subterranean demons of the sprouting grain, with the rain-giving cloud demons above the earth, and also with the bright celestial gods who dwell beyond the clouds. After having originated in this sequence, these elements became united into a cult dance whose combination of motives resulted in the mimetic play, the imitative and pantomimic representation of a series of actions. Thus, the mime itself is the original form of the *drama*, which now takes its place beside the epic as a new form of poetry. What the epic portrays, the drama sets forth in living action. This accounts for the fact that, even in its later independent development, dramatic literature draws its material principally from the epic, or from the saga which circulates in folk-tradition as an epic narrative. Moreover, as may be noticed particularly in the history of the Greek drama, the transition was made but slowly from the individual rhapsodist, who sufficed for the rendering of the epic song, to the additional players necessary for setting forth the narrative in action.

How essentially uniform this transition is, in spite of widely divergent conditions, is illustrated by the origin of the religious plays which grew out of the Christian cult. In reading the gospel, the priest assigned certain passages, originally spoken by participants in the particular event, to sacristans or priests associated in the ceremony, and the chorus of worshippers represented the people present at the event. In spite of, or, we might better say, because of their more recent origin, these Easter, Passion, and Christmas plays represent an early stage of development. In them, we can still follow, step by step, the growth of dramatic art out of church liturgy, and the resultant secularization of the religious play. Heightened emotion results in an impulse to translate the inner experience into action, and thus dramatic expression is given to certain incidents of the sacred narrative that are particularly suited for it. This tendency grows, and finally the entire scene is acted out, the congregational responses of the liturgy passing over into the chorus of the drama. Common to the responses of the congregation and the chorus of the dramatic play, is the fact of an active participation in that which is transpiring. Though this participation is inner and subjective, in the one case, and objective, in the other, the response of the congregation to the priest in the liturgy is nevertheless preparatory to the chorus of the drama. It is inevitable, however, that this change should gradually lead to a break with liturgy. The portrayal of the sacred action is transferred from the church to the street; the clergy are supplanted by secular players from among the people. Even within the sacred walls folk-humour had inserted burlesque episodes—such, for example, as the mimic portrayal of Peter's violence to the servant Malchus, or the running of the Apostles to the grave of Christ. These now gained the upper hand, and finally formed independent mimetic comedies. The serious plays, on their part, also drew material, even at this time, from sources other than sacred history. The newly awakened dramatic impulse received further stimulus from various directions. The old travelling comedy, wandering from market to market with its exhibitions, now of gruesomely serious, now of keenly humorous, action, was a factor in the creation of the modern drama, no less than were the amusing performances of the accompanying puppet-show. Added to these, as a new factor, was the short novel, a prose narrative cultivated with partiality particularly since the Renaissance; there was also its elder sister, the imaginary märchen, as well as the epic of chivalry in its popular prose versions, and, finally, that which more clearly approximates to the religious starting-point, the saint legend—all of these united in giving impetus to the modern drama.

Now, the similarity of this development to that of the ancient drama is so marked that, even where details are lacking, we may regard the nature of the transitions as identical so far as their general features are concerned. Indeed, we should doubtless be justified in assuming that in whatever other localities a dramatic art was perfected, as, for example, in India, the course of development was essentially the same as that which has been described. True, the development cannot proceed to its termination apart from an advance in cult and poetry such as was attained but rarely. Its sources, however, are always to be found in universal human characteristics which were operative in the very beginnings of art and cult. The two factors upon which the later drama depends may be detected even in the corroboree of the Australians. The corroboree is a cult dance whose central feature is a regulated imitation of the actions of totem animals, accompanied by song and noisy music. This imitation of animals also leads to the insertion of humorous episodes. Indeed, even in the corroboree, these episodes are frequently so numerous as to crowd out completely the cult purpose—an early anticipation of the secularization which everywhere took place in the art that originated in cult. In numerous other details as well, the continuity of development is apparent. Suggestions of the animal dance occur in the satyric plays of the Greeks. This same satyric drama took over the phallus-bearing choral dancers from the vegetation festival. In striking correspondence, as K. Th. Preusz has pointed out, and indicative of analogous customs, are the phallephoric representations found in ancient Mexican cult pictures. The puppet-show, which was perhaps not the least among the factors leading to the secularization of the drama, was not only universally to be found during the Middle Ages, but in India it made its appearance at an early period. It occurs even among peoples of nature, as, for example, among the Esquimos. Among these peoples, the doll and its movements always represent an imitation of man himself and of his pantomimes. But, though the tendencies to dramatic representation and, in part, even the beginnings of the drama, reach back to the early stages of art, the developed drama was the product of a later period, and was dependent for its rise upon almost all the other verbal and mimetic arts. The drama, however, may always be traced back to deity cult. The religious hymn which extols the deeds of the gods is a direct incentive to the translation of these deeds into personal action. The motives for the dramatic elaboration of liturgy were present particularly in those deity cults which combined soul cults with ideas of a beyond, and which centred about the life, the sufferings, and the final salvation of the gods, and the transference of these experiences to the human soul. The development of the mediæval Easter and Passion plays may be traced, step by step, from their origin. It is this development, particularly, that throws clear light upon early Greek and Indian drama, whose beginnings in the mystery cults are rendered obscure by the secrecy of the cults. These latter dramas, in turn, clearly indicate that the original source of dramatic representations is to be found in the very ancient vegetation ceremonies, which, in part, were transmitted to the heroic age from a period as early as that of demon cults. After the dramatic performance has been transferred from the temple to the market-place and the drama has become secularized, the further course of development naturally differs both with the conditions of the age and with the character of the culture. Nevertheless, however, the epic narrative, the mimetic representation, and the older forms of the song may have coöperated in the development of the drama, the latter, like the epic, steadily descends from the lofty realms of the heroes and gods, down to the dwellings of men. In the portrayal of human strivings and sufferings, moreover, the centre of interest shifts from the mysterious course of external events to the secrets of the human soul. But herewith again the drama transcends the boundaries of the heroic age. Its beginnings grow out of early deity cult. In its final stages, dramatic art, with its insight into human life as it is directly lived, becomes the vehicle of the idea of humanity in the entire scope of its meaning, comprehending both the heights and the depths of human life.

Closely bound up with the psychological motives underlying the development of the drama is the last of the musical arts—namely, *music*. We may refer to it as the last of these arts for the reason that it attained to independence later than any of the others. As a dependent art, however, accompanying the dance, the song, or the epic recital, it dates back to the age of primitive man. Musical art, also, received its first noteworthy stimulus from cult, as an accompaniment of the cult dance and the cult song. The strong emotions aroused by the cult activity caused a constantly increasing emphasis to be placed on the musical part of the ceremony, leading particularly to the development of melody. The polyphonic song of the many-voiced chorus of the cult members, and the music of the accompanying instruments which gradually assumed the same character, eventually developed into harmonic modulation. This introduced musical effects of a novel sort, such as were not possible for the accompaniment of the reciting rhapsodist and were attained only imperfectly by the common song. Thus, dramatic and musical art both sprang from the same religious root, the liturgic ceremonial, thence to pursue different directions of development. Later they again united in the case of certain particularly emotional parts of the dramatic action, first of all in the choral song, which is thus reminiscent of their common origin in liturgy.

With this exception, however, the emancipation of dramatic and of musical art from their common cult origin was succeeded by a long period in which they remained distinct. Hence it is certainly not without significance that the creator of the modern art-synthesis, the music drama, himself felt his achievement to be religious in character. Whether or not this may be affirmed as regards the content of the music drama, it is true so far as the fact of combining the two arts is concerned. But it is no less noteworthy that in this case also the separation of itself engenders the motives for the reunion. When the drama was transferred from the temple to the public market-place and then descended from the sphere of gods and heroes to the reality of everyday life, it lost, first its musical-melodic form, and then its elevated rhythm, thus giving way to prose. The liturgic song that survived in the cult, however, entered into reciprocal relations with the secular forms of the song, and a copious interchange of melodic motives ensued. With the same justification, perhaps, as in the case of the origin of the dramatic play in general, we may interpret the older developments by reference to the interchange between sacred and secular songs that took place in Christendom during the Middle Ages. The endeavour to combine dramatic with lyric and musical enjoyment gave rise to hybrid forms of art, to the musical play and the opera. This prepared the way for the further attempt to transcend these composite forms of art by creating a new unity of drama and music. Thus, the aim was to restore the original synthesis on a higher plane, not limited to particular religious cults but taking into account universal human emotions. Yet the entire development of this later art, as well as that of its component elements, the drama and the song, again carries us far beyond the limits of the heroic age. It extends over into a period in which, on the one hand, man supplants the hero and, on the other, the religious advance to a superpersonal god displaces those deities who suffer from the defects which they have inherited from their human prototypes and their demon ancestors—namely, the personal gods.

Along with the above-mentioned development of musical art there is also a second change, which appears on the surface to be antithetical to the former, but which in reality supplements it. This change consists in the separation of musical expression from the various elements with which it was originally connected, and in its entrance upon a free and independent development. In the recitative of the rhapsodist, in the liturgy of the temple service, in dance and song, the rhythmic-melodic elements are, to a certain extent, limited by the rhythmic-melodic possibilities of language. In part, it is true, they have freed themselves from this limitation—namely, in the instrumental accompaniment—and yet they fail to attain to independence so long as they are but means for intensifying the expression which emotion receives in language and mimicry. From this double bondage to the rhythmic-melodic powers of human expressive movements and to the thought content of language, musical art finally frees itself. While the musical instrument was at first a means designed to assist man in his endeavour to give direct expression to his emotions, man's activity in the case of 'absolute music' becomes limited to the mastery of the instrument itself. This renders available a wealth of new tonal possibilities, and adds an inexhaustible supply of new motifs for the expression of feelings and emotions. Musical art thus becomes purely a language of emotions. Free from connection with specific ideas, it in no wise restricts the experiences which the hearer may enjoy. It affects these experiences only in so far as the musical production is itself a portrayal of pure emotions. Inasmuch as music is not bound by concepts or ideas, its effect upon the hearer will be the purer and the more intense according as he is the more receptive to the particular emotions in question. In the form of the instrumental composition, therefore, music is the most subjective of the musical arts, as are landscape-painting and its related forms, though not in so pronounced a degree, of the plastic arts. Like these arts, and even more so, music is the expression of purely subjective feelings. Hence, it, as well as they, far transcends the boundaries of the heroic age, whose fundamental characteristic is attachment to the objective world. In the heroic age, the individual may indeed transfuse the outer world with his emotions, but he is never able to isolate his emotions from objects. Consequently, though art places its media at his disposal, he is unable to utilize them in giving expression, in its independence, to the inner life of personality.

CHAPTER IV

THE DEVELOPMENT TO HUMANITY

1. THE CONCEPT 'HUMANITY.'

THE question, Do we live in an enlightened age? was answered by Kant, with reference to his own time—which, as is well known, laid claim to the distinction—flatly in the negative. He added, however, that the age was doubtless one of increasing enlightenment. One might, perhaps, be even more justified in raising a similar question with reference to the relation of our own and of preceding ages to a universally human culture, and in answering: We are on the way to this goal, but are still far from having actually reached it. Indeed, in view of human imperfection, it may be doubted whether we will ever be able to reach it, unless the imperfection itself be included as an element in such a culture. The ambiguity of the word 'humanity' is such that it may signify human weaknesses as well as human sympathy and other virtues. It was in the latter, the more favourable, sense of the term that Herder, even in his day, attempted, in his "Ideas," to portray the history of mankind as an "education to humanity." This expression suggests that history manifests only a ceaseless striving toward true humanity; the goal itself lies beyond the reach of possible experience.

Now, a survey of the course of progress described in the preceding chapters may well cause us to doubt whether the presupposition from which Herder set out in his reflections on the philosophy of history is correct. The assumption that factors preparatory to the development to humanity are already to be found in the original nature of man—indeed, even earlier than this, in the general conditions of his natural environment—is not beyond question. Neither primitive nor totemic man shows the faintest trace of what we should, strictly speaking, call humanity. He gives evidence merely of an attachment to the nearest associates of horde or tribe, such as is foreshadowed even among animals of social habits. In addition, he exhibits but occasional manifestations of a friendly readiness to render assistance when danger threatens at the hands of strangers.

It is not until the heroic age that we encounter phenomena such as might properly be interpreted to indicate the gradual rise of feelings of humanity. But if we take into account the entire character of this age, we are more inclined to contrast it, precisely when it reaches its zenith, with all that we to-day understand by humanity. Consider, for example, the sharply demarcated State organizations of the heroic era, its depreciation of strange peoples, and its repudiation of universal human ties, brusquely expressed during times of war in its treatment of the enemy and, during times of peace, in slavery. The question as to whether and in how far the beginnings of our ideas of humanity reach back into the past and prevail at lower levels of culture, is confronted with a serious difficulty. Conceptions such as these are obviously themselves products of a long development and have been in constant flux. The concept 'humanity' suffers from an ambiguity which has attached to it ever since the time of its origin, and which has in no wise diminished as the word has acquired broader meanings. The word *humanitas*, which in later classical Latin was practically equivalent to our concept 'human nature,' in both its good and its bad connotations, acquired an additional meaning in the language of mediæval scholars. During this period of strong partiality for abstract word formations, the term came to be used also for the collective concept 'mankind,' that is, the Roman *genus hominum*—a concept independent of value judgments of any sort. Thus, the word passed over into our more modern languages with a twofold significance. Although the German language developed the two words *Menschlichkeit* and *Menschheit*, corresponding to the conceptual distinction just indicated, the two meanings were again combined in the foreign word *Humanität*. This is exemplified by Herder's phrase, *Erziehung zur Humanität* (education to humanity). For, in using this phrase to sum up the meaning of history, Herder meant that the striving which underlies all history was not merely for the development of the qualities of humanity (*Menschlichkeit*), in the highest sense of the term, but also essentially for their gradual extension to the whole of mankind (*Menschheit*).

But, whatever our opinion concerning the possible success of such striving and concerning the relation of its two phases, there can be no doubt that the concept 'humanity,' which has become common property among civilized peoples, combines an objective with a subjective aspect. On the one hand, 'humanity' means the *whole* of mankind, or, at any rate, a preponderant part of it, such as may be regarded as representative of the whole. On the other hand, 'humanity' is a value-attribute. It has reference to the complete development of the ethical characteristics which differentiate man from the animal, and to their expression in the intercourse of individuals and of peoples. This latter thought incorporates in the term 'humanity' the meaning both of 'mankind' and of 'human nature,' although it ignores the secondary implication of human imperfection which 'human nature' involves and takes into account only its laudable characteristics. Humanity, when predicated of an individual, means that he transcends the limits of all more restricted associations, such as family, tribe, or State, and possesses an appreciation of human personality as such; in its application to human society, it represents a demand for an ideal condition in which this appreciation of human worth shall have become a universal norm. This ideal, however, is subject to growth, and, like all ideals, is never completely realizable. Hence the following sketch of the conditions which succeed the age of heroes and gods cannot undertake to do more than point to the phenomena that give expression to the new motives that dominate this later period. Sharp demarcations are in this instance even less possible than in the case of the earlier stages of human development. The more comprehensive the range of human strivings and activities, the more gradual are the transitions and the more fully are the underlying motives—precisely because they involve the universally human—foreshadowed in the natural predispositions and impulses of man. Tendencies to esteem man as man, and a willingness to render him assistance, are not foreign even to the primitive mind. Even at the beginnings of human culture there are present, dimly conscious, those tendencies out of which the idea of humanity may finally develop. Moreover, every later advance seems to lead in the direction of this conception. The transition from tribe into State, the changing intercourse of peoples, and the spread over wide regions of the mental creations of a single people, of language, religion, and customs—all these phenomena are obviously steps on the way to the idea of humanity and to its permanent incorporation into all departments of human endeavour. Neither in its rise nor in its further changes, moreover, does this new idea entail the disappearance of previous conditions or of the psychical factors involved in their development. On the contrary, humanitarian culture takes up into itself the creations of preceding eras, and allows them to take firmer root. Thus, the idea of a cultural community of peoples has not weakened, but, so far as we may conclude from the past course of history, has strengthened and enriched, the self-consciousness of separate peoples and the significance of the individual State. The dissemination of cultural products has not resulted in their decrease. National differences have led rather to the increase of these products, and have thus enhanced the value attaching to the spiritual distinctiveness of a people and of the individual personality. That we may here, even more than in the case of the earlier periods of cultural history, speak only of *relative* values, needs scarcely be remarked. Humanitarian development includes a vast number of new conditions, in addition to those that underlie the preceding stages of culture. Since, moreover, the synthesis at which this development aims is everywhere still in the process of becoming, the way itself is for the time being the attainable goal. We may neither be said to be on the way *to* humanity, if we mean by this a condition in which none but humanitarian interests prevail, nor does a humanitarian age, in the sense of the exclusion of more restricted human relations, appear at all within the field of vision disclosed to us as a result of past history. As a legacy from the primitive era, man has permanently retained not only the general needs of individual life but also the most restricted forms of family and tribal organization. In like manner, it will be impossible for an age of humanity ever to dispense with the more limited articulations of State and society that have arisen in the course of cultural development. Scarcely any general result stands out as more certain, in a retrospective survey of our investigations, than the fact that, while every period discards as worthless a vast number of products, some of which were valuable to an earlier age, there are other products which prove to be imperishable. From this point of view, that which precedes is not merely preparatory to the further course of development but is itself the beginning of the development. The immediate beginning, however, is veiled in obscurity. The earlier age is ever unconsciously preparing the way for one that is to come. The clan of primitive tribal organization had no idea of a coming State, nor had the ancient demon worshipper any notion of a cult of rewarding and punishing celestial deities, yet State and deity cult could not have arisen except for clan and demon-belief. Similarly, the earlier modes of collective life possessed the idea of humanity only in the form of a hidden germ. Hence we may not properly describe these preparatory stages, which exhibit phenomena of a different and, in part, an entirely dissimilar sort, as a development to humanity. The term applies rather to an age in which the idea of humanity, having come to clear consciousness, exercises an influence upon the various phases of culture, and is entertained by a sufficiently large portion of mankind to insure its permanent effectiveness. But even with this limitation the development may not be regarded as one of uninterrupted progress. However widely disseminated the humanitarian idea may come to be, there will remain localities and levels of culture to which it has not penetrated. But, inasmuch as peoples of very different cultural stages enter into relations with one another, the possibility is open for such a turn of events as will obscure the idea of the development to humanity for long periods. That such deviations from the path of progress have frequently occurred in the past is certain; that they are never to occur in the future is scarcely probable. For this reason one can scarcely hope to do more than to show that, in spite of such retrogressions, the development to humanity forms a generally connected whole, and that here also psychological law is regnant.

That such law prevails is at once evident from the fact that of the two conceptions which we have found to be involved in the idea of humanity, the *external* and objective concept expressed by the collective term 'mankind' is historically the earlier; the concept referring to *inner* characteristics, and associated in the consciousness of the individual with clearly defined value-feelings, follows only gradually. We might express this relationship by the phrase, Mankind must prepare the way for human nature. This does not imply that isolated manifestations of the latter might not long precede the rise of the idea of mankind—indeed, must necessarily have preceded it, in so far as a predisposition is concerned. It means merely that human nature did not, as a matter of fact, attain to its complete development, nor was it able to do so, until after the idea of the unity of mankind had progressed beyond the stage of vague impulses or of recognition on the part of but a few individuals in advance of their age. In other words: The collective concept 'mankind,' as representing, not merely a generic term created by the intellect, but a real totality ultimately uniting all its members in a social whole, preceded the concept 'human nature,' as connoting a recognition of universal human rights to which each of the members of the human race may lay claim, and of duties which he, in turn, owes to human society. The case could not be otherwise. Unless the idea of mankind were already present in some form, even though this be at the outset inadequate, the requirement that an individual give expression to humanitarian sentiments would be impossible, since there would be no object of the activity. If we consider the sequence of the various phenomena involved in the development to humanity, we find a striking agreement between history and the results to which our analysis of the concept 'humanity' has led us. The earliest of the phenomena here in question dates far back to the beginnings of the events known to us through historical monuments, and consists in the rise of *world empires*. Though the term 'world empire' is sometimes used to refer merely to a great kingdom that results from the absorption of a number of separate States, such a use of the word does not do justice to its meaning. The idea of world empire really comes into existence only at the moment when such a kingdom lays claim to embracing the terrestrial part of the universe, and therefore the whole of mankind, however much this claim may represent a mere demand which has never, of course, actually been realized. The very fact of the demand, however, itself involves the conscious idea of a unity embracing the whole of mankind. Moreover, the endeavour to realize this ambition follows with inner necessity in the case of all political organizations that call themselves world empires, particularly at the period of their zenith and of an increasing consciousness of power. This leads to further important results, which, though at first doubtless not consciously sought, nevertheless later increasingly become the object of voluntary endeavour. Though externally retaining the traditional political organization, the world empire required an extension of the institutions of law and of administration that had thus far prevailed in the more limited State. A similar change gradually took place in connection with intercourse and its fostering agencies, and subsequently in connection with language, customs, and religious beliefs. Thus, it was the world empire that first prepared the way for *world culture*, only meagre beginnings of which existed in the period of a more restricted political life. The extension of wants and of the means of their satisfaction was first evident in the field of commerce, though a similar tendency came more and more to prevail in the various departments of mental life. Pre-eminent among these interests was the one which is the most universal and is based on the most common needs, such as are experienced by all members of human society, namely, *religion*. Thus, as one of the last of the creations possessing universal human significance, *world religion* makes its appearance. The preceding age did not progress beyond national religions. However much the mythological elements of cult, in particular, may have travelled from one people to another, these elements were assimilated by the national religions. Inasmuch as these religions continued, on the whole, to preserve their own identities, the fact that any elements were of foreign origin very soon disappeared from the folk-consciousness. Not until the period which we are now discussing do we find religions that lay claim to being universal. Even though this claim may remain a mere demand, just as in the case of the world empire, it is precisely as such that every historical world religion has asserted its influence. This striving for universality is far keener in connection with world religion than it is in the case of world empire and world culture. In comparison with this endeavour to become universal, the fact that no period ever witnessed merely a single world religion is relatively unimportant, though not to be overlooked in considering the spiritual needs of mankind Disregarding subordinate religions and such as are of less significance for culture as a whole, there are at least *two* great world religions, Christianity and Buddhism. These have asserted themselves side by side, and will presumably continue further to maintain themselves, inasmuch as they correspond to sharply defined characteristics of universal world culture. Finally, world culture and the world religions form the basis of *world history,* a third element in the collective consciousness of mankind. If we understand by 'world history,' not the political or cultural events that simultaneously run their independent courses, but the historic consciousness of mankind itself, combining the idea of mankind as a unity with that of the development of this unity in accordance with law, then world history, in this, the only accurate meaning of the term, is the last of all the factors involved in the idea of humanity. Since the individual who is developing in the direction of the ideal of humanity mirrors all other aspects of human nature, world history ultimately becomes for him the gradual realization of the idea of humanity. Thus, world empires, world culture, world religions, and world history represent the four main steps in the development to humanity.

2. WORLD EMPIRES.

Even in the midst of the spiritual forces dominating the heroic age there are phenomena that foreshadow a development transcending the limits of this period. Of these phenomena, none is more prominent than the striving for world dominion. The first battles of early political organizations, and the victories over conquered peoples, led to an enhanced consciousness of power on the part of the individual State. This consciousness found expression, first in strife between neighbouring dominions, and later, as soon as one of these had gained the supremacy, in the establishment of an empire including many separate States. Such an impulse to transcend the limits of the single State is so natural and so directly prefigured in the motives to individual action that we come upon it wherever any historically active political organizations have arisen. In the realms of western Asia, such attempts are to be found from the time of the Sumerian and Accadian States down to the struggle of Babylon and Assyria for the rulership of the world. Egypt had a succession of dynasties which at first glance might seem to simulate a unified history, but which in reality represents the transference of supreme power from one State or city to another, and along with this the growing ambition for a single all-embracing dominion. The same phenomenon appears in the struggle of the Greek and Latin tribes for hegemony, and also in the foundation of the great Persian kingdom of the Achæmenidæ; the latter gave way to the world empire of Alexander, which, though of short duration, was never again equalled in magnitude; succeeding it, came the world empire of the Romans, the last that could properly lay claim to the name.

It is in Egypt, on the one hand, and in the succession of West-Asiatic kingdoms, on the other, that the first stages of this development of a world kingdom out of the dominance of one powerful State over a number of vassal States are clearly exhibited. The struggle for supremacy, in which vassal might elevate himself to the position of ruler and lord be reduced to vassal, and in which newly immigrant peoples often took a decisive part, immeasurably enhanced the striving to extend the sphere of dominion. This development reached its culmination when the supreme ruler of a power that dominated a very considerable number of vassal States expressly asserted the claim of being *ruler of the world*. The fact that such a claim was made wherever a supremacy of this sort came into existence under conditions of relatively limited intercourse, testifies to the immanent necessity of the development. Wherever the domain of such an empire approximated the limits of the known world, the universal State was conceived as including also the rest of the inhabited earth. This conception came to expression in the title which the ruler regularly assumed. He laid claim to being the king of kings, the overlord of the world, the ruler of the 'four quarters of the earth.'

Through a reversal of that process of transference by which the characteristics of the terrestrial State were carried over, in deity cult, to the divine State, the ruler of the terrestrial State now himself became a god. This accounts for the surprising uniformity with which the idea of a god-monarch arose wherever that of a world monarch was developed. In the pre-Babylonian realms of the Euphrates and Tigris valleys, the ruler erected his own image, as an object of worship, in the temple; in the land of the Pharaohs, the heads of the sphinxes placed in front of the temples bore the features of the monarch. Even Alexander the Great commanded that the Egyptian priests greet him as a son of the god Amon Re; after acquiring the authority of the great Persian kings, he demanded from those about him the external signs of divine adoration. Similarly, the Roman emperors of the period from Diocletian down to Constantine. In spite of their inclination toward republican offices and customs, which by their very nature militated against such ceremonial, these emperors accepted the idea that the world ruler should be worshipped in cult. As the god-idea gained increasing power, however, deity cult itself presented a counteracting influence to the fusion of the ideas of world ruler and deity. A rivalry arose between god and ruler. The king whose omnipotence led to his deification repelled the ruler of heaven, and the ruler of heaven and earth, on his part, refused to tolerate any rival of earthly origin. This led to a temporary compromise in which the ruler, though not himself regarded as a deity, was nevertheless held to be the son of a god, as well as the agent who executed the divine will. Or, after the pattern of hero myths, and in remote resemblance to ancestor cult, the ruler was believed to enter into the heaven of gods upon his death, so that it came to be only the deceased ruler who received divine adoration. The later rulers of Babylon, for example, called themselves the sons of Marduk, who was the chief god of Babylonia, and the features of this deity were given to the image of Hammurabi. The Roman emperors, on the other hand, from the time of Augustus on, were accorded divine reverence after death. When the king, realizing the exalted character of divine majesty, finally came to feel himself entirely human, these practices vanished. The emperor now became either the mere representative of the deity or one who was divinely favoured above other men. Hence the development terminates in a formula of royalty which has even yet not disappeared—the formula, "by the grace of God."

The development which we have described progressed continuously from beginnings that were almost contemporary with those of States until it eventuated in the world State. What, we must now ask, were its motivating forces? We cannot ascribe it to a craving for power which overmasters the ruler of the single State as soon as he has successfully conquered a foreign territory and a foreign people. Doubtless this factor was operative, yet it was obviously an effect rather than a cause, although an effect which, in the reciprocal relations of impulses, itself forthwith became a cause. But the immediate and decisive factors that led to the idea of establishing a world State, are to be found only partly in the motives underlying the extension of the single State into a world State, and in the results connected with the attainment of this ambition. These motives and results were, in the first instance, of an external nature. They consisted in the fact that the world State enjoyed increased means of subsistence and power by reason of the tribute which it received from subjugated provinces or from vassal States. Tributes of grain and cattle, of precious stones and metals, and especially of valuable human material, were placed at the command of the Pharaoh, or of the Babylonian or Persian monarch, for the building of his canals, his temples, and his palaces, for military services, and for an officialdom more directly subject to his will than were free-born natives. Everything which the single State required for its maintenance was demanded in a heightened degree by the world empire. Thus, it was the concentration of the means of subsistence and power that led to the displacement of the single State by the world empire, just as it was the same influence, on a smaller scale, that gave to the State its ascendancy over the earlier tribal organization. In extending its authority over wider and wider territory, the world empire itself finally perished as a result of the increasing difficulty in unifying its forces. It either broke up into separate States or a similar process of expansion started anew within the same boundaries, beginning now with one of the erstwhile vassal States and now with a new tribe that migrated into the territory. The first of these changes is illustrated by the Babylonian-Assyrian empires; the other, by the catastrophes suffered almost contemporaneously by the realm of the Pharaohs, through the influx of the Hyksos, and by Babylon, at the hands of the conquering hordes of the Hittites. The same phenomena recur in the partition of the empire of Alexander the Great and in the downfall of the Roman world empire. Unless world empires degenerate into a mere semblance of universal dominion, as did the Holy Roman Empire, they obviously become the more short-lived in proportion as history comes to move the more rapidly. Hence the Napoleonic attempt to revive the old idea in a new form became a mere episode. The single State finally triumphed over the world empire, and everything goes to show that the idea of an all-embracing world empire is little likely to recur unless the continuity of history is to be seriously interrupted.

It thus appears that the idea of establishing a world empire is not to be accounted for solely in terms of a constant striving to augment the means of power. Such endeavour prevails now, no less than formerly, in every State that has in any way attained to an independent development of its power. At the present time, however, none but at most an occasional Utopian dreamer adheres to the idea of creating an all-inclusive world State. Even where this occurs the idea is completely antithetical to that of earlier times. The ideal which is at present proposed for the distant future involves, not the extension of any single State into a world State, but rather the dissolution of existing States and the establishment of a society of universal peace among nations, such as would render entirely superfluous any instruments of power on the part of the State itself. But we have further evidence that the impulse to increase the means of power could not have been the only, nor even the decisive, factor in the development of the idea of a world empire. This evidence is to be found in the fact that, while a world empire never existed except as an idea, the age in which this idea dominated history regarded the world empire as a reality. Hence there must have been other motives, of an ideal nature, to bridge over the chasm between idea and reality in such wise as to identify the former with the latter. Though it is possible to urge, in explanation, that the knowledge of the real world was at that time limited, this does not solve the problem. Even though the Babylonian king might have felt satisfied to call himself the ruler over the four quarters of the earth because practically all countries of which he had knowledge in the four directions of the wind paid tribute to him, this of itself is not adequate to account for the fact that he regarded the universality as absolute and not relative. Over and above the fact of a limitation of knowledge, there was requisite particularly the idea of the *unity of the world*, and the application of this idea to the reality given in perception. This idea of unity is similar to that of the absolute unity of the world-order whose centre is the earth, an idea that dominated the astronomical conceptions of antiquity. Both ideas, that of a world empire embracing the whole of mankind and that of a universe whose centre is the earth and whose boundary is the crystal sphere of the heaven of fixed stars, sprang from the same mythological world-view that also found expression in the conception of a divine State projected from earth into heaven. To these gods, with a supreme deity at their head, belonged the rulership of the world. Whenever a change in the city that formed the centre of the terrestrial world empire resulted in a new supreme deity, the conditions of the earthly kingdom were all the more faithfully mirrored in the divine kingdom, for the other gods became, as it were, the vassals of this supreme deity. This mythological picture, projected from the earth to heaven, was necessarily reflected back again to earth. Herein lies the deeper significance of the idea that the ruler of the world empire is himself a god, or, at the least, a person of divine lineage and the representative of the supreme guardian deity of the kingdom. It is precisely because of this connection with mythological conceptions that world empires were but transitory. The period of their zenith and, more particularly, the period in which they possessed a fair degree of stability, coincided absolutely with the time at which deity myth was at its height. In the age of a waning deity belief, it was only the influence of numerous elements of secular culture, combined with a high degree of adaptability to the conditions of individual States, such as the Roman mind acquired under the conjunction of unusual circumstances, that enabled the idea of a world empire to be again carried into realization, within the limits which we have set to the term. Proof of the inner connection between the idea of a world empire and a mythological conception of the world, is to be found even in the case of Diocletian, the last powerful representative of the idea of a world kingdom. Diocletian not only invested the Roman emperor with the attributes of the Oriental world ruler of ancient times, but also claimed for himself the worship due to an earthly Jupiter.

3. World Culture.

Inasmuch as the world empire belongs essentially to the age of deity cults, it is not so much a realization of the idea of humanity as a preparation for it, presaging a development beyond that of the single State. That this is the case manifests itself even in the temporal sequence of the phenomena. For it is at most anticipatory elements of the idea of humanity that are embodied in the world empire. With the disintegration of world empires, however, partly as their after-effect and partly as the result of their dissolution, we find phenomena of a new sort—those comprehended under the term *world culture*. In so far as the rise of world empire involves factors that lead to world culture, these affect primarily the material aspect of the life of peoples—world intercourse, the resulting multiplication of needs on the part of peoples, and the exchange of the means for the satisfaction of these needs. The spiritual phases of culture, which outlast these external and material phases, make their appearance more particularly at the time when the world empire is approaching its end. Since, however, it is these spiritual phases that are of predominant significance, world culture as a whole is to be regarded as an after-effect of world empire rather than as a direct result toward which the latter has contributed. The reason for this is not far to seek. It lies in the one-sided striving for the acquisition of external means of power, and in the consequent despotic pressure which the world empire, particularly in ancient times, brought to bear upon its separate members. It is also connected, however, with the fact that the dissolution of world empires usually brings in its wake migrations and a shifting of peoples. Even within the culture of the ancient Orient, the spread of the elements of myth and saga, as well as of the products of art and science, came especially with the destruction of earlier world empires and the reconstruction of others. The empire of Alexander the Great led to what was perhaps the greatest epoch of world culture in the history of civilization, yet the latter was conditioned, not so much directly by this empire, as by its disintegration at the time of the Diadochi. Similarly, the downfall of the last world empire that may properly lay claim to the name—the Græco-Roman kingdom—likewise resulted in a great cultural movement, due in part to the shifting of peoples which took place at this time, though more especially to the spread of Christianity. Here, again, the fact that the world empire was preparatory to world culture is substantiated. For the dying world empire employed even the last powers over which, in its final agony, it still had control, to pave the way for the world religion that was taking its rise.

Nevertheless, as a result of the tremendous resources which, in the beginnings of a higher civilization, were possessed by the world empire alone, there was *one* field in which the period of such empires was directly creative and in which it set an example to future ages. I refer to the technique of mass and to the monumental art connected with it. The streets, viaducts, and magnificent edifices of the period of the Roman emperors have long aroused the wonder and admiration of later generations, as monuments of a power that had unlimited means at its command. The constructions of the Egyptian, Babylonian-Assyrian, and Persian world empires lacked the artistic execution which the influence of Greek art made possible to the constructions of the Romans. We have now come to know, however, that the former were not surpassed by the latter in the immensity which resulted from the consciousness, on the part of the builders, that they had countless human forces at their disposal. The canals and roadways of the Egyptian and Babylonian monarchs, moreover, also give clear evidence that the needs of agriculture and commerce were provided for in a way that would have been impossible, in these early stages of world culture, except through the resources at the command of a world State. The extension of intercourse resulting from world empire is to be regarded as at least a partial factor in the transition to the institution of money. It exercised an influence also toward the development of a system of writing, whose purpose it was to communicate the decrees of government to officials and vassals, and to preserve a record of the deeds of rulers and of the laws enacted by them. In this wise, the material aspects of world culture exerted an influence upon the mental aspects, whose direct expressions are speech and writing.

As regards the relation of speech and writing, the two fundamental elements of all culture, the culture of individuals and world culture show an important difference. In the culture of individuals, of course, speech long precedes writing, verbal expression being crystallized into writing only after a relatively high level of culture has been attained. In world culture, on the other hand, writing paved the way for verbal intercourse. The reason for this difference lies in the fact that speech is a natural product of the direct intercourse of individuals who are sharing a common life. Writing, however, is an invention by which individuals seek to disseminate and to preserve the ideas embodied in speech far beyond the spacial and temporal bounds that limit oral communication. Hence, communication in writing is the first step from folk culture to world culture. The simplicity of the characters which it employs enables it to pass from one people to another and from one generation to the next even more readily than does the speech of commerce. For though the latter is of a more universal character than the many separate mother tongues, it asserts itself only with difficulty in competition with them. The history of cuneiform writing is especially instructive as regards the point under present discussion. The Semitic people, whose migration to Babylonia succeeded that of the Sumerians, lost all knowledge of the Sumerian language, but they preserved the written texts as sacred. In the course of folk migrations, cuneiform writing likewise penetrated to the coast regions of Asia Minor, although in this instance it was continually used to express new idioms not to be found in the land of its origin. Letters have been found representing a correspondence between certain Babylonian kings and Egyptian Pharaohs, and dating from the fifteenth century before Christ. These letters, called Tel-el-Amarna letters after the place of their discovery, are a remarkable testimony to the fact that the demands of commerce gradually cause speech to follow in the wake of writing, even though the means which the Babylonian employs to make his cuneiform writing intelligible indicates that his Egyptian correspondent possessed only a slight acquaintance with the Babylonian language.

It was not until a much later time that any language of intercourse and literature became sufficiently widespread to be called a world language, even in that relative sense which attaches to all universal terms of this sort. This occurred in the case of the *Greek* language, under the rule of the Diadochi. In this instance, again, the first advance in the direction of world culture followed, in the main, upon world empire. For, though we must admit that the empire of Alexander was of altogether too brief a duration for such a purpose, it is nevertheless true that it witnessed only the beginnings of a world dominance of Greek language and culture. Taking into account the narrow limits of the cultural world of that period of history, there has been no age since that of the Diadochi concerning which we would be prepared to say that it attained to so widespread a dissemination of a uniform culture. The striving beyond a national to a world culture which took place at that time was, of course, the fruition of far earlier tendencies. The fact that the Greek colonies retained the language and customs of the mother country was itself a preparatory step. Following the train of colonists were individual travellers, whose desire for knowledge led them beyond the regions where the Greek language was known. Even in that early day, Pythagoras and Xenophanes, Herodotus and Xenophon, Democritus and Plato made extensive travels throughout the lands bordering on the Mediterranean. Alexander's expedition to India, a country which had up to that time been regarded as a marvellous fairyland, marked the culmination of the journeys to remote regions which had, at the outset, been undertaken by individuals. Nevertheless, the spread of the impulse to wander remains of primary significance for the Hellenistic period. The warrior, the tradesman, and the physician share this impulse with the scholar and the artist. In the age of tribal organization, it was the tribe or clan that travelled to distant places, its object being to escape the pressure of want and the need threatened by the exhaustion of the hunting-grounds or the soil; in the heroic age, it was the people as a whole who left their homes, either because they were crowded out by enemies or because they were eager to assert their power by establishing cities and States; in the age under present consideration, it is the individual who is seized with the longing for travel, his purpose being to find elsewhere more favourable opportunities for the exercise of his vocation, or, perhaps, to see the world, and thus to enlarge his field of experience and his knowledge. The large and rapidly growing cities that spring up into centres of the new world culture attract the people of all lands, as do also the ancient and far-famed seats of intellectual culture. In Alexandria, Pergamus, Athens, and, finally, in Rome, there mingle representatives of all races—of the Greek, Egyptian, Syrian, Persian, and Italic peoples. Greek is the language of common intercourse. Alexandria, however, gradually displaces Athens as the chief seat of science. The latter comes to be fostered, not by Greeks, but, in large part, by individuals of other nationalities, particularly those of the Orient.

This new world culture possesses two distinctive characteristics. The first of these consists in a growing indifference to the State as such. The second, antithetical to the former and yet most closely related to it, is a high appreciation of the individual personality, connected with which is a tendency on the part of the individual to develop his own personality and to assert his rights. That which the public values undergoes a change. The emphasis shifts, on the one hand, from the State to a culture which is universally human, and thus independent of State boundaries; it passes, on the other hand, from political interests, in part, to the individual personality and, in part, to universal spiritual development. Thus, world culture is at once cosmopolitan and individualistic. As respects both these characteristics, however, the interest in humanity finds expression in a transcendence of the limits of a single people. Here, again, preparatory stages will be found far back in Greek culture. As early as the time of the Sophists, individuals, wandering from city to city as travelling teachers, proclaim the spirit of personal freedom and the dependence of all social institutions and ties upon the will of the individual. When we come to the Epicurean and Stoic schools, which reach over into the period of early world culture, the idea of humanity in both its aspects receives its classic expression, though with differing emphases, conditioned by the ethical and religious needs as a whole. Similar conditions prevail in the positive sciences. In natural science, which reached its first classical development in the Alexandrian period, an interest in universal natural laws, as discovered in astronomy and mechanics, occurs side by side with an absorption in descriptive observations of the most detailed sort. History fluctuates between attempts at an abstract schematization of the epochs of political development, after the pattern of the Aristotelian classification of the forms of the State, and biographical accounts of dominating personalities and their deeds. Similarly, philology combines the grammatical disputes of the Peripatetic and Stoic schools—disputes as yet unfruitful in their abstract generalities—with that minute pursuit of literary studies which has since given the period the discreditable name of 'Alexandrianism.' Art also manifests this *coïncidentia oppositorum*. The monumental edifices of this epoch exhibit a tendency toward the colossal, whereas sculpture is characterized by a painstaking and individualizing art of portraiture ; the drama portraying the pompous action of ruler and State, appears alongside of the play of civic intrigue and the mime.

As the result both of inner dissolution and of the aggression of new peoples who were just entering upon their political development, Hellenistic world culture underwent disintegration. It first split up into Greek and Roman divisions, in correspondence with the partition of the Roman world empire and that of the Christian Church connected with it. Except the fact of the separation itself, nothing shows more significantly how far both divisions were from possessing a world culture than does the decline of that indispensable means of common culture, language. The West preserved meagre remnants of the Latin civilization, the East, fragments of the Greek civilization. In the course of the centuries, the clergy of the West developed a class of scholars who were out of sympathy with the prevailing tendencies toward national culture. In the East, the barbarian nations, which the Church barely succeeded in holding together, exercised a benumbing influence upon culture ; cultural activity, therefore, sank into a dull lethargy. The ancient world empires, whose last brilliant example, the monarchy of Alexander, had formed the transition to the first great world culture, gave place, at this later time, to *world religion*. As the result of struggles which, though long, were assured of ultimate success, world religion subjected the political powers to its authority. Destined, in the belief of peoples, to be imperishable, this religion outlived the changing forms of the secular State, and was the only remaining vehicle of world culture, fragmentary as this may have been. But the inner dissolution to which the last of the great world empires, that of Rome, succumbed, overpowered also the Church as soon as the latter endeavoured to become a new world State and insisted on the duty of believers to render obedience to it. When this occurred, the world culture fostered by it necessarily proved too weak to assimilate the new tendencies which were beginning to manifest themselves. Conditions were ripe for the striving to achieve a new culture. In contrast with the ideal of the Church, this culture was concerned with the actual world, and therefore felt itself related to the cultural idea of antiquity. Thus arose the culture of the Renaissance. In it, we again have a world culture in the true sense of the word, even though it was shared, at the outset, only by the ambitious and the educated, as had, indeed, also essentially been the case with its prototype.

The culture of the Renaissance formulated its ideal by reference both to the past and to the future. It sought to revive the world culture of the Græco-Roman period, but yet to give to the latter a content suited to the spirit of the new age and to the tasks awaiting it. Hence the Renaissance was not merely a rebirth, as its name might suggest, but a new world culture. Though possessing many traits in common with the older culture of Hellenism, it bore, in an even greater measure, its own peculiar stamp. The most noteworthy feature common to the two was their combination of universalism and individualism—a feature that is, perhaps, characteristic of world culture as such. Apparently both universalism and individualism become more prominent with the course of time. During the period of the Renaissance, the cultivation—one might almost say the cult—of the individual personality probably reached the highest point that it had as yet attained. The human monster, who violated without compunction all laws of propriety and custom, and the ascetic zealot, who sacrificed himself for a visionary ideal, could both alike arouse admiration because of the uniqueness of their characters. Along with this emphasis of individual personality, there flourished social ideals of a religious and a political nature. It was under this influence that the reformation of the church began its work and that new political theories and Utopian accounts of a happy future for the human race made their appearance. In still another respect does the age of the Renaissance appear to be a genuine revival, in an enlarged world, of the Hellenistic period. Again the individual is overpowered by the impulse to travel, and, as a consequence, the age of great geographical discoveries is inaugurated. The voyages of the great discoverers—of Columbus, Vasco da Gama, and Magellan—were the result, for the most part, of personal initiative. And, though other motives may have lurked in the background, the discoverers themselves were chiefly inspired by that desire to wander which, more than a century earlier, had led the Venetian Marco Polo to travel alone in the distant lands of eastern Asia.

But, in certain essential particulars, the later period of world culture possessed a character all its own. The basis of culture was no longer a world State, but a world Church. No longer, moreover, was there an indifference to the State, as had been so generally the case in Hellenistic times. A heightened political interest was everywhere beginning to be manifest. That which long continued to give this period its unique stamp was the struggle between State and Church. The social impulses tended in the direction of a new political order, and to a certain extent, even at this time, toward a social reconstruction. The world culture of this period, moreover, sustained a completely altered relation to language, that universal vehicle both of mental life and of the material culture which grows up out of the intercourse of peoples. It was not a world language, such as results naturally from the authority of a world empire, that constituted the basis of the new cultural unity. On the contrary, the latter was dependent upon a multiplicity of languages, which gave expression to the mental individuality of peoples just as did the national States to the diversity of particular political and social interests. The influence of more extensive educational activities made itself felt. The forms of commerce and of the interchange of the mental products of nations were manifold, yet education rendered the means of material and intellectual intercourse common property so far as this was possible and necessary. Thus, world culture itself acquired a new foundation. A world language must of necessity be an active and a living language, and, in view of the fact that all social institutions are historically conditioned, it can attain its supremacy only through the influence of a world empire. Hence every world culture whose basis is a unity of language, in the sense of a world language, is doomed to be transitory. Fragments of such a culture may survive, but it itself must perish along with the language by which it is sustained and, more remotely, with the political power by which the language is upheld. All this is changed as soon as world culture is established on the basis of a multiplicity of national tongues as well as of national States. Then, for the first time, may world culture become more than merely an occasional epoch of history; thenceforth it may enjoy a permanent development. With this in mind, one may say that the period of the Renaissance laid the foundation for a new form of world culture, whose characteristic feature is that combination of humanistic and national endeavour which is still prevalent throughout the civilized world.

4. World Religions.

One of the most significant marks of the heroic age is the existence of national religions. Just as each race possesses its own heroes, so also does it have its own gods, who are reverenced as its protectors in wars with foreign peoples. True, gods and their cults may occasionally pass over from one people to another. Wherever there is an assimilation of foreign cults, however, all traces of origin disappear ; the gods who are taken over from other peoples are added to the company of native gods, and enrich the national pantheon. So far as these conditions are concerned, world empires bring few changes. At most, they expressly subordinate the gods of conquered lands to the god of the ruling city, and thus prepare for the idea of an all-comprehensive divine State corresponding to the universal terrestrial State. The decisive step in the completion of this development is taken only under the influence of the world culture that grows up out of the world empire. The special national deities that represent the particular interests of individual peoples then inevitably recede in favour of gods and cults sustained by universal human needs, in which case the cults are, on the whole, identical, even though the deities bear different names.

It is of importance to note the motives that led to the first steps toward the realization of a universal human religion. They were identical with the very earliest incentives to religion, such as prevailed among all peoples on the very threshold of the belief in demons and gods. For, after the disappearance of political interests, to which the national gods owed their supremacy, it was again *two* experiences that occupied the foreground—*sickness* and *death*. During the period of Hellenistic world culture, the occupation of the physician was held in especial esteem. Connected with this was the fact that the cult of Æsculapius, the god of healing, grew from small beginnings into a cult whose influence extended over distant lands. Even more marked was the increase in the influence of those cults that centred about a world after death and the individual's preparation for it. The origin of these cults was connected both with the needs of this life and with the desire for endless joy in the beyond. In view of their identical development, how could it have escaped notice that, whatever formal differences there might be, the Grecian Demeter, the Phrygian Cybele, and the Phœnician Astarte were alike in nature? Even more than was the case with the Greek mysteries, these Oriental cults carried over into the cults of the beyond, into which they developed, certain ecstatic and orgiastic elements of ancient vegetation cults. All the more readily, therefore, were the latter cults incorporated into the deity cults, inasmuch as these had as their concern the satisfaction of human needs generally. But conditions were ripe for a still further advance. As has been suggested, the national and State interests which fettered man to the actual world of his environment gave way to interests transcending this world. In proportion as this occurred, however, did the life of the present, deprived of its former values, relinquish all cherished desires in favour of that heavenly world possible to all men regardless of class, calling, or nationality. This change was antithetical to the innate fear of death, and yet was its own final product. All these cults thus became *redemption cults.* To be redeemed from the evil of the world—the desire of deeper religious minds—or, after the enjoyment of the good things of this life, to receive still greater happiness after death—a hope doubtless entertained by the majority then as now—such was the primary object of the cults of these supranational gods. National cults had fashioned the gods in the image of man, even though exalting them with all the power of the mythological imagination into the superhuman and the unapproachable. At this later period, all efforts were directed toward bringing these anthropomorphic gods nearer to man as regards the activities in which they engaged, and particularly as regards the experiences which they underwent. No figure in the later Greek pantheon better lent itself to such a purpose than did Dionysos. Like the female deities representing Mother Earth, this male deity originated in the ancient field and fertility cults. Later, however, he became more and more transformed by legend into the ideal of a striving and suffering deity, who, after a horrible death, arose to new glory. Related to Dionysos were other deities who likewise became supreme in the Hellenistic age—Mithra, Attis, Osiris, and Serapis. All of these were gods who had been redeemed from pain and anguish, and were therefore capable, in their sympathy, of redeeming man.

In its beginnings, Christianity also was one of these religions of redemption. Over five hundred years before its rise, moreover, there had already appeared in the Far East a religion in which the same thought occupied the foreground. I refer to Buddhism. With reference to the steps by which Buddhism attained its supremacy, our only data are the controversies of the philosophical schools that participated in the development. These controversies make it probable that the basal motives involved were similar to those that were later operative in the cultural world of the Occident. There were also essential differences, however, traceable to the fact that the various Brahmanic systems had a common religious substratum, and that Hindoo thought had attained to a fairly advanced stage of philosophical development. One fact is doubtless universal—the appearance of a redemptive religion marks the decadence of an old and the rise of a new period of culture. Beginning with the Hellenistic period, therefore, and continuing with increased strength during the Roman world empire, there was a transition from a national to a humanistic culture. World religion was a more decisive indication of this crisis than were any of the other elements of world culture, or than was even world empire, which prepared the way for world culture. The old gods could no longer satisfy the new age, unless, at any rate, they underwent marked transformations. The age required new gods, in whom national traits were secondary, as they were in life itself, and universal human characteristics were supreme. It was particularly the unique worth of the individual human personality, without regard to birth, class, and occupation, which this period of transition from the national to the humanistic ideal emphasized. Hence the obstacles which the surrounding world placed in the way of personal endeavour were inevitably felt the more deeply in proportion as the values of the narrower community life disappeared. A change in mood took place within the consciousness of the age, as it so often does within that of the individual, and this change was enhanced by the contrast of emotions. The world lost the values which it had thus far held, and became a place of evil and suffering. In contrast with it, there loomed up a yonder world in which the desired ideals were believed to meet fulfilment. This mood, of course, did not continue permanently. World religion was of inner necessity forced to adapt itself to the earthly life in proportion as State and society again acquired a more fixed organization. But, just as the strata of the earth's crust retain the effects of a geological catastrophe long after it has passed, so spiritual life continues to exhibit the influence of upheavals that have occurred in the transitions from age to age, even though the spiritual values themselves have undergone many changes. In this respect, world religion manifests a conserving power greater than that of any other product of mental life.

There are only *two* world religions, in the strictest sense of the term, *Buddhism* and *Christianity*. Confucianism, which might perhaps be included so far as the number of its adherents is concerned, is a system of ethical teachings rather than a religion. Hence, when we take into account the vast number of Chinese peoples, Confucianism will be found to embody a great number of different religious developments, the most important of which are the ancient ancestor cult and Buddhism, the latter of which penetrated into China from elsewhere. The faith of Islam is a combination of Jewish and Christian ideas with ancient Arabian and Turanian traditions. As such, it has brilliantly fulfilled the mission of bringing a cultural religion to barbarian or semi-barbarian peoples, but it cannot be credited with being an original religious creation. Judaism finally formed a supremely important element of Christianity, one whose influence would appear to have been absolutely indispensable. In itself, however, it is not a world religion, but is one of those vanquished cults which struggled for supremacy in the pre-Constantinian period of the Roman world empire.

But what, let us ask, were the powerful forces that gave these two great world religions their supremacy? Surely it was not merely their inner superiority, though this be in no way disputed. Nor was it simply propitious external circumstances, such, for example, as the fact that Constantine made Christianity the State religion. Doubtless there were a great number of co-operating factors, foremost among them being the desire for a purely humanistic religion, independent of nationality or external position in life. And yet this also could not have been of decisive significance—precisely such a longing was more or less characteristic of all the religious tendencies of this transitional period. Moreover, this leaves unexplained the peculiarities of each of the two great world religions. These are in complete accord as regards their universal, humanistic tendency, but are just as different in content as is a Buddhistic pagoda from a Gothic cathedral. As a matter of fact, these world religions are also cultural religions. Back of each of them is a rich culture, with characteristics peculiar to itself, even though its basal elements are universally human. Hence it is that these two world religions are not merely expressions of a striving for a universally valid religious and moral ideal, in the sense in which such a striving is common to mankind as a whole ; it should rather be emphasized that they reflect the essentially different forms which this striving has assumed within humanity. Buddhism, in its fundamental views, represents the highest expression to which the religious feeling of the Orient has attained, while Christianity, as a result of the conditions which determined its spread, has become the embodiment of the religious thought of the Occidental world. To appreciate this fact we must not allow our minds to be diverted to the tangled profusion of beliefs in magic and demons which Buddhism exhibits, nor to the traditional and, in part, ambiguous sayings of the great ascetic himself. If we would discover the parallels between Buddhism and Christianity, we must hold ourselves primarily to the ideas that have remained potent within the religion of Buddha. True, the worlds which these religions disclose to our view differ, yet in neither case had religious feeling up to that time received so exalted an expression. In Buddhism, as in original Christianity, human life is regarded as a suffering, and this underlies both the irresistible impulse to asceticism and repentance, and the hope for unclouded bliss in the future. The Christian of the primitive church looks forward to the speedy return of Christ, and to His inauguration of an eternal, heavenly kingdom. In contrast with this, it is as a prolonged migration through animal bodies, alternating with rebirth in human form, that the Hindoo thinker conceives that great process of purification by means of which sense is finally to be entirely overcome and man is to partake of an undimmed knowledge of the truth, and, with this, of supreme and never-ending bliss. This is the true Nirvana of Buddha. Nirvana does not represent the nothingness of eternal oblivion, but an eternal rest of the soul in pure knowledge, a peace which puts an end to all striving, just as does the heaven for which the Christian hopes. The difference between Nirvana and the Christian heaven is merely that, in the one case, the emphasis falls on knowledge, whereas, in the other, it is placed on feeling. This distinction, however, is not absolute. Buddha, also, preaches love of one's neighbour—indeed, sympathy with every suffering creature ; and the Christian, as well as the Buddhist, seeks the knowledge of God. Moreover, ideas of purification are necessarily involved in redemptive religions, and hence are to be found in Christianity no less than in the world religion of the Orient, though in a different form. The Occidental Christian, swayed by his prompter emotions, images in the most vivid colours the agonies of the damned and the purification of the sinners in need of redemption. The patient and peace-seeking Oriental entertains the conception of a prolonged suffering that leads gradually, through the light of knowledge, from the debasement of animal existence to a state of redemption.

A further feature which differentiates these kindred religious developments is their relation to the contemporary philosophy which affected them. Buddhism grew out of philosophy and then became a folk religion. In its spread, it became transformed from an esoteric into an exoteric teaching, continually absorbing older elements of folk belief. Its ethical basis never entirely disappeared, yet it became more and more obscured by a multitude of miracle-legends and magical ideas. Christianity, on the other hand, began as a folk religion and, in so far, as an exoteric teaching. But, in entering into the strife of religions and into the controversies of the thought-systems of the Hellenistic-Roman period, Christianity passed under the control of philosophy. Precisely because it lay outside the realm of philosophy, it was subjected to the influence of the various schools, though it was most decisively affected by Platonism and Stoicism. Inasmuch as philosophy itself had its setting in a superstitious age, it was the less able to purify Christianity from the belief in demons, miracles, and magic which the latter, as a folk religion, embodied from the very outset. Nevertheless, philosophical thought supplemented the real meaning of religious statements with an idealized interpretation. This gave birth to dogma, which consisted of a peculiar combination of esoteric and exoteric elements, and for this very reason assumed a mystical character. Hence it is that Buddhism, which sprang from philosophy, never possessed any real dogmas in the sense of binding norms of faith, whereas Christianity, which originated as a folk religion, fell a prey in its dogmatization to a theology which prescribed the content of belief.

These two world religions, which dominate the main centres of spiritual culture, do not, surely, owe their supremacy over other religious cults to the external conditions of their origin. Indeed, these conditions differ in the two cases. To account for the pre-eminence of the two religions we must look to the religious and moral nucleus which they possess in the sayings and teachings as well, also, as in the ideal lives of their founders. In spite of all differences, there is a similarity of character between the prince who wandered about as a beggar, preaching to the peoples the salvation which pure knowledge brings to him who renounces all external goods of life, and the man of the common people who pronounced blessings on the poor and the suffering because they are prepared above others to find the way to heaven. Another remarkable coincidence is the fact that the religious communities which they inspired sought to deprive them of the very characteristic which opens human hearts to them; they were real persons who lived and to whose deeds and sufferings their contemporaries bore testimony. What, as compared with them, are the redeeming gods in the pantheon of the various nations—Dionysos, Mithra, Osiris, or even Serapis, whose worship was established by the Ptolemies under the driving power of ideas of extensive political authority? The need of a living god whose existence was historically attested led irresistibly to the elevation of the man into a god. Thus, though in an entirely different world-setting and with a completely changed hero-personality, the process through which deities were created at the beginning of the heroic age was repeated. At this later period, however, it was not the universal type of idealized manhood that was regarded as the incarnate deity, but a single ideal personality. This purely human deity was no longer bound by national ties; he was not a guardian of the State and a helper in strife with other peoples, but a god of mankind. For every individual he was both an ideal and a helper, a saviour from the imperfections and limitations of earthly life. With this process of deification, the religions whose central object of cult was the suffering individual who secures for himself and for mankind redemption from suffering, opened their doors also to the gods and demons of earlier ages. Thus, there penetrated into Buddhism the Hindoo pantheon, together with the beliefs in magic and spirits which were entertained by the peoples converted to Buddhism. The Christian Church did not finally supersede the earlier heathen folk belief until it had assimilated the latter in the conceptions of demons and the devil, in the cult of saints, and in the worship of relics, the last-mentioned of which also constituted an important element of Buddhism.

In the case of Christianity, there was still another factor which prepared the soil for the new religion. This factor was due either to a direct transference or, as is probable so far as the main outlines of the history of the passion are concerned, to the real similarity of this event with the legends, prevalent in all parts of the earth, of the death and resurrection of a deity. Such legends everywhere grew up out of vegetation cults, which date back to the beginnings of agriculture. The hopes centred about a world beyond caused the cults based on these ideas to incorporate the soul cults. The latter then displaced the original motives of vegetation cults. In this way, higher forms of soul cult were developed, as exemplified by the ancient mysteries and by the related secret cults of other peoples. The exclusive aim now came to be the attainment of salvation from the earthly into a heavenly world. It was thought that this goal would be the more certain of attainment if, yielding to the old association of the mystical and secret with the magical and miraculous, the circle of initiated cult companions were narrowly limited. But how different is the form which this very ancient legend of a god who suffers, dies, and rises again assumes in the suffering and death of Christ! Jesus was a real person, whose death on the cross many had witnessed and whose resurrection his disciples had reported. Moreover, the cult of this crucified Saviour was not enveloped in a veil of secrecy. The redeeming god did not wish to win heaven merely for a few who had gained the privilege through magical ceremonies. The Christian heaven was open to all, to rich and poor, though especially to the poor, who were to receive in the beyond a rich compensation for the good things denied them upon earth. It is but natural that this new cult, with its vastly deeper and more vital significance, and with the strength which it nevertheless continued to draw from the old traditional legends, won for itself the allegiance of the new world with its strivings for a greater security in life as in death. Even some of the Roman soldiers, coming from their Saturnalian or Sacæan festivals, may, perhaps, have felt strangely moved upon seeing re-enacted, as a terrible reality, that which in their country was a playful custom, representing a survival of a once serious cult and ending in the mimic death of the carnival king. It was obviously in recollection of these very prevalent festivals that the coarser members of the crowd gave to him who was crucified the name "King of the Jews." The appellation was exactly suited to heighten the contrast between the joyous tumult of such mimic cults and this murderous reality.

The above scene was prophetic of the entire subsequent development of the new religion. That Christianity became a world religion was not due merely to the depth and sublimity of its spirit—these were hidden under a cover of mythological elements, from which Christianity was not free any more than were other religions. Christianity gained its supremacy, just as did Buddhism, in its own way, through a capacity to assimilate auxiliary mythological conceptions to an extent scarcely equalled by any of the previous religions. The very fact that the latter were national religions precluded them, to a certain extent, from incorporating alien ideas. It was not only mediæval Christianity that took over a large part of the earlier belief of heathen peoples. Even present-day Christianity might doubtless be called a world religion in this sense, among others, that, in the various forms of its beliefs and professions, it includes within itself, side by side, the most diverse stages of religious development, from a monotheism free from all mythological elements down to a motley collection of polytheistic beliefs, including survivals of primitive ideas of magic and demons.

But there is another phenomenon in which the spirit of

Christianity comes to expression even more significantly than in its capacity to adapt itself to the most diverse stages of religious development. Here, again, there is a similarity between Christianity and the other great world religion, Buddhism. The belief of Hindoo antiquity in a populous heaven of gods was very early displaced, in the priestly wisdom of India, by the idea of "the eternal, unchangeable" Brahma. We here have an abstract deity-idea from which every trace of personality has disappeared. It was under the influence of this priestly philosophy that Buddha grew up, and his esoteric teaching, therefore, did not include a belief in a personal deity. Meanwhile, the ancient gods had continued to maintain their place in popular belief, though their original character was obscured by rankly flourishing ideas of magic and demons. This state of affairs was due to the fact that there was no longer a supreme deity who could give to mythology a religious basis. In the religious movement which began with Buddha, however, the latter himself came to be a supreme deity of this sort, the old nature gods and magic demons becoming subservient to him. The god-idea had been etherealized into the abstract idea of a superpersonal being, but its place was taken by the human individual exalted into a deity. Christianity underwent the same crucial changes, though in a different manner. In the philosophy of the Greeks, the personal deity of popular belief had been displaced by a superpersonal being. Plato's "idea of the good," the Aristotelian *Nous*, which, as pure form, holds sway beyond the boundaries of the world, even the Stoic Zeus as the representative of the teleological character of the world order, and, finally, the gods of Epicurus, conceived as indefinite forms dwelling in nebulous regions and unconcerned with the world—all manifest the same tendency either to elevate the personal deities of the heroic age into superpersonal beings, or, as was essentially done by Epicurus, to retransform them into subpersonal, demon-like beings. In contrast with this tendency, Jesus, as the representative of a religious folk belief, holds fast to the god of ancient tradition, as developed in the Jahve religion of the Israelites. Indeed, it is in the conception of Jesus that this god receives his deepest and most personal expression, inasmuch as he is conceived as a god of love, to whom man stands in the relation of son to father. This conception of the relation of God to man Christianity sought to retain. But history is not in accord with this traditional view. Cult and dogma alike testify that in this case also the deity came to be superpersonal from an early period on. To cult, which is always concerned with personal gods, Christ became the supreme deity ; in the Catholic Church, there came to be also a large number of secondary and subsidiary gods, who sometimes even crowded the Christ into the background, as is exemplified particularly by the cult of the Virgin Mary. Dogma, on its part, cannot conceal the fact that it originated in philosophy, which is destructive of personal gods. For dogma ascribes attributes to the deity that are irreconcilable with the concept of personality. The deity is represented as eternal, omnipotent, all-good, omnipresent—in short, as infinite in all attributes that are held to express his nature. The conception of the infinite, however, contradicts that of personality, for the latter demands a character that possesses sharply defined attributes. However comprehensive our conception of personality may be, limitation is necessarily implied ; the concept loses its meaning when associated with the limitless and the infinite. Even though dogma may continue to maintain that belief in a personal God is fundamental to Christian faith, such a belief is nevertheless self-contradictory ; the union of the ideas 'personal' and 'god' must be understood as a survival within the era of world religions, where many such survivals occur, of the god-idea developed by national religions.

The truth is that the transformation of the personal god into a superpersonal deity is probably the most important mark of world religion. National religion displaced the subpersonal demon in favour of the personal god ; in world religion, the personal god is exalted into a superpersonal deity. At this point there is a very close connection between world religion and world culture. As the idea that the universe is bounded by a sphere of fixed stars must give way to the conception of the infinitude of the universe, so also does world culture transcend the limits imposed upon it by the preparatory world empire, whose own origin was the State. World Culture, as we have seen, comes to signify a cultural unity of mankind, such as includes the national States. Similarly, world religion strives toward the idea of a deity who is superpersonal, and who, though only in so far as he is superpersonal, transcends the world of experience. The foundations of this concluding stage in the development of religion had long been laid by philosophy. In religion itself, the culmination was actually attained with the recedence of the deity in cult ; in theology, it came with the ascription to the deity of attributes of absoluteness and infinitude, even though the deity-conception did not clearly emerge from a mystic incomprehensibility rendered inevitable by the combination of contradictory ideas.

Though the transition from a personal god to a superpersonal deity is the decisive characteristic that marks a world religion, there is closely connected with it a second distinctive feature. In Christianity, indeed, it was the latter that prepared the way for the idea of the non-personal character of God. The fact to which I refer is that, in addition to the non-personal deity, there is believed to be a personal god in the form of an exalted human individual. Cult continues to require a personal being to whom man may come with his needs and desires. And by whom could his trouble be better understood than by a deity who himself lived and suffered as a man? In Buddhism, therefore, as well as in Christianity, the god-man became the personal representative of the non-personal deity, not as the result of any external transference, but in consequence of the same inner need. The god-man is a representative in more than one respect. Cult honours him as the deity who dwelt upon earth in human form, and who represents the godhead ; it turns to him also as the human individual who represents mankind before God. Back of these two ideas of representativeness that dominate belief and cult, there is still a further, though an unrecognized, need for a representative. The religious nature requires that there shall be a personal god as the representative of him who has been exalted into a non-personal deity and has become inaccessible. The infinite god posited by the religious intellect is unable to satisfy the religious nature that is pressed by the cares and sufferings of finitude. Herewith the way is opened for a development whose course is determined by the changing relations into which the two aspects of the concept 'god-man' enter with one another. On the first stage, the divine aspect of the god-man overshadows the human character. At this period, it might appear as though world religion merely substituted a new god for the older gods. Though the superpersonal deity receives recognition in dogma, and the development, therefore, marks an important religious advance over the age of gods, the cult is directed to the person of the god-man. Then comes a second stage, in which the human aspect of the concept 'god-man' occupies the foreground. The god-man becomes an ideal human being who succours man in the afflictions of his soul, but who does so not so much by his divine power as by the example of human perfection which he represents. At the third stage, the god-man finally comes to be regarded as in every respect a man. It is recognized that, through the religious movement which bears his name, he indeed prepared the way for the idea that the deity is a non-personal source of being, exalted above all that is transitory. Nevertheless, the god-man is conceived as an ideal man only in the sense in which one may speak of any ideal as actual. Hence, the world religion derives its name from him not so much because of what he himself was as because of that which he created. From this point of view, it is eventually immaterial even whether or not Jesus or Buddha ever lived. The question becomes one of historical fact, not one of religious necessity. Jesus and Buddha live on in their religious creations. That these creations, to say nothing of any other proofs, point back to powerful religious personalities, the unbiased will regard as certain, though from this third point of view the question is of subordinate importance.

A world religion may lay claim to being such not merely on account of its wide acceptance, but also because of its ability to incorporate the elements of other religions. In a similar manner, and more particularly, a world religion is one that includes within itself elements representing past stages of its own development. Historically considered, religious elements are juxtaposed in such a manner that the religious life of the past is mirrored in the present. Hence the religion can at no time emancipate itself from its historical development. It is just as impossible to return to the religious notions of earlier times as it is to transform ourselves into the contemporaries of Charlemagne or even of Frederick the Great. The past never returns. Nevertheless, it is universally characteristic of mental development, particularly within the sphere of religion, that the new not only continues to be affected by the old, but that the more advanced stages of culture actually embody many elements of the past. That these be permitted to exist side by side with higher conceptions, and that there be no limiting external barriers in either direction, is all the more demanded by world religion inasmuch as the independence of State and society, which its very nature implies, presupposes, first of all, the freedom of personal belief.

Inasmuch as it possesses a universal human significance, religion cannot escape the change to which everything human is subject. This appears most strikingly in the undeniable fact that the fundamental idea of the two great world religions, Buddhism and Christianity, has in both cases changed. I refer to the idea of *salvation*. We do not, of course, mean to deny that an individual may either permanently or temporarily return to the religious ideas of the past with a fervour which again reinstates in him impulses that have long since disappeared. Nevertheless, the present-day idea of salvation is no longer identical with that which animated the primitive Christian Church when it looked forward to the return of its Saviour. Christianity is a religion of humanity. Precisely for this reason, it, in every age, took up into itself the feelings and aspirations representing the ideal spiritual forces of that age. All that was permanent in the midst of this change was really the religious impulse as such, the feeling that the world of sense belongs to an ideal supersensuous order—a feeling for which world religion seeks external corroboration in the development of religion itself. In distinction from national religions, which sprang from an infinitely large number of sources, a world religion requires a personal founder. To this personality is due also the direction of the further development of the religion. Thus, the final and most important characteristic of world religion is the fact that it is pre-eminently an *historical* religion. It is historical both in that it has an historical origin, and in that it is constantly subject to the flux of historical development.

5. World History.

The meaning attached to the term 'world history' clearly shows how firmly rooted is the anthropocentric view of the world in connection with those matters that are of deepest concern to man. World history is regarded as the history of mankind—indeed, in a still narrower sense, as, in the last analysis, the mental history of mankind. If facts of any other sort are taken into account, this is not because they are an essential part of the subject-matter, but because they represent external conditions of historical events. The justifiability of this point of view may scarcely be disputed. If the purpose of all historical knowledge is to understand the present condition of mankind in the light of its past, and, in so far as we also attribute to this knowledge a practical value, to indicate the probable course of the future, then the history of mind is the immediate source of historical knowledge. If this be true, it follows that the essential content of history consists in those events which spring from the psychical motives of human conduct. Moreover, it is the nexus and change of motives underlying such conduct that leads to events the inner continuity which is universally demanded of history.

But the very meaning which is universally associated with the term 'world history' itself includes *two* very different conceptions. For, even when the field of history is limited to the events connected with mankind, as those which are of greatest importance to us, there remains a further question. Is history to deal with the *whole* of mankind, or is it to be restricted merely to those peoples that have in any way affected the course of the mental history of humanity? As is well known, most of the works on world history have been confined to the more restricted field. For them, world history is an account of cultural peoples, whose activities are shown by a continuous tradition and by existing monuments to form a relatively connected whole. But there have also been more comprehensive works, which have felt it necessary to include at least those cultural and semi-cultural peoples who attained to some independent mental development, as did the peoples of the New World prior to the time of Columbus. Back of this uncertainty arising from the ambiguity of the concept 'mankind' lies a deeper-going confusion due to the no less ambiguous meaning of the concept 'history.' However much we may associate the word 'history' primarily with the traditional limits of historical science, we may not entirely put aside the broader meaning, according to which it includes everything which may at all be brought into a connected order of events. For we also speak of a history of the earth, of the solar system, of an animal or a plant species, etc. Now, with this wider connotation of the idea in mind, we cannot fail to recognize that the conditions that still prevail among certain races, and that doubtless at one time prevailed among all, are such that, while they would not concern historical science in its more restricted and familiar sense, they would demand consideration if the term were taken in its broader meaning. From the latter point of view, the condition of a primitive people of nature is no less a product of history than is the political and cultural condition of present-day Europe. But there is nevertheless a radical difference between the two cases. The historically trained European understands, to a fairly great extent, the external circumstances that have led to present conditions. He is conscious not merely of the present but also of its preceding history, and he therefore looks forward to the future with the expectation of further historical changes. The man of nature knows only the present. Of the past he possesses merely fragmentary elements, legendary in character, and much altered by the embellishments of a myth-creating imagination ; his provision for the future scarcely extends beyond the coming day. Hence, we should scarcely be justified in unqualifiedly calling peoples of nature 'peoples without a history.' In the broader sense of the term, they have a history, as well as have the solar system, the earth, the animal, and the plant. But they lack a history in the narrower sense, according to which historical science includes among 'historical' peoples only such as have had some special significance in the development of mental culture. That even this limitation is variable and uncertain need scarcely be mentioned. The past shows us many instances in which hordes that were previously unknown, and were thus, in the ordinary meaning of the term, peoples without a history, suddenly stepped into the arena of the cultured world and its history. The colonial history of the present, moreover, shows that the characteristics and the past development of races occupying regions of the earth newly opened to cultural peoples, have not been, and are not, without influence upon the course of history. It should also be remembered that between an historical tradition comprehending the entire cultural world and recollection limited to the immediate past, there are a great number of intermediate stages. These stages are dependent primarily upon the forms of social organization, though also upon other cultural factors. Peoples that have failed to advance beyond a tribal organization may frequently have traversed wide regions of the earth and yet have preserved at most certain legendary elements of the history of these migrations, although retaining myths, cults, and customs indefinitely. On the other hand, wherever a national State has arisen, there has developed also a national tradition, intermingled with which, of course, there have long continued to be mythological and legendary elements. But the tradition, even in this case, relates exclusively to the particular people who entertain it. Strange races are as yet touched upon only in so far as they have directly affected the interests of those who preserve the tradition. Indeed, such races continue to have but an inconspicuous place in tradition until the establishment of world empires and of the partly anticipatory colonial and trade interrelation of peoples. Hence it is not until the rise of world empires that we find the transition to world history in the sense in which the term is most commonly employed to-day. In so far as world history involves a transcendence of the history of a single people but nevertheless a limitation to the circle of cultural peoples who are more or less generally interrelated, it is a direct product of world culture. Such a history includes all peoples who participate in world culture and excludes all those who have no share in it.

Considered from a psychological point of view, the different meanings of the concept 'history' in its relation to the various stages of mental culture, clearly show a fluctuation between *two* ideas which, though opposite, nevertheless mutually imply each other. On the one hand, there is the purely objective conception of history. History, in this case, is regarded as a course of events of such a nature that the specific occurrences may be brought by an external observer into an orderly sequence of conditions and results. On the other hand, history has been conceived as a course of events, which not only exhibits an orderly sequence from an objective point of view, but which is also *subjectively experienced* as a nexus by the individuals concerned. In the one case, history is a reconstruction, on the basis of external observation, of the inner connection of phenomena ; in the other, it is the conscious experience of the latter connection. Mankind exemplifies all possible transitional stages between these two extremes—history as merely objectively given, and as experienced both objectively and subjectively. Indeed, it is even true to say that, as a matter of fact, none but such transitional stages actually occur. Even the horizon of primitive man includes a narrow circle of consciously experienced history. On the other hand, man is ever far from attaining to a self-conscious grasp of his own history in its entirety. Thus, that which is in a high degree characteristic of world religion is true also of world history. Within the conscious horizon of each individual very different levels of historical consciousness are represented, even in the case of the cultural peoples who participate more or less actively in the course of world history. Here, as in world religion, we find that what was developed in a sequence during the course of ages continues to remain, at any rate roughly speaking, in juxtaposition. Moreover, even apart from this, we never survey more than a segment of the entire nexus of historical factors. One of the most important tasks of the historian consists in tracing the chain of events back to motives which are, in part, inaccessible to superficial observation, and, in part, indeed, remain of a problematical nature even when we believe that, through inference, we have gained an approximately true conception of them. Nevertheless, it is not necessary that immediate knowledge be complete in order that there may be a consciously experienced nexus of events such as is demanded for the content of history proper. It is merely necessary that some interconnection be actually experienced and that its relations be directly apprehended. This knowledge, moreover, must possess sufficient power to influence decisively the actual course of events.

This narrower conception of history brings historical events into relation with the human *will*. The will is really a phase of conscious experience. It is necessary, however, to single it out for special discussion, because of the fact that popular opinion either regards it as the exclusive factor in history or else stresses it so one-sidedly that the causal view, required in principle even for individual consciousness, threatens to vanish entirely from the conception of historical life. Naturally, the will does not become an influence definitely affecting the course of events until individuals have become consciously aware of the interconnectedness of historical life. Whenever, therefore, an exaggerated importance is attached to the function of volition, the conscious intervention of individual personalities in the course of events readily comes to appear as the decisive feature that distinguishes the historical from the prehistorical stages of human development. But this is erroneous in both its implications. Even the life of primitive peoples of nature is not entirely unaffected by individual personalities, whose influence may be more or less permanently operative even after they themselves have been forgotten. On the other hand, the will acts of individuals constitute but one factor among the many which determine historical life. Moreover, inasmuch as every particular volition is conditioned by motives inherent in the general constitution of individual consciousness, it is subject to the same psychical causality that dominates human consciousness in general. The criterion for differentiating historic from prehistoric existence, therefore, is not the influence of a personal will upon the life of the group, but rather the fact that the conscious experience of historical continuity includes a recognition of the effect of individual personalities upon the destinies of peoples. The advance to such an insight is inaugurated by world empires, in which the vicissitudes of peoples first begin to form a unified history; it reaches its completion in world culture, which creates a common mental heritage for mankind, and thus engenders the consciousness of a universal community.

Of the various elements of world culture that give impetus to this development, the *world religions* occupy the foremost place. In extent and permanence they surpass not only the world empires but also all other forms of material and spiritual interchange between peoples. However much the traditions associated with world religions may be interwoven with mythological and legendary elements, they nevertheless constitute a bond whose primary effect is to arouse among peoples who may otherwise be widely different in culture and history, the idea of a universal human community. The peoples of Eastern Asia, for example, though exhibiting marked political differences, were united by Buddhism into a community of religious thought, in which they became conscious that, in spite of differences of race and of history, they possessed a similar religious and ethical temper. If we compare the Brahmanic doctrines with the sayings of such teachers as Confucius and Lao-tsze, we are struck particularly by the similarity of ethical trend as well as by the divergence of this trend from that of Occidental thought. In its idea of a community of faith, Islamism likewise brought the consciousness of unity to numerous peoples of barbaric culture—to a more limited extent than Buddhism, it is true, but for this reason all the more forcefully. Of Christianity, it is even more true that, from the very beginning, it took as its guiding principle the belief that in the eyes of God there is no distinction either of race or of class and occupation. Hence it has regarded missionary activity among heathen peoples as a task whose purpose it is finally to unite the whole of mankind beneath the cross of Christ. Thus, world religion destroyed the barriers erected by the preceding national religions, and took as its aim the unification of men and races into an all-embracing community. To the adherent of a national religion, the race that believed in a different god was strange and hostile; both characteristics, strangeness and hostility, were included by the Greek in the term 'barbarian.' The Christian speaks of heathen who have not as yet beheld the light of pure truth, but for him there are no barbarians. The god to whom the Christian prays likewise rules the heathen world, and to the heathen, also, the gospel is preached. True, we find a recurring limitation in that it is only the Christian who is a brother to Christians. Nevertheless, it is prophesied of the heathen that they will at one time be received into the brotherhood of the disciples of Christ. At the end of time, there is to be but *one* shepherd and *one* flock upon earth. Thus, in the missionary activity which the Christian recognizes as his calling, the assertion, All men are brothers, is based on the two ideas, All Christians are brothers, and All men are destined to become Christians.

It was on the basis of the Christian tradition that science first attempted to treat history, not as the history of a single people or, at best, as a number of histories of successive or contemporaneous races and States, but as true world history. At the outset, world history was objective in character. The underlying thought was that the whole of mankind was controlled by a single idea which governed all events, and that the task of humanity consisted in carrying this idea into realization. Augustine's *Civitas Dei* was the first attempt at a world history based on the idea of the religious vocation of mankind. That this exposition is limited to the legendary history of the Israelitic people, supplemented by the history of Jesus as transmitted in the Gospels, and by the Apocalyptic prophecies of a future world, should not cause surprise. The limitation is due to the fact that the idea of humanity is considered solely from the religious point of view. The Church, as the institution about which religion centres, is glorified by Augustine's work as the divine State. The adoption of this religious viewpoint causes the history of mankind to appear as a record, not of human experiences that come as a result of human striving and activity, but of events that are from the very beginning divinely foreordained.

Nevertheless, Augustine's remarkable work long continued to determine the general direction of conceptions relating to the history of mankind. Up to the eighteenth century, *religious* development was regarded as establishing the only connection between the various periods of history. The sole exception to this occurred in the case of Giambattista Vico. In his *New Science* (1725), Vico sought to combine the development of language and of jurisprudence with that of religion. True, the question regarding the origin of the State and the causes of changes in constitutions had concerned men from the time of the early Sophists on. Particularly during the Hellenistic period and at the time of the Renaissance, such inquiries were of focal interest, as a result of the great political changes that were then taking place. Yet, whenever the underlying laws of such changes were sought, it was the *single* State that formed the basis of investigation; by comparing its vicissitudes with those of other States, the attempt was made to arrive at a general law along some such line as the Aristotelian classification of States into monarchies, aristocracies, democracies, etc. There was hardly ever a suggestion that the historical sequence of civilizations and of States was a connected process intelligible in causal or teleological terms. Religion alone was conceived as a phenomenon which was, on the one hand, independent of the limits of a single people, and yet, on the other, subject, in its development, to law. The idea that Christianity was destined to be a world religion, together with the fact that it had originated historically and had spread widely, did not admit of any other interpretation. Within this Christian circle of ideas, moreover, the historical development and growth of religion were, quite naturally, brought into connection with the world beyond, in which the development was thought to await its completion. The religious philosophy of history thus terminated in a prophecy whose culmination was the final triumph of Christianity. The Age of Enlightenment, after effecting a unification of Christianity with the religion of reason, again made the world of historical experience the scene of triumph. This triumph was held to consist in the ultimate development of Christianity into a religion of reason—a conception in which the idea of the destiny of Christianity to become a world religion undergoes a philosophical transformation which recurs even in the writings of Kant.

Apart from this transformation, which was only partially complete even in the Age of Enlightenment, the idea of religious development that grew up in connection with

Christian thought involves *two* presuppositions. The first of these is that the pathway of mankind was *determined by God,* and not voluntarily chosen by man himself. It is not to religious thought that the characteristic features of the development must be ascribed. The development, moreover, is not immanent in religion ; it is the result of external causes. The second presupposition is that this development follows a preconceived *plan* ; it embodies a purpose—indeed, it expresses purpose in the very highest degree precisely because it proceeds from the will of God. Even the co-operation of individuals in the fulfilment of this plan is but the result of divine predetermination, or happens because God has made known His purposes to these individuals. Thus, this course of thought leads with inner necessity to the conception of *revelation.* This conception combines two essentially irreconcilable ideas, offsetting each by the other. The religious destiny of man is thought to lie outside his own control : it is imposed upon him from without, and is communicated to him in the form of an illumination which he receives from the supersensuous world. Thus, religious development itself becomes a supersensuous process, which falls beyond the possibilities of the ordinary means of human knowledge. As its goal lies in the supersensuous, so also is the development itself a supersensuous process that extends over into the world of sense.

But at this point the religious view of world history necessarily came into sharp conflict with the philosophical view, though the latter had in certain respects appropriated the idea, developed by the former, of a teleological direction of human destinies. The philosopher, always trusting the guidance of his own reason, might admit both a goal and a plan, but that these should be inaccessible to the *lux naturalis,* as the philosophy of the Enlightenment called rational knowledge in distinction from *lux supranaturalis,* or revelation, he could not concede. The logical outcome of this course of thought was an auxiliary concept which appeared to surmount the difficulty, and also possessed the happy characteristic of leaving every one free to retain, along with the natural light, as much or as little of the supernatural thought of an earlier period as he might deem wise. This auxiliary concept was that of *education*—a conception that would readily suggest itself to an age vitally interested in pedagogical questions. The thought here involved represents merely a special application to this particular instance of the idea that the world is governed by a personal deity. Thus it came about that, from the time of Locke and Leibniz down to that of Lessing and Herder, the favourite conception of history was that of an education of mankind. But it is significant that the very work whose title incorporates this idea, Lessing's *Education of the Human Race,* really ends by displacing it. True, as a result of Biblical tradition, the idea of education is here brought into connection with the thought that the Jewish race is the chosen people of God. Freed from this connection, however, and applied to mankind in general, the idea of education, in Lessing's work, becomes that of *self-education,* or, what is the same thing, that of a *development* determined by the general laws of mental life. Hence conditions were ripe for the further advance made by Herder, in his *Ideas on the Philosophy of the History of Mankind.* Though frequently lapsing, in his discussions of details, into the transcendent teleology of the preceding period, Herder nevertheless did away in principle with the restriction of the history of mankind to religious development, substituting for the latter the development to humanity.

Thus was determined the programme which historical science, at about the same time, accepted as its own—the programme of a universal history, whose task did not consist in presenting a loosely connected series of the histories of separate States, but in describing the common participation of peoples and States in the development of a universal culture. Furthermore, the way was cleared for the philosophical position that history is not, as was once thought, the expression of a predetermined plan whose purpose is that of a divine education, but that it is the result of laws immanent in historical life itself. Though variously expressed and partly obscured by surviving ideas of the preceding period, this is the fundamental conviction common to the nineteenth-century philosophers of history. It received its most complete expression in the writings of Hegel, not merely in his *Lectures on the Philosophy of History*, but in his entire philosophy, which reflects throughout a broad historical outlook. History had by this time come to be regarded as a strictly self-dependent development of ideas in which each advance proceeds with rigid logical necessity from that which went before. In other words, it was thought of as a development of reason in time, or, in the phraseology of a religious world-view, as the living development of God himself. God is no longer conceived as a transmundane being who guides the destinies of mankind according to a preconceived plan. On the contrary, He is represented as immanent in the world. His innermost nature is described as the world-reason, and this is said to be unfolded particularly in the history of mankind.

However superior this conception may be to the preceding semi-mythological and semi-rationalistic theory of a divine education, it is clearly apparent that it was the outcome of a continuous development, characterized, we may doubtless say, by strict logical necessity. Antecedent to it were, first, the conception that this world is a preparation for the kingdom of God, and, later, the thought that life is an education in accordance with a predetermined plan. That the Hegelian conception is the result of such a development is evident from the very fact that it continues to regard the destinies of mankind as guided by a plan. This plan has, from stage to stage, merely passed from transcendence to immanence, inasmuch as it is finally thought to be present to the mind of the philosopher who interprets the meaning of history. Hence this later philosophy of history resembles the earlier in still another respect. Ultimately, both are more concerned with the future than with the past, thus being at once history and prophecy. Even at the later period, the central question to whose answer everything else is preparatory concerns the final goal toward which mankind is striving. Hence it is that the philosophers of this age are led time and again to divide the total life of humanity into periods inclusive of past, present, and future, precisely as did the world-plan of Augustine, whose basal conception was the idea of redemption. Since these periods are not derived from the progress of events, but are for the most part imposed upon it in conformity to the dictates of logic, the course of history is mapped out by reference to logical categories. Each of the great cultural peoples is portrayed as representing a specific idea, and, disregarding everything that might disturb their sequence, these ideas are arranged in a logical series. Thus, Hegel begins his reconstruction of history with an account of the Chinese as the people who possessed the earliest civilization. He does so, however, not because Chinese culture was as a matter of fact the earliest, but because it has apparently been more stable than other cultures, as well as more closely bound up with rigid external forms. Correspondingly, all succeeding stages of history are arranged by Hegel according to the principle, on the one hand, of a progress from bondage to spiritual freedom, and, on the other, of a transition from finite limitation to a striving for the infinite. This philosophy of history should not be criticized for its lack of knowledge concerning the beginnings of culture. Its fundamental error lies in the fact that, in tracing the development of mankind, it is guided, not by the rich concrete actuality of events but by a logical schematism which is in large measure imposed upon history, and only to a far less degree abstracted from it. That which was once a plan prescribed by God for mankind here at length becomes a plan elaborated by philosophers.

Without question, therefore, a philosophy of history must henceforth adopt a different course. True, it cannot dispense with principles that are in a certain sense external to history itself. Yet the function of such a philosophy would appear to consist in considering historical life from the point of view of the purposes that come to realization within it, and of the values that are created on the various levels of historical culture. Such a teleology of history—indeed, in the last analysis, every teleology—must be preceded by a causal investigation, which begins, here as everywhere, by entirely ignoring purposes and values. Now, history is really an account of mental life. As such, it gives consideration to physical factors only in so far as they furnish the indispensable basis of mind. Hence the direct approach to a philosophy of history which aims, not to acquire a knowledge of reality from *a priori* concepts but, conversely, to derive ideas from reality, is a *psychological account of the development of mankind*. Although the concrete significance of the particular, as such, precludes the historian from disregarding it, everything that is merely particular should be ignored by one who is giving a psychological account of events. The aim, in this latter case, should be that of discovering the determining motives of historical life and its changes, and of interpreting these by reference to the universal laws of mind. Supplementing this aim should be the endeavour to gain, so far as possible, an insight into the laws that are immanent in history itself. Our first three chapters have attempted to give an account of the development of folk consciousness during the periods that, for the most part, preceded self-conscious historical life. But neither this account nor the bare outline which our final chapter gives of the beginnings of the development to humanity must pretend to be a substitute for, or in any way to represent, a philosophy of history. The difference between an investigation such as ours and a philosophy of history is precisely the same as that which distinguishes a psychological description of mental life in general from a philosophical interpretation. But, if anywhere, it is especially in the field of history that a psychological analysis, concerned primarily to understand life in its actual occurrence, must precede questions regarding the meaning of events and the value which individual historical characters possess as respects both themselves and their permanent influence. In other words, we may henceforth demand that any philosophy of history which seeks to contribute to our understanding of the questions just mentioned, should be based on a psychological account of the development of mankind.

The point that we would emphasize is not that the philosophy of history has failed, in the past centuries, to find a satisfactory solution of its problem, and that its failure was inevitable. To the historical mind there is a far more important consideration. This consists in the fact that, when freed from its original mythological and teleological connections, the general conception of a history of mankind developed during these centuries has given clear definition to the idea of humanity in its most universal form. Humanity, it has been shown, includes within itself all antecedent social phenomena—peoples and States, religion and culture. This entire social complex has been subsumed under the principle that law is immanent in all history.

INDEX

Prepared by Dr. Alma de Vries Schaub on the basis of the German Index compiled by Dr. Hans Lindau.

Printed in Great Britain by
UNWIN BROTHERS, LIMITED, THE GRESHAM PRESS, WOKING AND LONDON